THE
FIRST-TIME
MANAGER

· SEVENTH EDITION ·

THE
FIRST-TIME
MANAGER

SEVENTH EDITION

· LOREN B. BELKER ·

· JIM McCORMICK ·

· GARY S. TOPCHIK ·

HarperCollins
Leadership

An Imprint of HarperCollins

*To all managers who aspire to advance their skills for
the benefit of themselves and those they lead.*

© 2018, 2012, 2005, 1997, 1993, 1986, 1981 HarperCollins Leadership

The First-Time Manager

Published by HarperCollins Leadership, an imprint of HarperCollins Focus LLC.

Book design by Elyse Strongin, Neuwirth & Associates.

978-0-8144-3970-8 (eBook)

Library of Congress Control Number: 2018948463

ISBN 978-0-8144-3969-2

Printed in the United States of America
20 21 22 LSC 10 9 8

CONTENTS

Preface to the Seventh Edition   vii

Acknowledgments   viii

Introduction   ix

PART ONE

So You're Going to Manage People 1

1. The Road to Management   3

2. Starting Out   9

3. Building Trust and Confidence   19

4. Show Your Appreciation   23

5. Being an Active Listener   27

6. The New Manager's Job and Pitfalls to Avoid   33

7. Dealing with Your Superiors   39

8. Choosing a Managerial Style of Your Own   49

PART TWO

Tackling Your New Duties 55

9. Building a Team Dynamic   57

10. Management Versus Leadership   63

11. Managing Problem Employees   65

12. Hiring and Interviewing   71

13. Training Team Members   83

14. Managing Change: Dealing with Resistance   91

15. Disciplining the Employee   95

16. "Oh My God! I Can't Fire Anyone!"   105

17. Having a Legal Awareness   115

PART THREE

**Working with People, Building Relationships,
and Managing Risks 123**

18. No Secrets   125

19. The Human Resources Department   129

20. The Current State of Loyalty   133

21. Is There Such a Thing as Motivation?   135

22. Understanding Risk Inclination   143

23. Encouraging Initiative and Innovation   151

24. Improving Outcomes   157

25. The Generation Gap   163

26. Managing Remote Employees   169

27. Social Media in the Workplace   173

PART FOUR

Job Descriptions, Performance Appraisals, and Salary Administration   175

28. Writing Job Descriptions   177

29. Doing Performance Appraisals   181

30. Salary Administration   195

PART FIVE

Improving and Developing Yourself   203

31. Having Emotional Intelligence   205

32. Developing a Positive Self-Image   209

33. Managing Your Own Time   227

34. The Written Word   237

35. The Grapevine   241

36. Your Best Friend: Delegation   243

37. A Sense of Humor   249

38. Managing, Participating in, and Leading Meetings   253

39. Taking Center Stage: *The Role of Public Speaking in Your Career*   263

40. A Few Body Language Insights   269

PART SIX

The Complete Person   273

41. Coping with Stress   275

42. Having Balance in Your Life   279

43. A Touch of Class   283

Conclusion   285

Index   289

PREFACE TO THE SEVENTH EDITION

IT CONTINUES TO BE AN HONOR to be a part of this vitally important project that has had such a positive impact on hundreds of thousands of readers for more than thirty-five years. My first exposure to this book was when AMACOM Books approached me about updating it to create the sixth edition. Upon reading this classic, I arrived at four conclusions. The first was that this book is a fantastic resource that has clearly helped countless new managers. The second was that it would be impossible for people to read this book and not improve their ability to manage well, regardless of how long they have been managing. The third was that I would have thoroughly enjoyed sitting down with Loren Belker and Gary Topchik because both our philosophies of management and our general approaches to life are so well aligned. My final conclusion was that improving this extraordinary resource would be a daunting challenge. I felt as though I was being asked to polish an already brilliant gem.

Having never had the opportunity to meet Loren or Gary led me to feel an even greater obligation to bring their work forward respectfully, add some new insights, and not diminish the value they have provided. To paraphrase Sir Isaac Newton, if I have provided value "it is by standing on the shoulders of giants."

Respectfully,
Jim McCormick

ACKNOWLEDGMENTS

I WOULD LIKE TO ACKNOWLEDGE the managers I have encountered and observed throughout my career. Their skills have ranged from extraordinary to horrendous, though I have learned from all of them. To the team members I have had the privilege to lead I say thank you. You have all been sources of enjoyment and learning. To the aspiring managers I have had the opportunity to teach, I applaud you for your thirst for knowledge. Thank you to my editor, Ellen Kadin, for entrusting me with the legacy that is this book. And finally, I thank my agent, Maryann Karinch, who knows my skills better than I.

—JM

INTRODUCTION

BY OPENING THIS BOOK, you have set yourself apart and made the clear statement that you desire to improve your management ability. Our compliments to you for your desire to both improve your professional skills and your ability to make other peoples' professional lives more fulfilling. This book was created to assist you in that effort.

Just as you cannot lead a parade if no one is following, you cannot manage if you don't have a team to lead. Engrained in this book is the belief that a well-led team will always achieve results that are superior to those of an individual. Consistent with that conviction, this book was written by a team. Three of us have taken up the challenge—at different times and in our own ways—of seeking to provide you with the best guidance we can muster for a new or prospective manager. The results of this joint effort are better because of our collaboration. The same will be true for you if you take to heart the insights you will discover in this book.

The advice in this book centers around two overarching messages: Be thoughtful in your actions and always conduct yourself with class. You will never regret either.

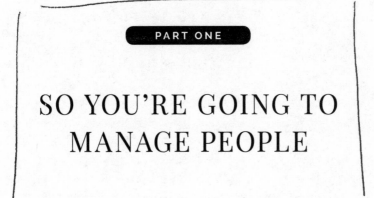

PART ONE

SO YOU'RE GOING TO MANAGE PEOPLE

Welcome to the exciting and challenging role of manager. Being successful is about valuing, understanding, and guiding the most complex of all systems—people. You will find it more of an art than a science and potentially more rewarding than anything you have ever done.

1

THE ROAD TO MANAGEMENT

THERE ARE MANY DIFFERENT WAYS that people become managers.

Unfortunately, many companies don't go through a very thorough process in choosing those who will be moved into a managerial position. Often the judgment is based solely on how well the person is performing in his current position. The best individual contributor doesn't always make the best manager, although many companies still make the choice on that basis. The theory is that successful past performance is the best indicator of future success. However, management skills are very different from the skills one needs to succeed as an individual contributor.

So the fact that an employee is a good performer, even though she demonstrates a pattern of success, doesn't necessarily mean the person will be a successful manager. Being a manager requires skills beyond those of being an excellent technician. Managers need to focus on people, not just tasks. They need to rely on others, not just be self-reliant. Managers are also team oriented and have a broad focus, whereas non-managers succeed by having a narrow focus and being detail oriented. In many ways, transitioning from the role of an individual contributor to a manager is similar to the difference between being a technician and being an artist. The manager is an artist because management is often nuanced and subjective. It involves a different mindset.

MANAGEMENT IS NOT FOR EVERYONE

Some companies have management-training programs. These programs vary from excellent to unfortunate. Too often, the program is given to people who already have been in managerial positions for a number of years. It's true that even experienced managers periodically should be given refresher courses in management style and techniques. But if a training program has any merit, it should be given to individuals who are being considered for management positions. The training program will not only help them avoid mistakes, it also gives trainees the opportunity to see whether they will be comfortable leading others. A management training program that helps potential managers decide that they are not suited for management has done both the prospective managers and the organization they are a part of a great favor.

Unfortunately, far too many organizations still use the "sink or swim" method of management training. All employees who move into supervisory positions must figure it out on their own. This method assumes that everyone intuitively knows how to manage. They don't. Managing people is crucial to the success of any organization; but in too many cases, it is left to chance. Anyone who has worked for any length of time has observed situations where a promotion didn't work out and the person asked for the old job back. The well-known saying, "Be careful what you wish for, because you just might get it" comes to mind. In many companies, the opportunities for promotion are limited if you don't go into management. As a result, some people go into management who shouldn't be there—and they wouldn't want to be in management if other opportunities existed for salary increases and promotion.

A series of management seminars was conducted for one company that used an enlightened approach to the problem of moving the wrong people into management. Everyone under potential consideration for a first-line management position was invited to attend an all-day seminar on what is involved in the management of people. Included were some simple but typical management problems. When these candidates were invited to attend, they were told by the company, "If after attending this seminar you decide that the management of people is not something you want to do, just say so. That decision will in no way affect other non-management promotion possibilities or future salary decisions in your current position."

Approximately five hundred people attended these seminars, and approximately 20 percent decided they did not want to move into management. After getting a brief taste of management, about a hundred people knew they would not make good managers, but they were still valuable employees. This is dramatic to consider. If this program is representative it suggests that 20 percent of people advanced into management would prefer not to be there. Far too many people accept management promotions because they feel (often rightly so) that they will be dead-ended if they reject the promotion.

THE OMNIPOTENT ONE

Some people believe that if you want something done right, you'd better do it yourself. People with this attitude rarely make good leaders or managers because they have difficulty delegating responsibility. Everyone has seen these people: They delegate only those trivial tasks that anyone could perform, and anything meaningful they keep for themselves. As a result, they work evenings and weekends and take a briefcase home as well. There is nothing wrong with working overtime. Most people occasionally must devote some extra time to the job, but those who follow this pattern as a way of life are poor managers. They have so little faith in their team members that they trust them with only minor tasks. What they are really saying is that they don't know how to properly train their people.

There is often a staff turnover problem in a team with this kind of manager. The employees are usually more qualified than the "omnipotent one" believes and they soon tire of handling only trivia.

You probably know of an omnipotent one in your own organization. It is a problem if you're working for one, because you'll have a difficult time being promoted. Caught up in your impossible situation, you're not given anything important to do. As a result, you never get a chance to demonstrate your abilities. Omnipotent ones seldom give out recommendations for promotion. They are convinced that the reason they must do all the work is that their staff doesn't accept responsibility. They can never admit that it is because they refuse to delegate. The trap of becoming an omnipotent one is being emphasized because you don't want to allow yourself to fall into this mode of behavior. If you notice that you are only delegating minor tasks, it is time to stop and make a personal assessment of your management style.

One other unvarying trait of omnipotent ones is that they seldom take their vacations all at once. They take only a couple days off at a time because they are certain the company can't function longer than that without them. Before going on vacation, they will leave specific instructions as to what work is to be saved until their return. They will direct their team to email, text, or call them regarding anything of significance even though they are supposed to be on vacation. The omnipotent one even complains to family and friends, "I can't even get away from the problems at work for a few days without being bothered." What omnipotent ones don't say is that this is exactly the way they want it because it makes them feel important. For some omnipotent managers, any joy in their retirement years is demolished because retirement means an end to their dedication to the job, their perceived indispensability, and possibly their reason for living.

THE CHOSEN FEW

Sometimes, people are chosen to head a function because they're related to or have an "in" with the boss. Consider yourself fortunate if you do not work for this type of company. Even if you *are* related to the boss, it's very difficult to assume additional responsibility under these circumstances. You doubtless have the authority, but today's businesses aren't dictatorships and people won't perform well for you just because you've been anointed by upper management. So, if you're the boss's son or daughter or friend, you really need to prove yourself. The reality is that your colleagues may even expect you to perform at a higher level than someone who does not have the advantages you have. You need to accept the higher standard they have set for you. That is just the way it is. You'll get surface respect or positional respect, but let's face it—it's what people really think of you, not what they say to you, that matters—and that affects how they perform.

In the best organizations, you're not chosen for a managerial position because of your technical knowledge, but because someone has seen the spark of leadership in you. That is the spark you must start developing. Leadership is difficult to define. A leader is a person others look to for direction, someone whose judgment is respected because it is usually sound. As you exercise your judgment and develop the capacity to make sound decisions, it becomes a self-perpetuating characteristic. Your faith in your own decisionmaking power is fortified. That feeds your self-confidence, and with more self-confidence, you become less reluctant to make difficult decisions.

Leaders are people who can see into the future and visualize the results of their decisionmaking. Leaders can also set aside matters of personality and make decisions based on fact. This doesn't mean you ignore the human element—you never ignore it—but you always deal with the facts themselves, not with people's emotional perception of those facts. This does not mean that you are blind to the emotional impact of your decisions but that you do not let those impacts take you off course. People are chosen to be managers for a variety of reasons. If you're chosen for sound reasons, acceptance by your new staff will, for the most part, be much easier to gain.

2

STARTING OUT

YOUR FIRST WEEK ON THE JOB as a manager will be unusual, to say the least. If you're a student of human behavior, you'll observe some surprising developments.

SETTLING IN

Don't believe that everyone is happy about your promotion. Some of your coworkers will feel *they* should have been chosen. They may be jealous of your new position and secretly hope you fail.

Others, the office "yes people," will immediately start playing up to you. As the chosen one, you can be their ticket to success. Their objective isn't all bad, but their approach is unfortunate.

Some coworkers will put you to the test early. They may ask you questions to see if you know the answers. If you don't, they'll want to see if you'll admit it or if you'll try to bluff your way through it. Some may ask you questions you cannot possibly know the answers to, just for the sheer delight of embarrassing you.

Most—you hope the majority—will adopt a wait-and-see attitude. They're not going to condemn or praise you until they see how you perform. This attitude is healthy and all you really have a right to expect.

Initially you will be measured against your predecessor in the position. If that person's performance was poor, yours will look great by comparison even if you're mediocre. If you follow a highly capable performer, your adjustment will be tougher. Before you begin thinking it's best to follow a miserable performer, consider the load of tough problems you'd be inheriting from your inept predecessor, which is why he is no longer there. It will be difficult but potentially quite rewarding, if you're up to the challenge. The highly capable predecessor is probably gone because she was promoted. In either case, you have a big job ahead of you.

One of your first decisions should be to refrain from immediately instituting changes in the method of operation. (In some situations, top management may have instructed you to go in and make certain immediate changes because of the seriousness of the situation. In such cases, however, it is usually announced that changes will be forthcoming.) Above all, be patient. Keep in mind that most people find changes threatening and are inclined to resist them either consciously or unconsciously. Sudden change often results in a fear response that will work against you and not serve you well as you seek to make a positive impact.

When you do need to make changes, whether soon after your promotion or later, be as forthcoming as possible in explaining what will be taking place and why. While change may be frightening to people the unknown is even more disabling. This does not mean that you disclose every detail. Determining what to disclose and what to keep to yourself is part of the judgment you need to have as a manager. But the more forthcoming you can be, the more you will help your team get past the resistance to change that is part of human nature.

In all settings, but particularly when implementing changes, answer questions as honestly as possible. If you are new to the position, don't be afraid to say "I don't know" if you don't. Your people don't expect you to know everything. They may just be probing to see if they can trust you. Trying to fabricate an answer to a question you don't know the answer to is always a bad idea, and will very likely cost you credibility and trust.

If you make changes immediately, you'll be resented. In addition to being disquieting to your team, your actions can be construed as being arrogant and an insult to your predecessor. Many young new leaders make their own lives more difficult by assuming they have to use all their newfound power immediately. The key word should be *restraint*. It is vital to remember that you're the one who is on trial with your subordinates, not they with you.

This is a good time to make an important point about your own attitude. Many new managers communicate rather well upward to their superiors, but poorly downward to their direct reports. However, your direct reports will have more to say about your future than your superiors. You are going to be judged by how well your team functions—the results your team delivers—so the people who now work for you are the most important people in your business life. Believe it or not, they're more important to your future than the president of your company. This bit of knowledge has always seemed obvious, yet many new managers spend almost all their time planning their upward communication and give only a passing glance to the people who really control their future.

USING YOUR NEW AUTHORITY

If there is one area where many new managers blunder, it is the use of authority. This is particularly true of new managers navigating their way through a self-directed "sink or swim" method of on-the-job training. This is due to the flawed belief that because you now have the authority of management, you have to start using it—and you must use and display it in a big way. This may be the biggest mistake that new managers make.

View the authority of the new position as you would a limited inventory. The fewer times you draw on the inventory, the greater is the supply that remains for when it is *really* needed.

The newly appointed manager who starts acting like "the boss" by issuing orders and other directives is off to a bad start. While you may not hear the remarks directly, the typical comments made behind the back of such a misguided manager might be, "Boy, is she drunk with power," or "This job has really gone to his head," or "He sure is fond of himself since he was promoted." You don't need this kind of problem.

If you don't draw down your inventory of authority too often, the authority you may have to use in an emergency is more effective because it is infrequently displayed. The people you lead know that you are the manager. They know that the requests you make carry the authority of your position. The vast majority of the time, it is unnecessary to use that authority.

There is a term in the creative arts called *understatement*. For the most part, it means that what is left unsaid may be as important as what is said. This is true with the use of authority. A direction given as a request is a managerial type of understatement. If the response you are seeking is not forthcoming, you can always clarify your request or add a bit of authority.

On the other hand, if you use all your authority to achieve a task, and then discover by the reaction that you have used too much, the damage is done. It is difficult, if not impossible, to de-escalate the overuse of authority.

In short, do not assume that you need to use the authority of your position. Perhaps the greatest by-product of this softer approach is that you are not building a negative image that may be nearly impossible to erase later.

HAVING THE PERSONAL TOUCH

Sometime during the first sixty days in your new management position, you should plan on having a personal conversation with each of the people in your area of responsibility. Don't do this the first week or so. Give your people a chance to get used to the idea that you're there. If you try to do it immediately, you risk overwhelming or intimidating your team members. When it comes time to talk, ask them into your office, to lunch, or out of the office for coffee for an unhurried discussion about anything that is on their minds. Do no more talking than necessary. This first discussion is not designed for outward communication with your team members; it is designed to open lines of communication from them to you. (Have you ever noticed that the more you allow the other person to talk, the higher you'll be rated as a brilliant conversationalist?)

Although the employees' personal concerns are important, it is preferable to restrict the discussions to work-related topics. Sometimes it is difficult to define these limits because problems at home may be troubling an employee more than anything else, but at all times you must avoid getting into a situation where you're giving personal advice. Just because you've been selected as the boss, it doesn't make you an expert on all the personal problems confronting your people. Listen to them; often that's what they need more than anything else—someone to listen to them.

Do not think for a moment that this can be done by email or by a phone call. Not a chance. Both methods are unacceptable substitutes for an in-person conversation. Neither allow the connection you are seeking to establish to occur. If you have staff working remotely, you may have to start with a video call if it is not possible to have an in-person conversation in the first sixty days. If you do have to resort to a video call make it clear that the conversation will be continued in-person as soon as possible.

GETTING TO KNOW THEM

The purpose of having a conversation with the members of your team is to give them the opportunity to open the lines of communication with you. It is important that you show a genuine interest in their concerns and learn of their ambitions within the company. Ask questions that will get them to expand on their points of view. You can't fake genuine interest in others; you're doing this because you care about the employees' well-being. Such attention is advantageous to both sides. If you can help employees achieve their goals, they'll be more productive. It is even more important that they see that they're making progress toward their goals.

So your goal in these early conversations is to let your team members know you care about them as individuals and you're there to help them achieve their goals. Let them know that if possible you want to help them solve the problems they are facing in their job. Establish a comfort zone in which they can deal with you. Make them feel that it is perfectly natural for them to discuss challenges with you. By discussing small problems and small irritants, you may be able to avoid larger problems.

You'll discover in your first few months as a manager that your technical abilities are not nearly as important as your human abilities. The majority of your problems are going to revolve around the human and not the technical aspects of the job. Unless your responsibilities are technically complex, you'll discover that if you have strong human skills, minor technical deficiencies will be overlooked. Conversely, even if you are the most technically competent manager in the office, without human skills you'll have great difficulty.

HAVING FRIENDS IN THE DEPARTMENT

One of the problems many new executives confront is handling friendships with people in the department who now report to them. This is a difficult situation to which there is no perfect answer. One of the most common questions new managers ask is, "Can I still be friends with the people who used to be my coworkers and now report to me?"

It is obvious that you shouldn't have to give up your friendships simply because you've received a promotion. However, you don't want your friendships to hurt your performance or the performance of your friends.

It is a mistake to allow your friendships to interfere with your method of operation. A direct report who is truly a friend will understand the dilemma in which you find yourself.

You must be certain that coworkers who were your friends before you became their supervisor receive the same treatment as everyone else. And that doesn't just mean not favoring them over other workers. They also must not be treated worse merely to prove to the others how unbiased you are.

Although it is certainly true that you can be friends with people, you cannot expect to be friends with them in the same way in the context of work. As a new manager, you will need to establish some expectations of how you will work with all of your team members, whether they are friends or not. You need to hold all individuals to the same standards of performance, behavior, and accountability. Also keep in mind that what might look like friendship to you can often look like favoritism to others.

There is a temptation to use your old friend in the department as a confidant, but you don't want to give the impression that you are playing favorites. In fact, you must not play favorites. If you do need a confidant, it is preferable to use a manager in another department or section of the organization.

You may want to consider having a conversation with a friend and former colleague about their moving to another department. Regardless of how hard you work not to display favoritism, it may be nearly impossible and best for both you and your friend if they do not report to you. This may be the best alternative if you truly value the friendship that is at risk because of your new role.

STRUCTURING YOUR ORGANIZATION

With time, you will want to consider whether you can improve the structure of your organization. Unless you are particularly familiar with your team members and their roles, it is best not to do this too soon. Restructurings tend to be very stressful for all involved. It is best to do them less often and well. While you can always correct a mistake in structuring your organization, it is best not to make the mistake to start with.

As you look at the reporting relationships within your team, you will need to pay particular attention to how many people are reporting directly to you. This number is referred to as your span of control. In recent decades, information technology has allowed organizations to have fewer but broader layers. This *flattening* of organizational structures has had many positive results. Executed well, it has allowed for more efficient communication and improved decisionmaking. As with anything, there needs to be balance when creating a flatter structure.

Less experienced managers sometimes make the mistake of an excessive span of control. It is easy to do. Nearly everyone would like to report directly to you. It gives them better access to the ultimate decisionmaker and brings with it a certain status within the organization. The problem is that you can only effectively manage a limited number of direct reports. When managers allow an excessive number of people to report to them directly, it becomes a free-for-all. They can find a line at their door every morning and an email inbox full of messages. They can spend their entire days trying to respond to all the needs and questions of their direct reports. They are rarely successful getting through all the requests for guidance and decisions, then start the next day behind; they rarely have time for any long-term thinking and planning. An excessively broad span of control is a setup for failure.

So, what span of control will work for you? There are a number of variables you need to take into account. One is the physical location of your direct reports. You can handle a little broader span of control if they are located in the same facility as you. The ability to meet with them in-person will ease communication. Another factor is the level of experience; a direct report who is a proven performer is not likely to require as much of your time. A new employee or one who has recently been moved into a new position or given additional responsibilities will probably require more of your time, at least for a while.

A good rule of thumb is not to have more direct reports than you can meet with once a week. By meet, this means actual one-on-one face time. The meeting may be in-person or a video call, but it needs to be a face-to-face, one-on-one meeting—not a staff meeting. Given that you have a lot to do in addition to meeting with your direct reports, five is a good maximum number. This allows you to have one of your one-on-one meetings each day of the workweek if that suits your purposes.

Be careful about letting these meetings slip—they are a vital part of your being able to manage well and efficiently. If your direct reports know they'll get face time with you every week, they will be able to save up items they need to discuss until that meeting. It is much more efficient to address issues in this setting then when passing in the hall, on a phone call from the airport, or by trading text messages or emails.

If your employees cannot count on having a regular opportunity to communicate directly with you, they will be more inclined to track you down whenever anything comes up that they think requires your attention. The negative results are twofold: a lot more ad hoc contacts that do not facilitate thoughtful decisionmaking and more issues being brought to you than necessary. If you can abide by weekly meetings with your direct reports and train them to hold as many issues as possible until those meetings, you will be surprised and pleased to see how many things they learn to resolve themselves that they otherwise would bring to you.

MANAGING YOUR MOOD

People who report to you are very aware of what kind of mood you're in, especially if you tend to have significant mood swings. Temper tantrums have no place in the work habits of a mature manager—and maturity has nothing to do with age. Letting your irritation show occasionally can be effective, as long as it is sincere and not manipulative.

All of us, from time to time, fall under the spell of moods that reflect situations outside the office that are troubling us. Many books on management tell us we must leave our problems at the door, or at home, and not bring them into the office. That attitude is naive, because few people can completely shut off a personal problem and keep it from affecting how they perform on the job.

There is little doubt, however, that you can minimize the impact a problem has on your work. The first step is to admit that something is irritating you and that it may affect your ability to work effectively with your colleagues. If you can do that, you can probably avoid making other people victims of your personal problem. If an outside problem is gnawing at you and you need to deal with an employee in a critical situation, there is nothing wrong with saying to the employee, "Look, I'm really not in the greatest mood today. If I seem a little irritated, I hope you'll forgive me." This kind of candor is refreshing to a subordinate. And it is far better to disclose that you are distracted than to risk a team member thinking he is the cause of your distant or agitated behavior.

Never think for a moment that others don't have the ability to judge your moods. By showing dramatic changes of mood, you become less effective. In addition, your direct reports will know when to expect these changes and what the telltale signs are, and they will avoid dealing with you when you're on the bottom swing of such a mood. They'll wait until you're on the high end of the spectrum.

MANAGING YOUR FEELINGS

You should work hard at being even-tempered. But it is not a good idea to be the kind of manager who is never bothered by anything—a person who never seems to feel great joy, great sorrow, or great anything. People will not identify with you if they believe you disguise all your feelings.

Keeping your cool at all times, however, is another matter. There are good reasons for keeping your cool. If you can always remain calm, even in troubled situations, you're more likely to think clearly and be in a better position to handle tough problems. But you can show feelings—without losing your cool—so that people won't think you're a management robot.

To be an outstanding manager of people, you must care about people. That doesn't mean taking a missionary or social worker approach toward them, but if you enjoy their company and respect their feelings, you'll be much more effective in your job than the supervisor who is mostly task-oriented.

This, indeed, is one of the problems companies bring on themselves when they assume that the most efficient worker in an area is the one who should be promoted to management. That worker may be efficient because she is task-oriented. Moving these kinds of workers into areas where they supervise others doesn't automatically make them people-oriented.

3

BUILDING TRUST AND CONFIDENCE

BUILDING CONFIDENCE IS A GRADUAL PROCESS. One of your main goals is to develop the trust and confidence of your employees, not only in their own abilities but in their opinion of you. They must have confidence that you are both competent and fair.

THE SUCCESS HABIT

Building confidence in employees is not an easy task. Your goal is to help them establish a pattern of success. Confidence is built on success, so your job as a leader is to give them tasks at which they can succeed. Especially with new employees, assign them tasks they can master. Build in them the habit of being successful, starting small if needed, with smaller successes.

Occasionally a team member will perform a task incorrectly or just plain blow it. How you handle these situations has a great impact on the confidence of your employees. Never correct them in front of others. Definitely abide by the credo, "Praise in public, criticize in private." It will serve you well.

Even when you talk to a team member in private about an error, your function is to train that person to recognize the nature of the problem so the mistake is not repeated. Your attitude about errors will speak louder than the words you use. Your statements must be directed toward correcting the misunderstanding that led to the error—*not* toward any sort of personal judgment. Never say or do anything that will make the employee feel inadequate. You want to build confidence, not destroy it. If you get pleasure from making team members feel foolish, then you'd better start examining your own motives, because you can't build yourself up by tearing someone else down. Examine the error based on what went wrong, where the misunderstanding occurred, and go on from there. Treat the small error routinely; don't make it bigger than it really is.

Let's briefly discuss the "praise in public" part of the credo. This concept used to be taken as gospel until managers found that it could also create problems. The individual on the receiving end of the praise feels warm and fuzzy about the compliment, but others who were not equally commended could react negatively. Their disappointment can then be directed at the employee who is praised. In addition, praising a team member in front of her colleagues can make her uncomfortable. This is why it is important to be cautious about praising in public. Why make life tougher for employees by creating jealousy or resentment among their coworkers? If you really want to praise someone expansively for outstanding performance, do it in the privacy of your office. You'll get the pluses without the negatives of resentment and jealousy from coworkers. On the other hand, if you have a group that works well together, respects the efforts of each member of the team, and is accomplishing its goals, praising in public will be a morale booster for the entire team.

For now, let's amend the credo to read: "Praise in public or private (depending on the preference of the individual and the dynamics of your team), criticize in private."

You can also build confidence by involving your people in some of the decisionmaking processes. Without delegating any of your supervisory responsibilities, allow employees to have input into matters that affect them. A new task about to be performed in your area presents the opportunity to give your subordinates some input. Solicit ideas on how the new task might best be worked into the daily routine.

When you request input, you send the important message that you value your employees' thoughts and ideas. You are also serving yourself well when you invite discussion. Your team members are likely closer to the situation than you are and may have insights that escaped you.

It is vital that you make it clear that you are genuinely interested in the input you are requesting. If your people sense you are going through an insincere exercise, you will be wasting time and risking a loss of trust.

Your challenge is that some of the input you get will not be useful. As a leader, you need to make it clear that you see value in the ideas being offered and appreciate them. When you get input you cannot implement, you will be wise to briefly explain why you will not be going in that direction. When you do, make sure you do not allow yourself to be critical of the advice or the person offering it.

Given this kind of participation, the new method is much more likely to succeed because it is everyone's method and not just yours. This doesn't mean your staff is making decisions for you; by involving your people in the process that leads up to your decision, you'll have them working with you rather than passively accepting new systems imposed on them. The result is likely to be a higher level of buy-in and less pushback.

THE EVILS OF PERFECTIONISM

Some managers expect perfection from their employees. They know they won't get it but they feel they'll get closer to it by demanding it. By insisting on perfection, you may in fact defeat your own purposes. Some employees will become so self-conscious about making a mistake that they will slow their performance down to a crawl to make absolutely certain they don't screw up. As a result, productivity goes way down and employees lose confidence.

Another drawback to being a perfectionist is that everyone resents you for it. Your direct reports believe that you are impossible to please and you prove it to them daily. This also shatters employee confidence. You know what the acceptable standards for work performance are in your company—no one can blame you for wanting to be better than the average—but you'll have far more success if you get the employees involved in helping decide how to improve performance. If they have ownership in the plan, you have a significantly better chance of achieving your goal.

You can also build confidence by developing esprit de corps within your own area. Make sure, however, that the feeling you build is supportive of the prevailing company spirit and not in competition with it.

THE IMPORTANCE OF BUILDING TRUST

In addition to allowing mistakes and helping individuals see their errors, giving praise and recognition, involving others in the decisionmaking process, and avoiding perfectionism, you, the manager, can build trust in many other ways.

You can share the vision of the organization and the department with your team members. Doing this gives them a clearer picture of what the goals are and how they are helping to meet them.

You can give individuals clear directions. This shows that you know what you are doing and are keeping things on track.

You can share examples of how you have succeeded and what mistakes you have made. Doing that builds rapport and makes you real to your team.

You can talk to each of your team members to learn what each one wants from the job. By doing this, you are demonstrating that you really care and you are serious about helping them advance professionally.

All of these additional strategies, and others that you devise, can build a trusting environment.

4

SHOW YOUR APPRECIATION

IN CHAPTER 3, THE IMPORTANCE OF GIVING positive feedback or praise was emphasized. It is one of the best methods for motivating individuals and building a positive work environment. Many managers do not give their direct reports praise, which is a big mistake. Praise lets employees know that you care about what they are doing. It also lets employees know that their work is important. If you think about it, it probably takes only seconds to give someone praise and it costs nothing. It does have a big impact on most employees, though. You can praise people face-to-face, over the telephone, with an email, or in a text message. Face-to-face is always the best method for giving feedback, but if you have employees in other locations or cannot get to them in a timely manner, use the telephone, email, or a text. The nice thing about doing it with a text message is that the team member is likely to receive it almost immediately. Most of us can't resist checking a new text message as soon as it is received.

Some managers might not show their appreciation because they never had appreciation shown to them by others, but you can stop that cycle. Show appreciation. Some managers feel that employees are supposed to perform well because they are getting paid to do well, so there is no reason to praise them for doing so. This is not good reasoning. Those managers should bear in mind that if they praised their employees, they might perform even better. Considering it costs nothing and takes very little time, why not do it? Your goal as a leader is to inspire your team members to perform at the top of their ability. Praising them in an appropriate way when it is deserved is part of providing this inspiration.

There are many managers, especially newer ones, who are uncomfortable giving praise. This is to be expected because it may be a new skill for them. In order to become more comfortable expressing appreciation, you have to do it. The more you practice it the easier it will become. Consider some of the following points when giving praise or showing appreciation:

✍ **Be specific.** If managers want certain behaviors repeated, they need to be specific in the type of positive feedback they give. The more detailed the manager is, the more likely the behavior or action will be repeated. Don't just say, "Great job last week." Say, "You really handled that difficult situation last week with diplomacy and good judgment."

✍ **Describe the impact.** Most team members like to know how their work ties into the bigger picture or the larger scheme of things such as meeting the objectives of the unit, department, or organization. If it did, let them know how their contributions had a positive effect beyond your team.

✍ **Don't overdo it.** Some managers go to extremes and give their team members too much positive feedback. When this occurs, the impact of the feedback is diminished and the praise may seem insincere. Make sure the praise is on target and deserved or it will lose its value.

THE ACTUAL SKILL

Giving praise or appreciation involves two steps. First, you specifically describe the behavior, action, or performance that deserves the appreciation. For example, "You did a good job with the new design for the cover of our products catalog." Then you describe why it deserves your appreciation and the business impact of the contribution. For example, "The new design will very likely increase sales."

To underscore this point, at a group of thirty attendees in a management seminar, the following two questions were asked:

1. What is the best example of enlightened management you've ever seen?
2. What is the worst example of management you've experienced?

It was no surprise that nearly all the responses had to do with some form of appreciation either received or denied when the staff member felt it was deserved. What was surprising was the depth of emotion displayed about the subject.

One answer was a classic: A young man recounted that he was asked to drive a pickup truck fifty miles to an outlying facility to make an important repair. At 10:30 p.m., when he had just returned home, the phone rang. It was his manager. "I just called to make sure that you got home okay. It's kind of a bad night out there." The manager did not even ask about how the repair went, which indicated her complete confidence in the young man's ability. The manager inquired only about his safe return. The incident had taken place more than five years earlier, but to the young worker, it was as fresh as though it had just happened.

In a poll conducted by a major company in the United States, employees were asked to rank work attributes they considered important. Salary came in sixth. What came in first, by a wide margin, was "a need to be appreciated for what I do."

If appreciation is important to you in your relationship with your manager, realize that it is equally important to the people you manage. When people deserve appreciation, do not withhold it. It does not cost you or your organization and is in many ways more valuable than money.

5

BEING AN ACTIVE LISTENER

ONE OF THE BEST-KEPT SECRETS OF successful management is the ability to listen actively. Active listening means letting the other person know that she has been heard. You do this by involving yourself in the conversation, making clarifying statements, asking questions, summarizing what you have heard, and using appropriate visual and vocal cues. The best listeners are active ones.

New managers should be concerned about their ability to communicate and listen actively. Many new managers have the mistaken idea that the minute they are promoted everyone is going to hang on every word they say. That is the wrong approach. The more they listen, the more successful they will be. How much listening is enough? As a starting point, make sure that you are doing at least twice as much listening as talking.

Active listening is one of the most valuable traits a new manager can demonstrate for two important reasons: First, if you do a great deal of active listening, you will not be thought of as a know-it-all, which is how most people perceive someone who talks too much. Second, by doing a lot of active listening and less talking, you'll learn what is going on and gain insights and information you would miss if you were doing all the talking.

Most people are not good active listeners, and it is valuable to understand why.

THE POOR LISTENER

Many people believe that the most beautiful sound in the world is their own voice. It's music to their ears. They cannot get enough of it, and they require others to listen to it. Typically, these people are more interested in what they themselves are going to say than in what others are saying. Indeed, most people can remember nearly everything they have said and hardly any of what the other person has said. People listen partially—they are not being active listeners. They are too busy thinking of the clever things they are about to utter.

If you don't remember anything else about this chapter, you'll do yourself immeasurable good by recalling this statement: *If you want to be thought of as a brilliant manager, be an active listener.*

Many managers, both new and experienced, do too much talking and not enough listening. You learn very little while you are talking, but you can learn a great deal while listening. New managers often think that now they're in charge, everyone is hanging on their every word. But the more you talk, the more you run the risk of boring and even alienating others. The more you listen, the more you learn and show respect for other peoples' ideas, experience, and opinions. It seems like an obvious choice, especially for a manager of people.

Another reason people are not good listeners is the comprehension gap. Most people communicate at between 80 and 120 words per minute. Let's assume a hundred words per minute as the average speaking speed. People can comprehend at a much higher rate. Those who have taken a rapid reading course, and who maintain the skill, can comprehend well over a thousand words per minute. If someone is speaking at a hundred words per minute to a listener who can comprehend a thousand words per minute, there is a nine hundred-words-per-minute comprehension gap. A speaking speed of one hundred words per minute doesn't demand our full attention, so we tune out the speaker. We think of other things, and periodically we check back in with the speaker to see if anything interesting is going on. How many times have you seen people checking their emails or texts while in a meeting or a presentation? While they are not fully engaged, many people are still capable of being reasonably attentive while performing another task. But if we become more interested in what we're thinking about than in the speaker's words, it may be quite a while before we tune back in to what the person is saying.

Everyone has a need to be listened to. What a wonderful service we provide, therefore, if we are great active listeners. The manager who is a skillful active listener fills an important need for every employee on the staff.

THE ACTIVE LISTENER

Active listeners possess several traits and skills, all of which can be developed over time. For one thing, they encourage the other person to talk. When active listeners finally talk, they don't turn the conversation back to themselves. They continue the other person's line of communication. They use certain phrases or gestures to signal that they are truly interested in what is being said.

Looking at someone who is talking to you indicates that you're interested in what the person has to say. Occasionally nodding your head affirmatively indicates that you understand what the talker is saying. Smiling at the same time indicates that you are enjoying the conversation.

When discussing a problem with an employee, other thoughts are likely to enter your mind. You need to take control of those thoughts. While the person is discussing the problem, try to anticipate where the thought is going. What questions are likely to be asked? If someone is suggesting solutions to a problem, try to think of other solutions. Ideally, you should focus 100 percent on what the person is saying, but the comprehension gap is a reality. By controlling your stray thoughts, you can stay focused on the subject at hand, rather than on some extraneous idea.

If you are vexed by a particularly persistent thought while you're listening, you may want to stop the conversation briefly by saying, "Give me a moment to get this thought out of my mind so I can fully focus on what you're saying." Then write down the idea and get back to active listening. This will allow you to be fully present in the conversation and avoid sending the nonverbal message that your thoughts are elsewhere.

The same method works well if you find your ability to listen is being hampered by a reply you're formulating in your mind. If you find yourself breathlessly waiting for an opportunity to break into the conversation so you can reply to something that has been said, you're not actively listening. Again, you want to take a moment to respectfully interrupt the conversation, make a note of your thought, then refocus.

A well-placed comment indicates to the talker that you have a genuine interest in what she has to say.

- "That's interesting."
- "Tell me more."
- "Why do you suppose she said that?"
- "Why did you feel that way?"

In fact, just saying, "That's interesting. Tell me more," will make you a brilliant conversationalist in the minds of everyone with whom you come in contact.

The height of active listening is restating what you believe you've heard. Restating is powerful for two reasons. It sends a clear message that you are engaged in the conversation and it significantly reduces the chance that you are mistaken in your understanding of what is being said.

To utilize restating, you simply inject yourself after an important point has just been made by saying something like, "Let me see if I understand what you are saying," then provide your version of what you think you just heard. Once stated, you then ask the person you're listening to if you got it right. By doing this, you are sending a clear message that you are placing value on what the person is saying.

Being an active listener also means that all three forms of communication are in accord. That means that the words you use, your facial expressions, and your tone of voice all give the same meaning. The speaker will receive a confusing message if you say, "That's interesting. Tell me more," but have a frown on your face or are speaking in a sarcastic tone. Another mixed message is to respond well verbally but look away from the speaker or become distracted by a stray thought, intended reply, or document. Would you have confidence that this listener is really interested in what you are saying?

CONVERSATION TERMINATORS

Once a manager achieves a reputation for being an outstanding listener, the staff lines up to discuss many matters. Some people will overstay their welcome. They may even think talking to you beats working. You need to have some tools in your managerial toolbox to wind up these conversations.

The verbal conversational terminators are known to just about anyone who has held a job:

- "I appreciate your coming in."
- "It was nice talking to you."

- "You have given me a lot to think about."
- "Let me think about that a while and get back to you."

There are also some more subtle conversation terminators that you may have heard. You should be aware of them for two reasons: First, so that you can immediately recognize them when a more experienced executive uses them on you, and second, so you can use them when they seem appropriate.

If you've ever had a conversation in someone's office and, while you're talking, watched your host reach over and rest a hand on the telephone receiver even though the telephone hasn't rung, that's a conversation terminator. It says, "I hope you leave soon, because I want to make a phone call." Another technique is for the person to pick up a piece of paper from the desk and glance at it periodically during your conversation. By holding the paper in his hand, your host is saying, "I have something to take care of as soon as you depart."

Another conversation terminator is the one where the host turns in her chair behind the desk to a side position as though about to get up. If that doesn't work, she stands up. That always gets the message across. This approach may seem too direct, but sometimes it becomes necessary.

Occasionally, you'll have an employee who is having such a good time visiting with you that all the signals are ignored. In that case, a verbal terminator that always works is, "I have really enjoyed the conversation, but I am sure we both have a lot we need to get done." That is not rude when someone has ignored all other invitations to depart.

When an employee or colleague comes into your office who you know in advance is not going to pick up any of your signals, you can announce at the beginning that you have only a limited amount of time and if that is not enough, then the two of you will need to schedule a time to meet later. You will find this strategy works quite well. Your visitors will usually say what they need to within the allotted time frame.

It is important that you recognize these conversation terminators. Of course, you should try to keep your conversations meaningful enough to preclude their use on you and your use of them on others. There are many more, but you'll compile your own list and find that different people have their own favorite conversation terminators.

LISTENING SUMMARY

People enjoy being around someone who shows a genuine interest in them. Good listening skills carry over into many aspects of both your professional and personal life. The interesting thing is that you can start out using these techniques because you realize people will like being with you. There is nothing wrong with this attitude. You become well liked and your team members get a manager who makes them feel good about themselves.

Everyone gains from such an arrangement. You may need to work hard on your active listening skills, but eventually they'll become second nature. At first, you may consider this type of behavior to be role-playing. But after a while you'll be unable to tell when the role-playing has stopped and it's actually you: After practicing these new listening habits, you become very comfortable with them and they become part of your regular behavior. You'll derive a great deal of personal satisfaction from being the kind of person others enjoy being around. You'll also be a much more effective manager.

6

THE NEW MANAGER'S JOB
AND PITFALLS TO AVOID

SO WHAT REALLY IS THE MANAGER'S JOB?

There are many ways to answer that question, but the most helpful is to look at management much the same as an actor would look at a role. As a manager you need to play many roles—coach, standard setter, performance appraiser, teacher, motivator, visionary, and so forth. You select the appropriate role based on the situation you're in and the objectives that you want to accomplish. Often, new managers are given the advice to "just be yourself." This is actually bad advice. It will prevent you from using the different roles that will make you a successful and effective manager.

Another mistake many new managers make is believing that their role is to be directive—that is, to tell others what to do, how to do it, and make sure it gets done. This may be part of the job or necessary to do sometimes. What enables you and your employees to succeed in the long run, however, is helping your employees to become self-directed. This means that you must get their support and commitment, share power with them, and remove as many obstacles to their success as possible.

THE MANAGER'S MAJOR RESPONSIBILITIES

Most management experts agree that managers have certain main responsibilities no matter where they work or who works for them. These chief responsibilities include hiring, communicating, planning, organizing, training, monitoring, evaluating, and firing. The better and more comfortable you become with these responsibilities the easier the job of managing becomes. These eight responsibilities are addressed throughout the book, but let's define them here:

1. *Hiring* is finding individuals with the skills or potential skills and commitment and confidence to succeed on the job.
2. *Communicating* is sharing the vision, goals, and objectives of the organization with your employees. It also means sharing information about what is happening in your department, unit, group, or business community.
3. *Planning* is deciding what work needs to be done to meet the goals of your department that, in turn, meets the goals of the organization.
4. *Organizing* is determining the resources that are needed to perform each job or project and deciding which staff members do what.
5. *Training* is assessing the skill level of each of your employees to determine skill gaps, and then providing instructional opportunities to close these gaps.
6. *Monitoring* is making sure that the work is being done and that each of your employees is succeeding with projects and assignments.
7. *Evaluating* is assessing the performance of individual team members, providing them with valuable feedback, and comparing their performance to the levels needed for that person and the team to be successful.
8. *Firing* is removing people from the team who are not able to make the contributions necessary for themselves or the team to be successful.

GENUINE CONCERN

One way to perform your job well is to give full attention to the needs of the people in your area of responsibility. Some leaders make the mistake of thinking that the concern they show for their employees will be interpreted as a sign of weakness. Genuine concern, however, is a sign of strength. Showing interest in the welfare of your people doesn't mean you'll "cave in" to unreasonable demands. Unfortunately, many new managers fail to recognize this fact. They are unable to differentiate between concern and weakness.

Your concern must be genuine. You cannot fake it. Genuine concern means seeing that your people are properly challenged, that they're appropriately recognized, that they're rewarded when they perform well, and that they receive accurate and timely feedback on their performance.

You can't start off by complacently telling yourself, "I'm going to be Mr. Nice Guy." You must seriously take on the burden of responsibility for these people. In fact, you and your team are mutually responsible for one another. You must see to it that the objectives of the company and the objectives of your team members are not at cross-purposes. Your people should realize that they can achieve their own objectives only by doing their part in helping the company achieve its overall goals.

Your team members look to you for leadership. You serve as interpreter for the employees, as you are a primary source of information on the organization's broader strategies and goals. A vital part of your role is keeping your people informed. Trying to keep your people in the dark or being stingy with information will work against you. Your team members will just look elsewhere in the organization to fill the information void you have created. They will not only receive the message that you don't respect them by your unwillingness to provide information they need to be successful, they also may receive incorrect information since they come by it indirectly or secondhand.

PITFALLS TO AVOID

Most first-time managers do not supervise a large group of people. Therefore, there may be a temptation to become overly involved in the work of your handful of employees. As you advance, you will likely be responsible for more people. It is impossible to be involved in every facet of the work of thirty-five people, so begin now to distance yourself from the details of each task and concentrate on the overall project.

One of the dangers for a first-time manager is that you now may be managing someone who does your old job, and you may consider it more important than other tasks. It is human nature to think that what we do is more important than what others do, but that doesn't work when you're the manager. It is not a balanced approach to management. You must resist the temptation to make your old job your occupational hobby, simply because it is familiar and comfortable.

Often, your first managerial job is a project leader or lead position. You manage others, but you still have tasks of your own to perform; you wear two hats. If this is your situation, you must stay interested and involved in the details for a while. When you move into a full-time management position, however, don't take an occupational hobby with you, lest it distract you from the bigger picture.

Of course, don't carry this advice to the extreme. When some people move into management, they refuse to help their staff at a "crunch and crisis" time. They read management journals while their staff is frantically meeting deadlines; they are now "in management." This is just plain stupid. You can build great rapport with your staff if, at crunch time, you roll up your sleeves and help resolve the crisis.

As you transition into your management role stay aware of the most common management mistake—delegating responsibility without authority. You have likely experienced it. Can you think of a time when you were given an assignment but not the authority to be successful? The result was that you were either not able to complete the task or you went back to your supervisor to request the authority you needed. The bottom line is that you were placed in an unwinnable situation.

It is likely that your supervisor did not do this intentionally. He just may have not thought through the authority you would need. Similarly, you will likely not do the same intentionally to the people you are supervising. As you assign tasks to the people you now lead ask yourself whether you are delegating enough authority for them to succeed. You may even want to discuss the question when you make the assignment.

You will succeed as a manager when your people are successful. Part of setting them up for success is making sure you delegate authority with responsibility.

A BALANCED VIEWPOINT

In all management matters, maintain a sense of balance. You have undoubtedly encountered managers who say, "I'm a big-picture guy; don't bother me with the details." Unfortunately, this trait is true of many managers. They become so big picture-oriented that they are oblivious to the details that bring the picture together. They also may be insensitive to how much effort is required to complete the detailed work.

Other managers, including many first-time managers who have been promoted from a line position, are so enthralled with detail that the overall objective is lost. Balance is required.

7

DEALING WITH YOUR SUPERIORS

CHAPTER 6 DISCUSSED A MANAGER'S ATTITUDE toward employees. It is also important for managers to pay attention to their attitude toward superiors. Their future success depends on both their subordinates and their superiors.

If you've just had a big promotion, you may be feeling grateful toward your boss. You may also be pleased that senior executives were perceptive enough to recognize your talent. But your new responsibilities demand a new level of loyalty from you. After all, you are now a part of the management team. You can't be an effective team member unless you identify with the team.

LOYALTY TO THEM

Loyalty to employers has become less common. Blind loyalty has never been a good idea, but being loyal doesn't mean selling your soul. Presumably, your company and your boss are not out to rip off society. If they are, they're not worth your loyalty. More important, you shouldn't be working for them.

So let's assume you're convinced that your company's purpose is honorable and you're pleased to be associated with its goals. The kind of loyalty we're talking about has to do with carrying out policies or decisions that are morally valid. Let's assume your position with the company allows for some input into decisions having to do with your area of responsibility. You must make every effort to see that such input is as thoughtful and broadly based as possible. Don't be the kind of narrow-sighted manager whose recommendations are designed to benefit only your own area of responsibility. When this happens, your advice will be discredited and eventually will no longer be sought because it does not reflect a broad perspective.

If you make recommendations that are broadly based and consistent with the greater good of the company, your advice will be seen as more valuable and be sought more often. The important thing here is that your contribution to the decisionmaking process can go beyond your own managerial level.

On occasion, a decision or policy will be made that is directly contrary to the opinions you've expressed; you'll be expected to support that decision or policy, and you may even have to implement it. If you don't already know, ask your boss why the decision was made. Explain to her that you would like to understand the reasoning behind the decision so you can better implement it. Find out what important considerations went into formulating the policy and the processes that led to the decision.

The philosophy of following the leader blindly no longer holds in today's world. Nonetheless, many managers and senior executives may wish blind loyalty still existed.

If you are going to do an outstanding job of managing, you have a right to understand the reasons behind major company decisions and company policies. Perhaps your managers follow higher authority blindly and guard information about top management as if all of it is top secret—and you're the enemy.

If this is their approach, they are making the mistake mentioned in Chapter 6 of not providing the information you need to be effective. Again, the information void will be filled, but this time by you. Unfortunately, you are going to have to adapt to their preference for withholding information. If it is a policy that affects other departments you need information about, you may be able to find out from people at your own organizational level in those departments. If a friend in Department X has a boss who shares information freely with employees, it may be relatively simple to find out what you want to know from your friend.

YOU HAVE A RESPONSIBILITY

When working and communicating with your manager, you have many responsibilities in building a good relationship with this person. You need to do the following:

✍ Keep your manager informed of your plans, actions, and projects.

✍ Be considerate of your manager's time and try to schedule appointments or meetings at your manager's convenience.

✍ Be well-prepared. Present your arguments and concerns logically and objectively and have examples and facts to back up what you're saying.

✍ Be willing to listen to your manager's point of view. Your manager may have experience or information you are lacking that led you to a different conclusion.

DEALING WITH AN UNREASONABLE MANAGER

We do not live in a perfect world. As a result, at some time in your career, you may be in the uncomfortable position of reporting to a difficult manager—someone who is not doing a good job of managing or may be unpleasant to be around. Unfortunately, you cannot fire an incompetent or unreasonable boss, as much as you might like to.

Let's be candid. If a long-term manager is difficult, you have to wonder why the situation is allowed to exist. If everyone in the organization knows this person is miserable to work for, why does senior management allow the situation to continue?

On the other hand, if everyone else in the department thinks the manager is doing a great job and you're the only one having a problem, that's a far different situation. If you are new to the department, you might give it some time by not reacting too quickly. The problem may resolve itself if you do excellent work and are not highly sensitive. You may find it is style and not substance.

If your manager is really causing problems for you or your direct reports, however, you definitely need to do something about it, and you do have some viable choices. Depending on the political environment and culture of your organization, different strategies may work better than others. Right off the bat, you should try to communicate directly with your boss. Tell her what's up. Explain in a professional and diplomatic manner how her behaviors, policies, or actions are having a bottom-line business impact. Make it about the organization, not the person. Start the discussion with a constructive, nonjudgmental statement such as, "We may be missing some opportunities to be more effective."

For example, suppose your manager is giving different instructions to your staff than you are. This is causing shipping delays and customer complaints—bottom-line concerns. Even if he doesn't like hearing it, your boss should appreciate your directness in pointing out this problem.

Supervisors often don't realize that they may be doing something unhelpful. They need feedback. You should always try to meet with your boss on a regular basis to discuss any issues that need addressing. If your manager doesn't think these meetings are necessary, you should insist. Try to explain how regular communication can prevent problems from springing up and help make you both more effective.

On another note, if you have not been assigned a mentor, you owe it to yourself to find one. You need someone within the organization who is well-respected and aware of the organization's political dynamic. You need someone who can guide you and share insights gained over time.

Let's say you have the type of boss who does not like to get feedback from employees. What do you do now? Here is where understanding the politics and culture of your organization comes in and where your mentor can be of great assistance. You may need to get someone else to speak to your boss. It could be someone on the same level, a mutual friend you have in the organization, human resources—if their reputation is good and they play fair—or you may have to take the biggest risk of all and jump levels to have that person's boss handle the situation. Keep in mind that when you do this, you will probably sever your relationship with your boss forever, but you may have no other choice. You are undertaking this action for your team or the overall benefit to the organization.

You do have one final option. You may have to say to yourself, "The boss is difficult. She has been difficult for many years; no one seems to care or is willing to change her behavior. This may not be the best place for me since my boss has a great influence on my success. Perhaps I need to find a position in another department or in another organization."

DRIVING GOOD PEOPLE AWAY

It is true that many companies take advantage of a downturn in the economy to drive their people harder, recognizing that it's more difficult for people to leave. There are reasons why such an attitude is shortsighted. First, top-flight people can always find other jobs, no matter how tough the economy. The lesser-talented people are the ones who cannot. So, this maladjusted company attitude drives away the more talented and retains the less talented. That is a recipe for mediocrity. Second, in a tough economy, appreciating all of your staff, including the very talented managers, places the organization in a stronger position to compete effectively. A company with a capable and valued staff will prevail every time over a company that treats its employees merely as units of production. The long-range prospects for the latter style are not good.

One of the surest ways to eventually drive good people from your company is to perpetuate bad management. This may sound obvious, but many new managers can't wait to start treating their people the way they've been treated. They may be taught the more humane management approach, but they go with what they know. They are anxious to take their turn "dishing it out" after all these years of "taking it."

The lesson of the unreasonable boss is to be the kind of leader you wish you had, not to carry on the tradition. Do not adopt the management style you hate and get even with people who had nothing to do with the unprofessional management under which you have suffered. If you're working for an unreasonable boss, do society a favor and say, "Let it end with me."

KNOWING YOUR MANAGER'S
PERSONALITY STYLE

There have been countless books and articles written on the topic of managing your boss. The main premise of all these writings is the same: If you know the personality style of your manager, you will be able to manage this person by knowing what your manager needs and wants and how he likes to work and communicate. If you can be responsive to their style, you will have fewer problems at work.

There are four basic manager personality types. Some have a distinct personality style while others are combinations of two or three styles. Read the descriptions that follow and see if you can identify your manager's style. If you can, you will be more successful working with your manager.

✍ **The Monopolizers.** These managers like to be in charge of everything and are fast decisionmakers who stick to their decisions, are very organized, and are bottom line oriented. They are "my way or the highway" types. If they were doing target practice, their saying would be "ready, fire, aim" (as opposed to the usual saying of "ready, aim, fire"). If you work for monopolizers, make sure you are clear and direct with your communication, have all your facts ready, and are prepared to do what they say. Sometimes monopolizers project an image of being inclusive and empowering managers who want to incorporate all the team members' opinions into their decisions. With managers who project this style, watch the outcome more than the process—they may indeed be committed monopolizers once you get past the participative outer layer.

✍ **The Methodicals.** These managers are analytic types who like to take their time gathering information and data before making a decision. They are very steady and predictable and overly concerned with accuracy. If they were doing target practice, their saying would be "aim, aim, aim." They hate to make decisions and are always looking for more or different information. If you work for methodicals, be patient! Realize that they are trying to make the best decision based on all data. When you give your opinion or your suggestion, make sure that you have analyzed it carefully and can explain your reasoning and logic to them.

✍ **The Motivators.** These are the bosses who are fun to be around. They are charismatic and seem to have good relationships with everyone in the organization. They have high energy, creativity, and a competitive spirit. However, they often talk more than necessary. They like to get things started, but completing them is another story. If they were doing target practice, their saying would be "talk, talk, talk." They just love to talk and have fun and sometimes work gets the backseat. When communicating with motivators, make sure to do a lot of chit-chatting. Ask them how their weekend was, how the kids are, and so forth. Before they can get down to business, they need to socialize.

✍ **The Mixers.** You probably have a relaxed and laid-back work environment if your supervisor is a mixer. Mixers have a strong sense of dedication, are loyal team members, patient, sympathetic, understanding, dependable, and great at keeping the peace. Their Achilles' heel is that they shy away from conflict and do not like change. They favor the status quo. They may also be more concerned with how people are doing than with getting the work out. If they were doing target practice, their saying would be "ready, ready, ready." They are always there for you. The needs of others come before their own. When working with Mixers, put on your feelings and teamwork hat. You will need it!

Figure 7-1 summarizes the four personality styles described above.

FIGURE 7-1. YOUR SUPERVISOR'S STYLE	
MONOPOLIZER	**METHODICAL**
• in charge	• analytical
• direct	• wants lots of information
• quick decisions	• prizes accuracy
• organized	• slow decisions
• be ready with the facts	• be ready to support your position
MOTIVATOR	**MIXER**
• fun to be around	• dedicated & loyal
• charismatic & social	• patient & understanding
• high energy	• conflict-adverse
• may not follow-through	• dislikes change
• be ready for small talk	• needs you to be a team player

Be attentive to the last bullet in each category. It gives you insights as to how you will need to be ready to respond to a person with that style.

YOUR SUPERVISOR'S PREFERENCES

Your work life will be easier and more enjoyable if you are attentive to your supervisor's preferences. As an example, if your supervisor tends to focus on the big picture and has little tolerance for details you will just frustrate yourself and her if you insist on discussing small details. Similarly, if your supervisor is detail-oriented you will need to be prepared to provide detailed information when you are working with him. Otherwise you will likely be asked to come back with more information and run the risk of being seen as poorly prepared.

Here are the four important aspects of your supervisor's preferences to which you need to be attentive:

1. How she processes information.
2. The level of detail your supervisor prefers.
3. His level of immediacy, meaning how concerned he is about having all the latest information right away or if he prefers that new information be presented after it has been contemplated.
4. The topic that interests her and the topics for which she has little interest.

Figure 7-2 will help you with this process.

FIGURE 7-2. YOUR SUPERVISOR'S PREFERENCES	
HOW DOES HE OR SHE PREFER TO PROCESS INFORMATION?	**WHAT LEVEL OF DETAIL DOES HE OR SHE PREFER?**
• verbally • in writing • graphically • in presentations	• extensive detail • overviews and summaries • big concepts
WHAT IS HIS OR HER INNATE LEVEL OF IMMEDIACY?	**WHAT DOES AND DOES NOT INTEREST HIM OR HER?**
• wants new information right away • prefers you to process and consider information before you share it with them • would rather receive information at a regular time in the day or week	• what fascinates him or her • what does not interest him or her • what causes him or her to "check-out"

First go through the graphic with your supervisor in mind. You may even want to openly discuss the topics with your supervisor. Doing so will send a clear message that you are serious about being responsive to his preferences to facilitate successful interactions. Having thought through your supervisor's preferences it is now in your best interest to keep them in mind when you are interacting with him.

Do not limit this process to your direct supervisor. There are likely other people in your organization with whom you need to work successfully. Ask yourself the same questions about them then adapt your methods accordingly. By doing so you will be seen as responsive, efficient, and effective.

8

CHOOSING A MANAGERIAL STYLE OF YOUR OWN

IF YOU LOOK AT THE HISTORY of management styles, you'll notice that two styles have dominated. Managers were either autocratic or diplomatic. Today, however, the best managers know that there are more than two styles of managing and they need to be good in multiple styles. Before discussing the necessity of having an "aware" managerial style, let's look at the autocratic and diplomatic styles.

THE AUTOCRAT VS. THE DIPLOMAT

It is difficult to believe that we still see the old-fashioned autocrat in management today. You have to wonder why this is so. Partly it has to do with the fact that so many managers are given no training. They are left to find their own way, so they begin acting as they think they should. They think in terms of being a "boss." Autocrats also believe that if they take a softer approach, employees will take advantage of them, thinking that a softer approach will be seen as a sign of weakness.

Another possibility is that it takes more time to be a diplomatic manager. These managers spend time with people explaining not only *what* is to be done but also *why* it's done. The autocratic type of boss doesn't want to be bothered. This person's attitude is "Do it because I said so." The diplomat realizes that the more people understand what and why, the better they perform.

Autocrats want to make every decision and view the staff as providing robotic responses to their commands. The autocrat pushes the buttons, the staff snaps to, and it happens. The diplomat knows that the time spent up front getting everybody involved pays off with huge dividends down the road.

The autocrat engenders fear while the diplomat builds respect and even a degree of affection. The autocrat causes people to mutter under their breath, "Someday, I'll get even with this SOB." The diplomat causes people to say, "He respects us and cares for us. I'd walk the last mile for him. All he needs to do is ask."

The autocrat believes the diplomat is a wimp. The diplomat believes the autocrat is a dictator. The difference is that the autocrat uses authority constantly, while the diplomat uses it judiciously.

People working for the autocrat believe they are working *for* someone, while those reporting to the diplomat believe they are working *with* someone.

THE NEED FOR AWARENESS

As a new manager, you should use the "awareness approach" when selecting an appropriate managerial style. In order to be *aware*, you must use the right amount of *control* and *encouragement* for each of your employees.

Control is:

- Telling employees what to do
- Showing them how to do it
- Making sure that the work is done

Encouragement is:

- Motivating
- Listening
- Running interference so employees can do what is expected of them

Some employees need high amounts of control and encouragement, and others need little. Then there are those who fall somewhere in between. In order to use the awareness approach in selecting a managerial style, you have to determine what each of your employees needs from you. That is, how much control and encouragement do they need from you?

The amount of control or encouragement each employee requires will depend on what she is working on or what is occurring in the department. For example, if an employee needs to learn how to operate a new piece of equipment, she will need a lot of control. If there are talks of downsizing and cutting back throughout the company, your team members will need a great deal of encouragement.

The following graphic and descriptions will help you see the connection between what your staff needs from you and how much control or encouragement you give them; in other words, are you being aware of their needs?

- **Type A.** This is someone who is very motivated to do well but lacks the skill or knowledge to succeed. Being aware, you know this person needs mostly control from you.
- **Type B.** This is someone who has lost motivation but has the skills to do the job. Being aware, you know this person needs lots of encouragement.
- **Type C.** This is someone who performs very well and is also motivated. Being aware, you know this person needs little control and encouragement.
- **Type D.** This is someone who lacks both ability and willingness to perform. Being aware, you know this person needs lots of control and encouragement.
- **Type E.** This is someone who has medium amounts of skill and motivation. Being aware, you know this person needs medium amounts of control and encouragement.

ASSESSING YOUR PEOPLE

To apply this to your team, first you need to assess your people based on the two criteria we are using—their level of motivation and their level of skills and knowledge that relate to their responsibilities. First you assess them then you plot them on the graphic. The more motivated they are the closer they are to the top of the graphic. The more they possess job-related skills and knowledge the closer they are to the right of the graphic.

YOUR RESPONSE

Looking at Figure 8-1 and where you have plotted your people, you are now aware of how to respond. The closer to the left the person is indicated, the more control you need to exert. The closer to the bottom of Figure 8-1 they are indicated, the more encouragement you need to provide.

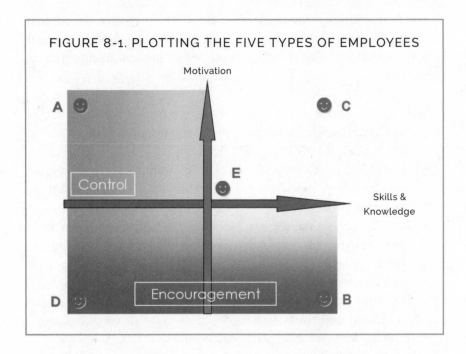

FIGURE 8-1. PLOTTING THE FIVE TYPES OF EMPLOYEES

Let's look at a workplace scenario and see how aware you can be. Suppose you're heading a large independent project at a telecommunications company. One of the employees assigned to you, Andy, is used to working independently on his assignments. Andy likes calling all the shots and really enjoys his work. He always gets excellent results and his internal clients are thrilled with his performance. Working on your project, however, you notice that he finds it difficult to plan and communicate and make decisions with the other team members. In addition, Andy disparages the whole concept of working as a team and says it is a waste of time. He has expressed his unhappiness with being on this new project.

Being aware, what type (A to E) is Andy and what does he need from you as his manager? The answer: Even though Andy is an experienced employee in his regular work, this is not true on your project. Andy needs control and encouragement. He needs guidance in how to work with others in a team environment and support for the difficult transition he is making. Andy's type is D for this project, although he is probably a C type on his own assignments.

Here is a suggestion that will make managing much easier for you. On the way to work, think about all your direct reports every few days. Think about what their type is on all the different assignments and projects that you have them doing. Then be aware. Think about what they need from you. If you are already giving it to them, you have the perfect scenario. If you are not, decide what you need to do differently. You'll find this one suggestion will make a huge difference for you as a manager. Try it.

MANAGEMENT IS SITUATIONAL

No single management style is always appropriate. A situation you are facing may dictate a different style than you would commonly use. When you are confronted with a short deadline emergency for which absolutely no defects are acceptable, you may need to be more directive than usual. By contrast, the start of a major project where you need all team members to agree to the methods that will be used may require you to be more hands-off than normal as you allow a consensus to surface. While you will develop a baseline management style with time, you will need to adapt it in some situations based on the nature of the challenges you are facing.

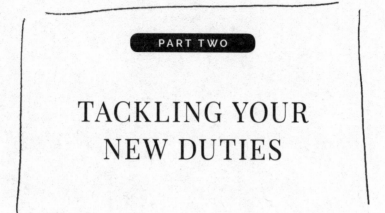

PART TWO

TACKLING YOUR NEW DUTIES

As a manager you will need to become proficient at spotting and cultivating talent. It is like being the coach of a sports team where your success depends on recruiting the best you can get and then making them better.

9

BUILDING A TEAM DYNAMIC

IN RECENT YEARS, GETTING WORK DONE through teams has become standard practice in many organizations. This is true for a couple of reasons. One reason is synergy. Generally, it has been proven in workplaces that groups make better decisions than an individual working alone. Another reason for having teams is that communications technology and limitless information sources make it unlikely that a manager can know as much as all of the employees. The manager can no longer be the expert. In many fields and occupations, managers have people working for them who have specific expertise far beyond theirs. It is not possible in these instances to tell people what to do. The manager needs to support and guide employees and let them come up with work-related answers.

If you really want your team to succeed and perform at the highest levels possible, you need to build a team dynamic. A team dynamic is the willingness and the ability to work in an interdependent fashion where team members need to rely on other team members to accomplish their work or to achieve the goals of the team. In order to build a team dynamic, the following six factors are essential:

1. Open communication
2. Empowerment
3. Clear roles and responsibilities
4. Goal clarity

5. An effective leader
6. A reward and accountability system for both individual team members and for the entire team

OPEN COMMUNICATION

Consider this scenario: A young manager-to-be accompanied her mentor, an experienced manager, to observe a high-performing team in operation at a manufacturing company. When she first walked into the room, she said to her mentor, "Oh boy, this is a dysfunctional team! Listen to the way they're arguing with each other." The mentor replied, "Pay attention, this is actually a great team."

It took the manager-to-be several minutes to understand what the older manager meant. This team was in conflict. The members were strongly disagreeing with one another on the best way to improve their product. It is often a good sign when this kind of friction exists. A team that cares passionately about its task is very positive. It had open, honest communication. That is a team dynamic!

EMPOWERMENT

You get a strong team dynamic when you empower your team members by giving them the right to make decisions concerning the work they are doing. Of course, you set boundaries of time, money, choices, and so forth. But once you give the team the final power of decisionmaking, you will notice that a confidence, camaraderie, and feeling of strength emerge. Make sure you do not empower teams that are not ready for it. That can be disastrous, and many new managers make this big mistake. They probably do it because they want to get into the good graces of the team. Make sure the team is ready for empowerment or you and the organization will suffer from the consequences of its poor decisions.

CLEAR ROLES AND RESPONSIBILITIES

Can you walk up to any one of your team members and have this person clearly define his role and responsibilities on the team? Can you walk up to any one of your team members and have this person clearly define the roles and responsibilities of every other team member, including yourself as the leader? When team members can do this, they know what is expected of them and what is expected of every other team member. They also know on whom they can count for help with their work. All of this leads to an effective team dynamic.

GOAL CLARITY

Does everyone you manage know the goals of both your team and the entire organization? Make sure they do. Keep it simple—ideally down to one sentence for each. Your team's goal statement could be something like, "Our goal is to provide our internal customers with accurate, timely, and valuable market data at the lowest cost." This is perfect—it covers it all. Once you have worked with your team to develop your simple goal statement, make sure everyone knows it and has it memorized. You may want to post it in prominent locations, always include it at the top of meeting agendas, or include it below the signature on your internal emails.

When I was in Singapore to train some new managers based on this book I came across an excellent example of an organization with goal clarity. Over the employee entrance to a large hotel in the downtown area was a goal statement that presumably applied to everyone who worked there. In illuminated foot-high letters were four words that made everyone's task clear: Creating Memorable Hotel Experiences. I applaud the brilliance of such a simple and memorable goal that applies to every member of the team. The corporate website for the organization that operates the hotel identifies those four words as the corporate vision that is applied to their thirty properties on three continents. It is not surprising that the hotel I passed by has impressively high online ratings.

Why is this important? Organizational goal clarity keeps everyone moving in the same direction. It gives them the standard against which they can make decisions and decide on a course of action. The simple standard is whether the decision or outcome they are considering works for or against the goal. If it supports the goal, proceed. If it works against the goal, stop.

Goal clarity facilitates a number of valuable outcomes:

- It allows your people to make more of their own decisions.
- Fewer issues will need to be escalated to you to resolve.

- Decisions will be made more quickly.
- Your organization will be more agile, making it better able to adapt quickly to changes.
- Your organization will be more efficient.

Obviously, your team members will be confronted with situations that are not black-and-white as to whether they support or work against the goal. These will have to be brought to you. But often in their daily efforts, they will be able to make unhindered progress by just using the goal statement as their guide.

Once you've settled in and gotten to know your team and its role, work with the team to develop a simple and clear goal statement. It will fuel a much more empowered and entrepreneurial team dynamic.

EFFECTIVE LEADERSHIP

Read the following list. Check off the items that you currently do. Develop an action plan for any items not checked. When you are able to check off all the items, you are doing your part in building an effective team dynamic. As leader, you should do the following:

- Set clear goals for each team member and for the team.
- Give clear directions for those who need it.
- Share examples and experiences of your personal successes and mistakes in order to relate to the team.
- Emphasize the positive rather than the negative in your talks with your team.
- Give continual feedback to each team member and to the team— both positive and constructive.
- Use small successes to build team cohesiveness.
- Practice what you say.
- Express your and the organization's appreciation through rewards, if available.
- Develop a constructive relationship—you and the team are working together toward the same goals.
- Make change happen for the better by encouraging creativity and innovation.
- Encourage self-reliance and professional development.

- Encourage team members to express their views during conflict and share yours with them.
- Help your team see its connection to the larger organization, customers, and the community.

REWARD AND ACCOUNTABILITY SYSTEM

This last factor for building a strong team dynamic is the responsibility of the organization and the managers working together. Many organizations preach teamwork. You walk around the building and see posters with happy groups of people working and playing together. You read company mission statements and they say something about being the best team. People are assigned to teams, yet teamwork is lacking. Why is this? It is because the organization and its managers do not hold people accountable for working in teams or reward them for it.

If we truly expect people to cooperate with each other for the common good of the organization, we cannot just evaluate them, rate them, or give them performance appraisals solely for their individual contributions. We have to do all of that for their team contributions as well. When team members understand that you are holding them accountable based on how well they perform as team players, they quickly get the message that teams count. It beats those posters! You have to do the same thing with the reward system. That is, reward people for both their individual and team contributions.

Some managers claim that it is not a good practice to reward some team members more than others. They say that you will never have high-performing teams if you do that. Those managers should take a look at the most successful professional sports teams. They have team members who earn more than others based on the roles they play or their achievements. It works, and their team dynamic is likely strong. Look at many successful and effective work teams. You will often find individual team members making higher salaries or getting special rewards for their individual contributions. It works in those situations, and there is a strong team dynamic on those teams as well.

10

MANAGEMENT VERSUS LEADERSHIP

IT IS COMMON TO SEE THE WORDS *management* and *leadership* used in place of one another. This is understandable but doing so causes an important distinction to be lost. As a manager you need to both manage and lead but it is vital that you understand the difference.

At the risk of oversimplifying the difference, management is about controlling and leadership is about inspiring. Figure 10-1 expands on the distinctions.

FIGURE 10-1. MANAGEMENT VS. LEADERSHIP	
MANAGEMENT	**LEADERSHIP**
• More top down and directive	• More bottom up and participative
• More structured	• Less structured
• Focuses on methods	• Focuses on exceptions
• More directive	• More of a coaching dynamic
• More focused on correcting	• More focused on affirming
• Determines methods	• Establishes goals then lets team members determine their methods

The more you grow as a manager the more you will be able to use leadership methods. Doing so needs to be among your goals. As the workforce becomes better educated, informed, and transient, managers who are not also inspirational in their methods will be at a disadvantage.

11

MANAGING PROBLEM EMPLOYEES

NOT EVERY EMPLOYEE YOU MANAGE is going to be successful on the job. Someone who is performing poorly may require additional training, a transfer to another area where the employee may shine, or ultimately, outright dismissal. Too often, in large companies, managers unload their problem employees onto another department. This is not being fair to your fellow managers, unless you really believe that the employee will do better in a new department where there is a better match for her skills. In some companies, I have even seen managers promote their poor performers, just to get rid of them. When asked by the manager of the other department how the prospective candidate is performing in the current job, these managers are not always completely candid in their reply. I think the only correct policy in this situation is to be open and honest. Someday you may be looking at people in other departments as candidates for promotion into your own department, and the best way to reduce the chances of getting someone else's rejects is to never deliver that kind of cheap shot yourself.

You can probably relate to the following story involving a first-time manager. After reviewing performance appraisals of people one level below the job he was attempting to fill in his division, he selected three likely candidates. As is customary, he called the managers of these candidates and got a glowing report about one in particular. He promoted the candidate to his department and it ended up being a complete disaster. He had to terminate the candidate after a short period of time because of poor performance. The first-time manager then confronted the person who had made the recommendation and asked for an explanation, never dreaming he had been deceived. The answer he got was that the employee had not been satisfactory and the manager was tired of dealing with that employee. Because the previous manager was not candid, the first-time manager was tricked into doing the dirty work.

Of course, there is a great temptation to pay back such a manager in kind, but the solution is to make sure no one ever does that to you in the first place. Retaliation in an intra-company operation is not beneficial to anyone and will likely catch up with you if you pursue it.

REHABILITATION

There is nothing wrong, however, in attempting to rehabilitate an unproductive employee if it's done with the full knowledge of everyone involved. In the situation just described, for example, had the fellow manager sat down with the first-time manager and indicated that the employee was not doing a good job *but* there were strong reasons for wanting that employee to have another chance, the first-time manager might have taken the person. There have been many efforts like this one that have been successful. The job and the employee were not a good fit, but the employee had talent; the move to another area where that talent could be better used turned a less-than-satisfactory employee into a productive one.

Generally, however, you'll be much more effective as a leader if you can solve your own problems in your own department and not unload them onto another department. Companies use many testing devices to put people into jobs that align with their natural skillset. These devices range from simple five-minute tests to complex three-hour psychological evaluations. This is something your company either already does or should consider implementing. To emphasize my point again, you must always be conscious of the advantages of fitting employees to jobs at which they have the best chance to be successful. It is much easier to move people into jobs for which they are suited than to keep them in jobs they perform poorly, where you must then try to "educate" them. It just doesn't often work.

SERIOUS PERSONAL PROBLEMS

Some subordinates have personal problems that hinder their attendance and performance on the job. You would be quite naive to believe that alcohol, drugs, or serious family difficulties are not going to affect your management responsibilities.

Just because you're a manager doesn't mean you're equipped to handle every problem that comes your way. Many enlightened companies recognize this fact and maintain employee assistance programs. These programs are usually community supported, unless the company is large enough to justify an onsite service. Employee assistance programs have professional resources available, offer connections with chemical dependency programs, and know the services that exist within the community.

It's foolish for you as a manager to believe that you have the capacity and the resources to solve all problems. If you try to handle a situation beyond your professional competence, you run the risk of making the situation worse. As a manager, your responsibility is to see that the job is done within the boundaries of sound management principles. An employee's personal problem can interfere with accomplishing that objective. Although rescuing a human being is also a legitimate objective, doing so professionally and successfully is likely beyond your personal expertise.

Also, under the eyes of the law in most states, a manager is viewed as someone who is not qualified to give personal advice. The following case occurred several years ago in a computer manufacturing company in Salt Lake City. An assembly-line worker was late about half of the time, sometimes by as much as forty to fifty minutes. In addition, her performance was going downhill quickly. After a few weeks of this behavior, her manager spoke to her about it. The employee apologized and said that her young son's daycare center often opened late. She said she could not just leave her son on the doorstep and come to work. She also said she worried about her son all day because she did not know how good the center was and this was affecting her performance.

The manager replied, "Take my advice. Send your child to the daycare center where I send my children. It opens one hour earlier. If you do this, and I strongly suggest that you do, you will no longer be late and you will not have to worry about his care." The employee heeded the advice of the manager. Without going into the gory details, something unfortunate happened to the employee's young son at this new center. The employee, with the assistance of legal counsel, sued the company and won.

The court ruled that a manager is not qualified to give personal advice. The manager should have referred the individual to human resources or to a qualified service such as employee assistance. Switching daycare centers was up to the employee. Of course, you must listen to your employees and be supportive of what they're going through. Keep in mind that all your team members have challenging lives outside of work and they all have made adjustments to be at work.

You will probably need to have a candid discussion with the problem employee, but you will have to define your *overall* objective first. Your objective is to straighten out a work problem. You need to insist that troubled employees solve their problems, and you can direct them to the employee assistance program. You have to make it clear that if they choose not to solve the problem, they may be dismissed from employment. Take care not to do this in a cruel, uncaring way, but be sure to be firm so there is no misunderstanding.

You must be willing to listen, but not to the extent that problem employees spend a great deal of time in your office talking when they should be working. There is a fine line between being a good listener and allowing people to get away from their work for two hours while they drink coffee and pour out all their problems to you.

Sooner or later in your management career, you'll hear every conceivable problem (along with some inconceivable problems). People are involved in the totality of life; they have problems with spouses, partners, children, parents, lovers, coworkers, themselves, religion, diets, feelings of self-worth, and so on.

A cardinal rule in dealing with human frailties, one that will save you endless aggravation, is: *Don't pass judgment.* Solve the work problem, and point employees to resources where they can solve their personal problems. In some cases, you may demand that they solve the problem because of the negative impact it is having on their work performance.

HOW TO MANAGE CHALLENGING
BEHAVIOR TYPES

As a new manager, you are likely to run into many different types of employees whom you find challenging. When faced with managing them, you must deal with their behaviors. If you let these behaviors slide, you're giving the message that it's okay to keep behaving that way. Also, the rest of your staff will lose trust and confidence in you. They will feel you don't have the ability to handle difficult employees or you don't care.

The best way to confront these challenging behaviors is to tell the employees what behaviors they need to change and why. Then you need to listen to them—they may have good reasons for behaving the way they do. Next, get them to agree that they will change and discuss how you will monitor their behavior. Make sure to give positive feedback when they show signs of improvement. Of course, you want to come to this meeting prepared with examples of what you mean in case they doubt what you are saying or are not sure what you mean. Be positive. Make it clear that you want them to succeed. Explain how they will likely be more successful if they're able to change some of their problem behavior. It will be much easier for you if they do. Having to put someone into a discipline procedure can be a nightmare for everyone. You may have no other choice, but it should always be your last alternative. We will talk more about discipline in Chapter 14.

Here are a few of the types of employees that most new managers find particularly challenging. There are many others. Be on the outlook for them. Use the suggestions discussed here for confronting their unacceptable behavior.

- ✍ **The Attacker.** This person always disagrees with what you say or with what other team members say. The Attacker tries to undermine you and block the efforts of the group or department from achieving its goals.

- ✍ **The Comic.** This employee thinks her main job at work is to entertain others. Laughter in the workplace is great, but when done to excess it distracts from getting the job done.

- ✍ **The Deserter.** This individual either mentally or physically leaves the team. The Deserter drops out and stops contributing or even performing at work.

- ✍ **The Limelight Seeker.** This employee likes to take credit for the work done by others and goes around bragging about how crucial he is to the success of the organization.

- ✍ **The Moonlighter.** This employee treats her regular job as secondary to some other interest. At one company with about 3,500 employees, a manager had trouble figuring out one of his employees, named Joy. From August to January, Joy was the busiest employee you could imagine. She was always on the telephone or her computer or holding meetings in the conference rooms. But from February through July, Joy sat around with nothing to do. Take a wild guess what Joy was up to. She ran the company's football pool and made it her full-time job!

✍ **The Not-My-Jobber.** Employees like this do nothing unless it's in the job description. If you asked them to drop something at HR on the way to lunch, they will refuse. After all, where does it say that is one of their responsibilities or goals?

✍ **The Bleeding Heart.** These employees feel they have given their lives for the company, received nothing in return, and want everyone to know it. The Bleeding Heart usually has no life or no enjoyable life outside of work.

✍ **The Complainer.** This type likes to moan and complain about everything. It could be the workload, the other employees, the boss, the customer, the drive to work, the day of the week, the weather, and so on. Complainers are dangerous because their negativity easily spreads to others.

There are obviously many other types of challenging employees. As a manager, you need to expect all kinds of difficult behaviors and deal with them effectively as soon as possible.

12

HIRING AND INTERVIEWING

NOTHING YOU DO AS A MANAGER is more important than hiring well. Nothing. You cannot afford to take shortcuts in hiring decisions. One bad hiring decision can cost you hundreds of hours trying to address the problems created by that decision. If you are uncertain or uncomfortable about a prospective team member, trust your instincts. Do whatever is necessary to either further qualify or disqualify the candidate. Once you've made a job offer, your options are significantly limited. You need to be very confident you have the right person before you offer the job. Your certainty needs to be based on hard facts, research, reference checks, testing, and whatever other tools are available to you. This is not an area where you can afford to go on intuition alone. Hiring decisions are the most important decisions you will make as a manager.

There are probably as many different hiring practices as there are companies. It would be impossible to cover all the various methods, so let's make a couple of simple assumptions. Let's say the human resources department does the initial screening, but you have the ultimate decision-making authority as to who comes to work in your area of responsibility.

THE USE OF TESTS

With greater federal, state, and sometimes city participation in hiring procedures, your company may not do much testing of prospective employees.

There are many legal requirements to follow when testing. But testing is among the best ways to determine if candidates really have the skills they claim they do. There are many companies that pay their job candidates for their interview time because they keep candidates onsite an entire day in order to test them.

The quality of prospective employees will vary a great deal. When unemployment rates are high, you'll have a larger number of prospects to choose from. The reverse will be true when unemployment rates are low. There are even situations where available employees are so few that you'd consider hiring just about anyone who appears at your desk. So, there are forces beyond your control. We're focused here on situations you can control.

THE MISSING INGREDIENT

Almost without exception, managers say the most important ingredients in hiring a new employee are experience, qualifications, and education. They rarely come up with the missing ingredient: *attitude.*

You can hire an employee with all the experience, education, and qualifications you could hope for, but if the person has a bad attitude, you have just hired a problem employee. On the other hand, you can hire a person with less experience, education, and qualifications, and if that person displays an outstanding attitude, in all likelihood you will have an outstanding employee. Every experienced manager will agree that attitude is the most important element in an employee.

THE SCREENING PROCESS

Most managers do too much talking and too little listening during the interview process.

The interview with the prospect is a two-way sizing up. Naturally, the prospect wants the job, so most candidates will give you the answers they believe will maximize their chances.

Don't ask questions that are so difficult the prospect can't possibly answer them. Here are some questions to avoid that managers who pride themselves on being tough interviewers might ask:

- "Why do you want to work here?"
- "What makes you think you're qualified for this job?"
- "Are you interested in this job because of the salary?"

Dumb questions like these will make you a rotten interviewer. You must strive to put the prospect at ease so that you can carry on a conversation. Your aim is to get to know the prospect better, and that means not creating a confrontational tone during the interview. Rather, make statements or ask questions that will relax the applicant. Hold the tougher questions—but not the previous three questions—for later in the process. Consider the following sample interview.

MS. VALENCIA'S JOB INTERVIEW

The objective ought to be to find out if the applicant meets the job qualifications and *has a good attitude*. It makes sense to spend the early part of the interview engaging the applicant in some nonthreatening small talk.

Most applicants are nervous. They have a great deal riding on the results. The goal is to put the person at ease. By not immediately going to the business at hand, you let people know you're interested in them as individuals, apart from the job. It is important that you develop a comfortable relationship. If this person is going to work for you, it's the beginning of what could be years of daily contact. Even when candidates don't get the job, they will feel kindlier toward you and your company because you've shown a sincere interest in them.

Note: A company has many "publics": the general public, the customers, the industry it is part of, government agencies with which it interacts, its employees, and those who seek employment with the company. In one case, a woman who was a substantial patron of an upscale department store thought it would be fun to have a part-time job there. She resented the treatment she received when she applied for a job, and vowed never to set foot in the store again. That cost the store thousands of dollars a year from her purchases alone, not including the purchases all her friends would have made had she not shared her negative experience with them.

When the small talk is over, you might consider using this approach: "Ms. Valencia, before we start talking specifically about the position you've applied for, I'd like to tell you a little about our company. Because, while we're considering you, you're also considering us, so we want to answer any questions you may have about our company."

Then go ahead and tell her something about the company. Tell her what your purpose is, but don't spend too much time on statistics. Talk more about the company's relationship with its employees. Tell her anything in this area that is unique. You want her to get a feel for the company and its people. The purpose of this discussion is to give her a feel for the company she wishes to be a part of. It also gives her more opportunity to relax and feel comfortable.

We now arrive at the critical point in the interview. You want to ask questions that will give you some clues about this person's attitude. Most people-oriented managers (and that is most of them) cannot stand a vacuum, so if the applicant doesn't respond promptly, they tend to move in and try to help out. It's an act of kindness, but in this case it interferes with obtaining the crucial information you need to make a proper selection.

QUESTIONS TO ASK AND WHAT YOU CAN LEARN

Some sample questions to ask are:

- What did you like best about your last job?
- What did you like least about your last job?
- Tell me about your last manager.
- How did your last job allow you to grow professionally?
- How would you have restructured your last job if you could?

These are sample questions. You might devise some of your own that seem more appropriate for you, but until you do, consider using the ones suggested here.

Let's examine each question and what "right" and "wrong" answers can tip you off about employee attitude. If the answer to the first question—*What did you like best about your last job?*—mentions items such as the challenges of the job, the fact that the company promotes from within, that the company encourages and assists with educational opportunities, or that self-starters are appreciated, you have indications of someone who has recognized what is important in a sound working environment.

However, if the person's answer mentions things such as the office being closed every other Friday, which makes for nice long weekends; that the company provides many social activities, including both a bowling and a golf league; and that employees receive a paid vacation the first year with the company, you may have an applicant who is looking for a place to socialize. This person may be a social butterfly, and while there is nothing wrong with enjoying the company of others, that should not be the main reason for seeking the job.

Now let's discuss some potential answers to the second question about the items liked least on the last job. If the answer involves things such as being required to work overtime occasionally, being asked to come in on a Saturday, or being expected to give up a Saturday to go to a community college for acquiring skills that will be helpful on the job, (even though the company paid the seminar fee), those are not the answers you want to hear.

However, if the answer mentions that the company had no formal performance appraisal system, that the granting of raises didn't seem to bear any relationship to quality, or that there wasn't anything the person really disliked, but just feels there might be better opportunities elsewhere, those are thoughtful "burn no bridges" responses that suggest the candidate may be achievement-oriented and have good judgment.

Let's now move to the third question about the candidate's last manager. You'll note that the question is more open-ended. If the applicant really trashes her last supervisor and is generally negative, such as, "I don't think I ought to use the kind of language it takes to describe the SOB," that is a negative answer.

If we assume that the relationship with the last supervisor was terrible, but she answers, "Well, as with many bosses, we had our differences, but I liked and respected her," that is a diplomatic description of what may have been a bad situation. Job prospects who trash a former company or manager, even if deserved, say more about themselves than about the object of scorn. There is no way such an approach will advance the candidate's prospects for the job, so the insightful person will avoid negative comments about past working relationships.

The fourth question about how the applicant's last job allowed him to grow professionally can give you some insights into how candidates see their work. Someone who says they did not seek opportunities to grow professionally tells you they see work more as a job than a career. This is not bad but it is a valuable insight. If they tell you that the lack of opportunities for professional growth was a significant frustration you have a different insight on how they see employment. They are likely to be someone who sees work as a career and desires to advance. If they tell you they grew significantly they have given you an opportunity to discuss their professional goals.

The fifth question about how they would restructure their last position gives you a sense of how they see themselves fitting into a larger organization. A thoughtful and constructive answer tells you they see the bigger picture of how their contributions fit into the team. An answer that focuses on making their life easier at the expense of their colleagues is a danger sign. It tells you they may be focused on themselves to a fault.

QUESTIONS FROM APPLICANTS

You may also say to the applicant, "I've been asking you all these questions. Do you have any questions you'd like to ask of me?" The questions asked by the prospect can also provide clues to attitude.

What if questions from the prospect are along these lines?

- How many holidays do you close for each year?
- How much vacation do you give the first year?
- How long do you have to be here to get four weeks' vacation?
- What social activities does the company sponsor for the employees?
- What's the earliest age you can retire? How many years of service do you need?

Questions along this path indicate someone whose attitude is focused on getting out of work rather than into it. These samples are obvious, and again overdrawn to make the point. Some questions asked by the applicant may be subtler than this, but are still a tip-off of an undesirable attitude.

The following sample questions asked by applicants reflect a decidedly different attitudinal bent:

- Are people promoted based on performance?
- Can an outstanding performer receive a larger salary increase than an average performer?
- Does the company have regular training programs for employees, so they can broaden their work skills?

The thought may have entered your mind that the applicant is asking questions she thinks you want to hear. If that is so, it indicates you are not interviewing a dummy. Isn't an employee who can anticipate what the questions ought to be going to be a better staff member than an applicant who hasn't a clue?

An important strategy the manager brings to the interview process is silence. When a person does not answer right away, the silence may feel uncomfortable but if you jump in, you are not as likely to get the real answer.

The human resources department probably has oriented you in the types of questions that can and cannot be asked. You need to know the areas that you cannot move into because they are discriminatory, illegal, or both.

One forbidden question that comes to mind is, "Do you have to provide childcare for children?" This is one of the topics you cannot broach, and if the applicant asks about work hours, do not consider that a negative question. It may be triggered by a concern about childcare.

Another question from an applicant that should not be considered a negative has to do with health insurance. An employee asking about health benefits is showing responsibility. In short, it is the general tenor of questions that indicates an attitude problem. You must use your good judgment about which subjects denote attitude and which indicate responsibility.

As you obtain more experience with the interview process, you will become more skilled at it. In most job interviews, employee attitude is completely ignored. Typically, managers hold applications in their hands and say, "Well, I see you worked for the XYZ Company." Look that application over before you sit down with the applicant, not for the first time in the presence of the applicant. Then ask questions that reveal work attitudes.

THE EFFECTS OF UNEMPLOYMENT RATES

If your area has a high unemployment rate, you'll get better acting performances from prospective employees. People who desperately need steady work and a steady paycheck will take almost any kind of job. They will also be more adroit in selling the interviewer on why they should have the job.

With high unemployment, you'll also run into overqualified applicants. No doubt, you can empathize with these people in their current dilemma. But you should also realize that once other opportunities open up that make it possible for them to cash in on their full qualifications, you will lose these employees. First, if people are working below their capacity, they are not challenged in the job. Second, they will soon be looking for a better job.

Knowing the unwillingness of most managers to hire overqualified workers, some desperate applicants will shade their qualifications on the application, so that their greater education or experience is hidden. If you hire overqualified people, be prepared to lose them unless you will be able to advance them to a position more aligned with their qualifications.

GET A SECOND OR THIRD OPINION

Never hesitate to ask colleagues you respect to interview a candidate you are considering. Once you have narrowed the field of candidates down to a few, more input is always helpful. A second or third perspective can often provide you with observations or insights you missed. The more important a position, the more important it is that you make the right decision. Additional opinions will increase the chances that you get it right.

THE COMFORT-ZONE UNDERACHIEVER

A comfort-zone underachiever (CZU) is a person who is highly qualified but doesn't like being challenged. There are many of them around, but very few admit to it.

One of the main problems for CZUs is convincing you they genuinely want to work at a position that seems far below their capacity. They often get burned, in that they're not hired for jobs they want because they're overqualified. They soon discover that the way to handle this is not to list all their qualifications on the job application. The registered nurse who doesn't want to practice nursing may not indicate her training in that field. She may trim her list of qualifications to fit the clerical job she wants. Likewise, the schoolteacher who really can't stand young children in a classroom environment may not list all his credentials. Hiding previous work experience on the job application gets more difficult because the trained interviewer will zero in on any gaps. So, if our teacher really wants the job of maintaining the facilities grounds and gardens, his application might show him as a member of the school's "maintenance crew" rather than of its teaching staff.

Since you're interested in getting ahead and managing other people, you may have difficulty understanding applicants with this kind of personality. Don't underestimate them. They certainly aren't stupid. They see work from a different perspective than you do. It isn't a matter of who's right and who's wrong. Each attitude is right for the person involved.

Consider the forty-five-year-old CZU dentist who regrets the decision to spend the rest of his life looking into people's mouths and filling teeth. There are many unhappy people working at unsuitable jobs and we should respect CZUs for having the courage to change their situation. People resist change, and the combination of resisting change and knowing change is necessary leads to inner emotional conflict. That's what psychologists call avoidance: You're trapped by having to choose between two unpleasant alternatives because by doing nothing you're eating yourself alive.

The comfort-zone underachiever is trying to find "what's right for me." The jobs CZUs take may be temporary; they're at a crossroads in a period of reassessment. Often, they're looking for a job that won't divert them from their search. They are seeking a job requiring a minimum of attention, freeing them to think, to sort things out. Often, they'll go after a job that's highly repetitive in nature that can be done accurately without effort, thus enabling them to have their thoughts elsewhere. Certain jobs in your own company would doubtless drive you bananas in two hours, but there are people who enjoy doing those jobs; it's a matter of the proper fit.

WORK AND PLAY

The word *work* has a bad image for many people. To them, work is a form of punishment. If a person is a professional athlete and plays a sport for a living, it's work; but if a person plays the same sport for recreation, it's play. Perhaps it comes down to a distinction between have-to and want-to situations. That is why many people who are independently wealthy still work. For them, it's a want-to situation.

DESCRIBING THE JOB

In describing a job, you should include some basic information that everybody would like to have, so that they don't have to ask. Tell them the hours, starting salary, length of probationary period, and whether successful completion of the trial period generates a salary increase. You can also include a brief overview of the benefits package. By getting this basic information out of the way, you avoid cluttering up the open-ended questions that provide the attitude clues needed to make a hiring judgment.

Let's return to the sample interview with Ms. Valencia. In talking with her about the job, describe it in nontechnical terms—use terms she'll understand. The jargon and acronyms of your business may be commonplace to you, but they are a foreign language to new employees. The same situation exists with job descriptions. If they are written in technical jargon, they will mean very little to prospective employees.

JUDGMENT AND FOLLOW-THROUGH

While attitude and job skills are vitally important when assessing a candidate, few traits will better define a contributing team member than judgment and follow-through. A team member with both will be more self-directed and easier to lead. Without judgment he will be forever in need of assistance when he is confronted with decisions. Without follow-through he will require an excessive amount of your time and likely become resentful of being as closely monitored as will be required. Without both he will be not much more than a puppet you need to direct at every turn and monitor closely. Neither is a good use of your time.

So how do you assess judgment in the interview process? Give the candidate real life situations they may face on the job. Ideally these are situations where the best direction is not obvious. They may even be situations where there are multiple acceptable paths to take. Present them with the situation then ask them *not* how they would proceed but how they would make their decision on how to proceed. Get a sense of how they process information and make decisions. Get a sense of the extent to which they see information voids they would seek to fill. In essence, get a sense of their judgment skills. This should not be a brief part of the selection process: Because this is likely to be time consuming both in preparation and execution you will probably only take your last and best candidates through the process.

Follow-through can be assessed two ways. One is with input from former supervisors of the candidate if it is available. Do not ask the former supervisor directly if the person had follow-through. Ask if they were reliable when given a task. Ask if they met deadlines. Ask how closely they had to be managed.

The second way to assess follow-through is to ask the candidate about projects she was a part of that were not as successful as she wished they

were. Let her talk about all the factors involved in the less-than-ideal outcome. Ask her how she could improve the outcome given another opportunity. In the discussion you will get a sense of the extent to which her
follow-through was present. If she talks of missed deadlines ask her what
factors contributed to the misses. She may be able to identify external factors that were truly beyond her control. Or she may say things like, "I was
overtaxed or lost track of the timeline." The more you carry on the discussion the better you will get a sense of her ability to reliably perform.

While many factors are important in high-performing team members,
without both judgment and follow-through they will require much more
of your time than they should and distract you from doing the best job of
which you are capable.

MAKING THE HIRE

If you're considering several people for the job, be careful not to mislead
any of the prospects. Tell them that a decision will not be made until all
the prospects have been interviewed. They should appreciate the fairness
of that arrangement. Tell them that they will be called as soon as a decision has been reached. See that they are phoned that day and informed of
the decision.

THE ATTITUDE TALK

After the applicant is selected for the job, you should have your "attitude
talk" with the person. Following is an example of a good attitude talk.
You'll develop your own style after a while, but the basic thoughts remain
the same:

> "One of the reasons I selected you for this position is that you display
> the kind of attitude we want in this organization. Your application
> and tests indicate that you have the capacity to handle the job. Many
> of the people who applied had the qualifications to do the job, but
> the one reason you were selected above all the others is that you
> display the kind of attitude we are looking for. We believe that the
> difference between an average employee and an outstanding one is
> often attitude.

"Not everyone in this organization has a great attitude. What do we mean by *attitude?* The attitude we're talking about is one where you are not worrying about whether you're doing more than your share. It's an attitude of pride in doing high-quality work and gaining a sense of accomplishment at day's end. It's personal satisfaction in a job well done. We believe you display that kind of attitude, and coupled with your ability to handle the job, you will make an outstanding addition to our organization."

Let's analyze the reasons for some of the statements in this mini-speech:

When is an employee most likely to be receptive to ideas about the job? Likely at the start of a new position?

Do people generally try to live up to the image they think you have of them? They do. Recall the interview and the possibility that the applicant may have been displaying the attitude she thought you wanted. She now knows that attitude is exceedingly important to the company and to you as her manager. She now needs to display such an attitude on the job. Isn't that a win-win situation for both her and the company?

Why advertise the fact that there are people in the company who do not have a great attitude? If you remain silent about some who may have an undesirable attitude, your words become hollow indeed when this new employee runs into one of them. Since you mentioned it, however, now when she encounters a colleague with a bad attitude, your credibility is enhanced. She may think, "He told me there are some with a bad attitude like this. I'm here to help change it." Your credibility is fortified.

The exact timing of your attitude talk with a new employee is a matter of personal preference. Bringing the person back into the office after he has been notified he got the job can be an ideal time to congratulate the person and give the attitude talk. It should be reinforced the first day on the job too, but in a low-key way because there are so many things on the new employee's mind that day. He's nervous; he's concerned about how he's going to like the people he is going to meet and if they will like him. But that first day is when the new employee is most receptive to what is expected.

13

TRAINING TEAM MEMBERS

MANY NEW MANAGERS BELIEVE THEY MUST know how to perform every job in their area of responsibility. It's as though they feel that if some key person quits, they might have to get out there and personally perform the task. If you believe in that philosophy and carry it to its logical conclusion, then the chief executive officer of the organization ought to be able to perform every job in the company. That, of course, is ridiculous. It's just as ridiculous as believing that the president of the United States should be able to perform every task in the federal government. The president shouldn't even be able to perform every job in the White House. You don't have to be a master chef to recognize rotten chicken.

YOUR RESPONSIBILITY FOR TRAINING

You must know what needs to be done, not exactly how it's done. A lot depends on what level manager you are. If you are responsible for doing some of the work yourself and leading others in the same function, you will know how to perform the operation.

If you have thirty-five people performing a variety of tasks, however, you will not know how to perform each task—but you will have someone out there who does know how it's done. The administrator of a large hospital is not able to perform surgery, but that administrator knows the process by which skilled surgeons are secured and retained on the staff.

Many new managers are uncomfortable about what they cannot do. Don't be. You will be held responsible for the results you achieve—not for performing every task yourself.

Although this concept may be frightening to you at first, you'll get used to it and wonder how you ever could have thought otherwise. Your initial reaction will be, "I've got to know it all." If it's a big, varied operation, you can't possibly know it all. Don't sweat it.

TRAINING THE NEW EMPLOYEE

Some jobs require more extensive training than others, but even the most experienced person coming into a new situation needs some basic training. New employees need to be trained as soon as possible in their job, learn how things are done at your company, and understand how they fit into the overall organization.

In many ways, instructions given to employees on their first day are wasted. Their first day on the job is an opportunity for new employees to become acquainted with the people they'll be working with and their work setting. You should permit them to spend the first day just observing and then start the actual training the second day. Many workers go home from their first day on the job with either a bad headache or a backache— undoubtedly the result of nervous tension.

There are different philosophies on how a person should be trained. The most common philosophy holds that the person leaving the job should train a new employee. Automatically following that philosophy can be a mistake. Everything depends on why the employee is leaving and on the departing person's attitude.

TRAINING THE WRONG WAY: AN EXAMPLE

The following example shows the wrong way to train a new employee. It demonstrates the worst kind of judgment. The manager of an office consisting of several salespeople and one clerical person decided that the clerk should be fired for incompetence. He gave her two weeks' notice but asked her to work during that time. He then hired her replacement and asked her to train the new employee. The result was a nightmare for all concerned.

Small wonder. If the people leaving your company are less than 100 percent competent, you must never allow them to do the training. Why would you want those fired for incompetence to train their replacements? They're likely to put no effort at all into the training. And even if they do make an effort, they'll probably pass all their bad habits on to the new employees. Even people who are leaving voluntarily usually are not the best trainers. Most people who put in their notice are already focused on their next position. The training they do may be casual and incomplete. On the other hand, when a position opens up because the incumbent in the job is being promoted, that person is probably the best one to handle the training.

The manager who wanted the fired employee to train the replacement did not understand the clerical job. It was impossible for him personally to train the new employee—any attempt to do so would merely have displayed his ignorance. He therefore went to impossible extremes to "keep his cover." That is a serious managerial failure.

Don't misconstrue this suggestion to mean that a manager must personally know how to perform every job in the organization. In the example given, there was only one clerical position, so no one else was available. The manager took the easy route of having the departing clerical worker train the incoming one. Even if the manager couldn't explain the specific details of the job to the new employee, he should have been able to explain exactly what he expected from the clerical position.

THE ROLE OF THE TRAINER

Before starting a new employee on a training course, you must have a talk with the prospective trainer. You should never spring it as a surprise. Meet with the trainer in advance to discuss the outcome you are seeking. You may have some ideas on how the new person can do things more effectively than the person who was in the job. This is an ideal opportunity to implement the changes you have in mind. There is no better time to effect change than when the new person is starting. Even if you don't have any changes in mind, it is important that you and the trainer agree on the expected outcome.

Once the new employee is hired and a starting date has been established, notify the person you've selected as the trainer. The trainer may need to rearrange some schedules to accommodate the assignment.

Pick a trainer who is very good at explaining what is going on—one who can break the job down into its component parts and who doesn't describe it in technical terms that will be hard for the new employee to understand at first. The technical terms will be picked up eventually, but this "foreign language" must not overwhelm the trainee. You must outline to the trainer what you want to happen. If you'd like the first day to be casual, the trainer needs to know that.

Sometime during the latter part of the first day, you should stop by and ask the trainer and the trainee how things are going. What you say is not as important as your display of interest in the new employee.

At the end of the first week, call the new employee into the office for a chat. Again, what is said is not as important as the interest displayed in the new employee's welfare. Ask a couple of questions to determine if the instructions from the trainer are clear. Is the new employee beginning to get a handle on the job?

THE IMPROVEMENT SEED

This is also the time for planting the *improvement seed*. You might handle this discussion with the employee by saying, "As a new person on this job, you bring fresh insights to the position that the rest of us may not have. I encourage you to ask questions about what we do and why we do it. After you've been trained, we encourage you to offer any suggestions you can think of to improve what we're doing. What seems obvious to you as a new employee may not be so obvious to the rest of us." This sends the message that you are serious about continuous improvement and value input from a new team member.

The reason for emphasizing "after you've been trained" is to keep new employees from suggesting changes before they understand what is going on. What may seem like a good idea early in the training may be taken care of as the nature of the position becomes more clearly understood.

Everyone you manage must know that you are serious about continuous improvement. This also makes it less likely that they'll react negatively to new ideas.

You'll always have plenty of problems with people who defend themselves with the statement, "We've always done it this way." That argument is usually desperate; it tells you that the person using it either can't come up with a valid explanation of why something is being done or is just seriously threatened by change.

THE JOB DEFINED

During the training period, it's a good idea to break the job down into small parts and teach the functions one at a time. In showing new employees the entire function, you run the risk of overwhelming them. Of course, you should first explain the overall purpose of the job including how it fits into the broader operation.

FEEDBACK

It's important to develop a method of feedback that lets you know how well the trainee is doing after beginning to work unassisted on the job. The trainee should take over the job from the trainer on a gradual basis as each step in the process is mastered. The feedback method should apply to every employee. The system should be developed in such a manner that unsatisfactory performance always comes to your attention before too much damage is done. The process is vital to your success as a manager, but no strict guidelines can be offered for establishing it because it will vary according to the specifics of your operation.

The feedback must be internal. Hearing about the mistake from a dissatisfied client or customer means it is already too late. You want to correct the problem before the work gets out of your own area of responsibility.

QUALITY CONTROL

If it is possible to maintain quality control procedures your employees can relate to, so much the better. Don't expect perfection; that's an unrealistic goal. Determine what an acceptable margin of error should be for your area and then strive as a team to reach that goal and eventually exceed it. The goal must be realistic if you expect the cooperation of your team.

New employees need to know what is expected of them once they're operating on the job alone. If your ultimate goal for them is 95 percent efficiency, it would help them to know your interim targets. You might expect them to work at 70 percent efficiency at the end of thirty days, at 80 percent efficiency at the end of sixty days, and at 95 percent efficiency at the end of ninety days. This will depend on how difficult the work is. The simpler the job, the easier it should be to get to the ultimate quality goal. You need to determine the timetable and share it with the new employee.

By keeping employees informed of your expectations, you make them a part of the process. Encourage them to let the trainer know in advance if they are concerned about not reaching a targeted level of efficiency so they can work together to find ways to improve performance. Let trainees know that you and the trainer will respond constructively and not punitively. During the training process, you want the new employee to correctly see you and the trainer as coaches and supporters, not disciplinarians. Make it clear that your goal is his success.

Even when new employees take over the job on their own, you should have the trainer audit their work until you believe the work is acceptable and quality checks are not as crucial. Each mistake should be gone over carefully with the trainee. The trainer must be a diplomat who is good at talking about what went wrong without attacking the new employee. Don't make it personal. The trainer should not say, "You're making a mistake again." Rather, something like: "Well, this still is not 100 percent, but I think we're getting closer, don't you?"

END OF THE TRAINING PERIOD

At some point the probationary period must end. In most companies, this is usually after a specified number of weeks or months. Once the trainee demonstrates the ability to work unassisted, it's time for another formal interview between you and the trainee. This marks the completion of a phase in the new employee's career, and some attention should be paid to the event. This is an opportunity to express your satisfaction about the progress made up to this point, to note that the employee will now be working without a trainer, and to indicate how the work will be monitored both for quality and quantity. It is also an excellent opportunity to continue the discussion you initiated at the end of the employee's first week about things she may have discovered for improving the way she performs her job. Even if she does not have any suggestions yet, it reminds her to keep open to opportunities for improvement and makes it clear that your interest in her suggestions is genuine.

RECOGNIZE AND REWARD THE TRAINER

The conclusion of the training process is a good time to recognize and reward the trainer. If she has done a good job, find an opportunity to share that information with the trainer's colleagues. The trainer took on additional responsibility, and you will be well served to praise the trainer, sending the message to all team members that putting forth additional effort is valued. An affordable reward may also be in order, like a Friday afternoon off or a gift card.

14

MANAGING CHANGE: DEALING WITH RESISTANCE

ONE OF THE MOST IMPORTANT ASPECTS of a manager's job is managing change effectively. Managing change includes accepting change and supporting it, understanding why your team members may be resistant to it, and finding ways to reduce that resistance. When you are able to do all three of these, you have mastered one of the most critical competencies of any manager.

ACCEPT CHANGE YOURSELF

Have you ever worked for a manager who found it difficult to accept the changes initiated by the organization? This type of manager will openly express disagreement, call the decisionmakers fools who have no clue what they are doing, and try to convince you that most of these changes are terrible for the staff as well. This is a serious mistake on the part of a manager. It causes employees to lose faith in company decisions and ultimately in the company.

As a manager, not only do you have to be prepared to embrace change and be a champion of it, but also to accept and support changes that you may disagree with. It is best to admit that you do not like the change (as your staff may already know this), but state that you will actively support it and expect your staff to support it as well.

For example, let's say that the company has decided to go with a new Enterprise Management System (EMS) system but you feel the old system is currently giving you what you need. What would be the danger of not supporting the new decision? First, you are looking at the change only from your vantage point. There may be benefits you do not see that are real for others in the company. Second, you are sending a message that your opinion counts more than that of the organization. It is important as a new manager that you get your team members to align themselves with the goals and decisions of the organization. Ideally, it would be best if you were part of the decisionmaking process and upper management asked your thoughts and listened to your opinions. Then, perhaps, you could accept the change more readily, even if you disagreed with it. But whether or not you were included in the decisionmaking process, as a manager, you must actively communicate your support for company policies, procedures, rules, regulations, and decisions.

RESISTANCE TO CHANGE

As was mentioned in Chapter 2, most people are naturally resistant to change. There is often resistance even when an apparently good change is introduced in the workplace. What makes people so resistant to change? People basically fear the unknown and how they will react to uncertainties. Change may put a person's job at risk. Many may believe they do not have the skills to perform the responsibilities that the change may bring or they are unclear about the reasons the change is being introduced in the first place.

Resistance to change is also very subjective. That is, people have different threshold levels to change. Some of us who have had bad experiences with change, or grew up in environments where change was considered threatening, will obviously be more resistant when change occurs than those who have benefited from change in the past, or were taught to embrace change.

Resistance to change is subjective in another way. Changes affect people in different ways. For example, Michelle has always prepared documentation for any package she sends out so that she will be able to track it later on if necessary, or quickly answer any questions from customers, vendors, salespeople, and so forth. Brad has never done this; he thinks it is a waste of his time. When the company institutes a new policy calling for careful documentation of all outgoing packages, Michelle is unfazed. Brad reacts negatively to this new "busywork" and complains to everybody about it.

HOW TO REDUCE RESISTANCE

It is unwise to think that you can totally eliminate your team's resistance to workplace changes. As we already mentioned, people will normally be resistant. You will be more successful if you try to reduce the amount of resistance. The best strategy is to involve your employees in the change.

Above all else, provide as much information as possible. Because resistance to change is based on a fear of the unknown, you need to minimize the unknowns. *The fewer unknowns the less resistance.* This of course does not mean that all information will be well-received. But it is better for your people to have accurate information they do not like than no information or inaccurate information. As we all know, people will get information any way they can. If you are not providing it they will find other sources—and there is a high likelihood that what they find will be inaccurate. By being your team's source of accurate information you will be correctly seen as their best guide through the change.

Next explain why the change is occurring and point out any benefits to them. Often there are no benefits for them. The customer may benefit or some other department may flourish as a result. Sometimes, you just have to be honest and say something like "This will not help our team, but it will help make the entire organization more successful," or, "Not every change benefits our team, but others have and will."

Then, ask your employees how the change can be implemented in their group or your department. The more you involve others with the change the more readily they will accept it. Sometimes your most resistant employees, once involved, become your biggest champions for the change. Always try to identify the most resistant individuals from the beginning and get them on your side. Change occurs much more easily when you have their support.

15

DISCIPLINING THE EMPLOYEE

PERFORMANCE STANDARDS VARY BY THE KIND of business you are in, and may even vary by departments within the same company, because of the variety of tasks involved.

Every employee you are managing must know what the expected standards of work are. You create problems for yourself when you discipline an employee on the basis of vague work standards. Doing so will weaken your position in the process and easily lead to genuine misunderstandings. You can't get by with a nebulous approach to performance standards.

Let's assume you've done a satisfactory job of establishing standards for each job. In all probability, those standards are written into a job description. The job description indicates the elements of accountability that apply to the job, which allows you to measure the individual against those standards. Now you must have methods within your area of responsibility that allow you to be continuously aware of how people are performing in relation to the standards. You cannot operate on the assumption that unless you're hearing complaints from customers or other departments, the performance is acceptable. By the time such warning signals arrive, severe damage may already have been done.

PRIOR KNOWLEDGE

Your attitude about your team members' performance is crucial. The place and time to convey that attitude is when they first step into the job. They need to know exactly what is expected of them both during their training period and once they have completed it. During the training period, you'll accept less in the way of quality and quantity. Make sure that during training, you have things structured so the trainee's errors don't reach beyond your own department.

Feedback is critical to proper and effective discipline. You need to design your systems so performance that is below agreed standards comes to your attention quickly. It is vital that you know as soon as possible when performance is substandard so you can address it immediately. In the following discussion of discipline procedures, let's assume that you've set clear standards and that the employee knows and understands those standards. Furthermore, you have an adequate method of feedback so that you know when substandard performance is a problem.

NEVER MAKE IT PERSONAL

One of the oldest rules of management is that employee discipline should always be done in private. Never humiliate an employee, even in cases of dismissal. The employee must always be made to understand that what is being discussed is the performance, not the person.

Too many managers, at all levels of experience, turn a discussion of poor performance into a personal attack. In most cases, it's probably not done maliciously; this kind of approach is simply not thought through.

The following opening gambits often get the discussion off to a terrible start:

- "You are making far too many errors."
- "I don't know what your problem is. I've never had anyone screw up on this job like you."
- "Your performance is so substandard that we don't have a word to describe it."

These are outrageous statements, but attacks like these are uttered every working day somewhere. The managers may be right on target, but they have just made their problems worse than they need to be.

This approach will lead to employees feeling that they are being personally attacked. When attacked, our natural tendency is to defend ourselves, and the defensive barriers of the employee will almost certainly go up.

Now both parties to the conversation have to fight through these barriers to get back to the problem. Give employees the benefit of the doubt. You might say, "I know we both want you to be successful, so let's talk about how we can improve the results you are getting."

Address the substandard performance by viewing it as the result of some misunderstanding about how the work should be done. Perhaps the employee has missed something in the training process, and this has created a systems deficiency that is causing the work to fall below the agreed standards. By taking this approach, you inform the employee from the outset that you're talking about the performance and not the person.

GIVE AND TAKE

You should have a conversation, not deliver a monologue. Many managers do all the talking, which usually results in resentment in the party on the receiving end. You need to encourage the employee's participation in the conversation. Without it there is a good chance you won't solve the problem.

Be careful, now, and don't go overboard! Some executives, in their effort to be scrupulously fair, become so cautious and tactful that the employee leaves their office expecting to get a raise for outstanding performance. You have to make certain that your employee understands that the work is not up to standards. How you say it, though, is critically important.

When bringing the employee into your office, put him at ease. This may not seem like a big deal to you, but to an employee who may not have spent much time in your office, you're the boss and being called into your presence may be a frightening prospect. Therefore, do everything you can to make the other person comfortable.

Encourage the employee to participate in the discussion early in the game. You might start off with a statement like this: "Derek, you've been with us three months now and I think it's time we had a conversation about how you're doing. As you know, I have a great interest in your being successful on this job. How do you feel things are going?"

By using this approach, you encourage an employee who is not performing up to standards to bring up the subject himself. It seldom comes as a surprise to an employee to learn that specified standards are not being met. Surprise is likely only if the employee has never been told what is expected. If that is the case, you really have some serious problems—problems of training and communication.

As the employee describes how things are going, you direct the conversation to the standards that are not being met. For example, you ask, "Do you think you're getting close to the standards we've established for experienced employees?" If the answer is yes, you could ask, "Do you believe you're performing at the same level as an experienced employee?" If the answer is again yes, then the employee may be out of touch with reality. The point is to continue asking questions of this type until you get the kind of response that will lead you into a discussion of the quality of the work.

Obviously, if all your tactful efforts have not resulted in the employee bringing up the crucial subject, you have no choice but to insert it into the conversation yourself. To the employee who persists in asserting that things are going well, you could say, "That's an interesting observation you've made about the quality of the work, because that is not what I am seeing." Why do you suppose my information is different from yours?" You then have the matter on the table for discussion.

ELIMINATE MISUNDERSTANDING

As you proceed further into the conversation, use techniques that ensure the employee knows what's expected. Get feedback on what you've mutually agreed upon, so there can be no misunderstanding later about what was said.

It is always a good idea to write a memorandum at the conclusion of the conversation and place it in the employee's file. This becomes particularly important if you are managing a lot of people and it's possible that six months from now you won't remember the details of the conversation.

THE PRIMACY OF THE PERSON

There are problems about an employee's performance that cannot be separated from the person. When talking about the quality or quantity of an employee's work, it's obvious that the techniques discussed in this chapter can help in establishing firmly in the employee's mind that a difference exists between your criticism of the work and your view of the person. But with certain attitudinal problems, it's more difficult to make the distinction, and in many cases it can't be done.

Let's assume you have a highly satisfactory employee who can't seem to get to work on time. Disciplining unsatisfactory employees is easier than disciplining a problem employee like this one whom you obviously want to keep. What happens in these situations is obvious. If you allow the employee the privilege of coming in late every day, you're going to create a morale problem with the rest of the people who adhere to the office hours, no matter how superior that person's performance. (This obviously does not apply if your office has flexible work hours.)

In talking with the satisfactory employee about this problem, one of the better approaches is to explain the management difficulties you'd have if every employee ignored the working hours. You couldn't tolerate that situation. In addition, the employee is creating difficulties for himself. You can then go into the discussion in some detail and start working on a solution.

You may find that the employee is dealing with a recurring problem that is difficult or even impossible to solve. A common example is child-care challenges. Sometimes childcare facilities have restrictive policies or change them so that it impacts an employee's ability to be timely. If the employee's child is sick, he may have to take the child to a different child-care center. If the facility for sick children is out of the way, it can make it impossible for the employee to be on time. You may need to solve this kind of problem by changing the employee's hours. Having him start half an hour later may solve the problem.

Let's follow through with the problem of the tardy employee, because it happens often enough that you'll eventually have to face it.

Most conscientious employees who are doing a satisfactory job will react positively to your statements. You may notice that for the next ten days or so they are getting to work on time. At that point, you may be feeling good about your success in managing people. You'll find, however, that when the pressure is off, the reformed employee may start coming in late again. You can't take a casual approach about this and assume it was just an unusual set of circumstances. All your subordinates must be made to know you expect them to be on time every day.

The first time this happens after your initial conversation, you again have a discussion with the offender. This doesn't have to be a full-blown dialogue of the same length and detail as the first one; all you need to do is reinforce what you said previously. There may be a sound reason for the recent lateness, and it could be that the second conversation is all that is needed. If you can get to the point where the employee is coming to work on time for approximately six months, you may assume you've changed that person's work patterns enough so that you no longer have a serious problem.

DISCIPLINE FOR A GOOD EMPLOYEE GONE BAD

Let's look at a step-by-step case study regarding the use of employee time that is as challenging an employee-disciplinary situation as you are likely to face. Kelly, one of your direct reports, does executive coaching for your consulting firm. She goes to client sites and works with senior managers one-on-one, helping them with their managerial skills and giving advice on project implementation. She usually spends one day a week at a client site for a month or two. You have always gotten the best feedback from the clients about Kelly. She is always in high demand. You consider her to be one of your best staff members.

Then, things change. You begin to receive feedback from these same clients, and new ones, that her short breaks of five or ten minutes are turning into an hour or more a couple of times a day, and these breaks are not during lunch. After a couple of weeks listening to these comments, you set up a meeting with Kelly and tell her of the complaints you are getting about her. You explain that it makes her and your company look unprofessional when she leaves a senior executive hanging, and that these client companies are paying big bucks for your services. You also explain that the executives have scheduled their day around her being there.

Kelly doesn't believe she is taking such long breaks and flatly denies it. You try to open the floor to her and have her discuss anything that is troubling her, work related or personally, but she just keeps saying that everything is perfect and that she cannot imagine that she is taking such long breaks. You decide on an action plan. Kelly will notify the client when she needs five or ten minutes (she's a smoker), look at her watch, tell the client what time it is and what time she will return.

You think the problem is over. But it isn't. You continue to receive the same complaints from clients, so you have a couple of additional discipline sessions with Kelly, which lead nowhere. You even suggest that Kelly visit an outside counselor, at company expense, if she wants or needs to talk to someone. She refuses your offer. The same behavior continues. You give her one last opportunity to change. You tell her if you get one more complaint on the same issue she will be gone. You get several more and Kelly is terminated.

The situation just described is one that many people would view as a failure of management skills. That's wrong. Not every personnel problem can be solved by accommodation. In the case study described here, you did everything you could to remedy the situation. You gave Kelly every opportunity to address her behavior, to open up to you concerning whatever problems she may have; you worked out a plan for her to follow, and you gave her several chances to change her behavior. Since nothing you did worked, the only solution you had was to get someone to replace her, no matter how valuable an employee she was at one time.

OTHER PROBLEMS

It's likely that you'll have other problems of a similar nature, such as people spending too much time on the internet for non-work-related activities, consistently overstaying the lunch hour, or just failing to show up. Needless to say, you don't run a sweatshop, and everyone will have some issue at one time or another. What is critical is dealing effectively with chronic offenders who create management problems for you and the organization.

One of the most challenging problems for a manager to handle is personal hygiene. For example, suppose you have a young woman in your department who has an unpleasant body odor. Other employees are making sly comments about her. Even worse, they are avoiding her. This is unacceptable because their work depends on communicating with her often during the day. Her body odor has become a business issue and so you have to deal with it.

Rather than do it yourself, you may want to arrange to have someone in human resources talk directly to the employee. The reason is not to avoid a difficult situation, but rather to spare the woman embarrassment every time she sees you, along with the misery of being constantly reminded of the uncomfortable conversation. By having someone in human resources talk to her away from her work area, you might solve the problem and also be able to salvage an otherwise satisfactory employee. If the embarrassment is too great in a delicate situation like this, you may lose the employee.

A SIMPLE PERFORMANCE-IMPROVEMENT TOOL

There is a simple but effective tool that can help you provide a problem employee with a clear understanding of what he needs to do to improve his performance. When things are not going well, it is particularly important that there be absolute clarity. For the greatest impact, create this tool while you are having a one-on-one meeting with the underperforming employee.

The tool requires a single sheet of blank paper. Regular copy paper is perfect. Fold the sheet into thirds as if you were going to put it into an envelope, then unfold it. Draw a horizontal line at each of the two folds. You now have a blank sheet of paper divided into three approximately equal sections.

Explain to the employee that you are creating an improvement plan for him. At the top of the first section write *Strengths*. Title the middle section *Areas for Improvement* and the lower section *Goals*. Now ask the employee to help you fill in the three sections. Obviously, you need to have a good idea of what you want in each section, but the employee's input is critical and can offer valuable insights.

You are creating the plan with the employee's input. It is your job to filter the employee's suggestions as appropriate. If he suggests something you don't agree with, use his suggestion to fuel a conversation.

Let's say the employee states that one of his strengths is his ability to work well in a team setting, but you believe this is not the case. You may want to start by saying, "Now tell me why you say that." His input may cause you to revise your opinion—or it may not. If not, tell him that based on your observations and feedback from some of his colleagues, you would like to include an ability to work effectively in a team setting in his areas for improvement. Keep the tone constructive and emphasize that the goal of this exercise is to help him succeed. To be successful, he needs to have an accurate understanding of what he needs to work on.

With an area for improvement identified, now agree to a specific goal related to this issue to put in the goals section. An example may be a rating of 3.5 or better out of 5 on the anonymous peer ratings that are done at the conclusion of each team initiative. Each goal must have a date associated with it for the achievement of that goal.

Keep the goals simple and clear so they leave no room for misunderstanding. Quantify them as much as possible. Examples would be a minimum error rate or a maximum number of days missed.

You will often find that the employee is really tough on himself in assessing his areas for improvement and reluctant to identify his strengths. He will also commonly bring up topics that may not have occurred to you. Done well, this process can be constructive and nonthreatening.

Of course, the most important part of the exercise is the goals. The goals give the employee a clear understanding of what he needs to achieve within the agreed-upon time frame.

Once there is agreement on the plan, both you and the employee sign and date it at the bottom of the page. Now, provide the employee with a copy and agree to the specific date and time you will meet again to review his progress. Allow no more than a month until the next meeting. If the situation is particularly dire, meet again even sooner.

You have now made your life much easier. When you meet again it will be abundantly clear whether the employee is improving. Reviewing the goals and his performance will be a straightforward process. Ideally, the employee will have achieved all of them. Even if he has, you still want to go through this process at least one more time to make sure the team member stays on track. Should he achieve all his goals a second time, there is value in going through the process a third time. The difference is that this time you will probably wait longer until you meet again.

If the employee is improving, lengthen the time between meetings. If he is not improving or is deteriorating, shorten the time.

If after a few updated improvement plans and follow-up meetings you are not seeing sufficient progress, your path is clear. The employee has made it apparent that his skills and the position he is in are not a match. This is why this is a powerful tool. Used correctly, it leaves little room for misunderstanding. You either have a team member who is improving or one who needs to move on. It also significantly increases the chances that the employee will see the need to try something different if his performance has not improved sufficiently.

DISCIPLINARY TECHNIQUES

Let's assume you have a highly satisfactory employee whose work sharply deteriorates. Needless to say, you're continually communicating with the employee about the deterioration. You want to retain the employee, but you find that your words are not being taken seriously. In a situation like this one, you may recommend zero salary increase for the employee for that year, with a full explanation as to why you're doing it. Inform the employee in advance that if the work doesn't get better, there'll be no increase in pay. Having made that threat or stated that possibility of action, you must then follow through on it so that you don't lose credibility. This is exactly when you want to use the process of improvement plans and one-on-one meetings described above.

Another disciplinary technique you can use is to put the employee on probation. Make it clear that the person's work deterioration needs to be corrected, and you want to give the employee every opportunity to correct it. You must make it perfectly clear that the substandard level of work being delivered cannot be allowed to continue. Putting an employee on probationary status makes it quite clear that her job is at risk and performance must improve.

New employees in a company often start on probationary status, either in line with standard company policy or as individual cases. Many companies use a ninety-day probationary period. Employees doing satisfactory work at the end of that time are taken off the probationary rolls and become regular employees. It's also customary to give a modest salary increase in recognition of satisfactory completion of the probationary course. If the work is not satisfactory at that point, the employee should anticipate being terminated. Again, it should never come as a surprise. If it is a surprise, you have not done a good job of communicating with the employee.

16

"OH MY GOD!
I CAN'T FIRE ANYONE!"

IF THERE'S ONE MOMENT THAT LIVES forever in a manager's memory, it's the first time a direct report must be fired. It's not a pleasant task. Firing someone can be traumatic for both parties in the drama. If you've done your job properly, the event will not come as a surprise to the person who is about to get the ax. But you can set the bar higher. Your goal, when dismissing an employee for poor performance, is to have him actually thank you for removing him from the position. Really. This cannot be achieved every time, but it is the goal you want to target.

Simply stated, if you have communicated openly with the employee and made her a part of the attempted performance-improvement process, it is very likely she will realize that her skills are not a match for the job. Before we get into the details of this process, let's cover some basics.

The first is that sudden firings are nearly always wrong, except in cases where an employee has been dishonest or violent. Most companies have strict guidelines as to what offenses call for immediate dismissal.

Second, never fire someone when you're angry. Never take such radical action on an impulse. When a direct report pushes you over the edge and you feel like "showing her who's boss," don't give in to your emotions. If you do, you'll regret it.

As you read this chapter, the thought may occur to you that some people don't deserve the time and consideration that it takes to terminate someone. If those thoughts are surfacing, change your focus. Dismissing someone effectively is one of the most important and challenging responsibilities you have as a manager. Focus on investing the time necessary to do it well because you want to improve your skills.

Since most companies have guidelines on the termination process, you need to ask your manager or human resources department if you are not sure what they are. It is best to err on the side of excess deliberation rather than on the side of excess haste. In fact, some managers adopt the philosophy of never firing a direct report until everyone in the office is wondering why they haven't taken the step already. A manager who takes that approach is not leading well.

TRYING TO MAKE IT WORK

The situations requiring dismissal that you are most likely to encounter in your managerial career have to do with poor performance or the employee's inability or unwillingness to abide by the company's standards. Sometimes the employee is just not suited for her position. Despite your best efforts, she may have been a bad hire or promotion. She may get to a satisfactory training performance level but will never advance beyond that point to the performance level the job requires.

Firing is not the first thought that should come into your head. Turnover is expensive. If you do ultimately have to let the underperformer go, you may incur costs related to the dismissal such as severance pay, transitional health benefits, and possibly outplacement assistance. In addition, you will have to invest time in replacing her. Doing all you reasonably can to bring her performance up to acceptable standards needs to be your first priority.

You must first satisfy yourself that the training was done well and clearly understood. Was there any kind of personality barrier between the trainer and the trainee that impeded the flow of adequate information?

Go back over the employee's aptitude tests, job application, and other initial hiring data on the chance that you may have missed something. Meet with the employee to discuss her current level of performance, the required level of performance, and how she can get there. Assess whether she desires to improve or if she finds her current performance acceptable.

This is the stage in the process during which you want to move toward one of two outcomes. The first and most desirable is to work with her to bring her performance up to speed. The second outcome is to have her thank you when she is dismissed.

The key to both of these outcomes is communication. It's time to be very direct. Make it abundantly clear to the employee that her job is at risk. This is not a time to be subtle. Just as important, make it clear that you want to see her be successful and will do all you can to assist her if she is committed to that success.

This is a time for goals and agreed actions to be in writing. Nothing fancy is necessary—a single page is sufficient. Once you and the employee have agreed to the steps she will take to improve her performance, put them in writing along with the date by which the action will be completed.

You need to be clear and unambiguous: "Your average daily errors are five. We need to cut that down to three errors per day by the end of the month." Your precise specifications serve a dual purpose. If the employee meets the goal, you may be on the way to solving the problem *and* retaining the employee. Failing that, you're ready to start the termination process.

Agreed actions may include things like a few additional days of training, assignment of a mentor, or a full day for her to observe someone in a similar role who is particularly effective. Written goals need to be specific. Include quantifiable levels of performance and the date by which they will be achieved.

Before the conversation is over, do three more things:

1. Have the employee sign a copy of the sheet to take with her.
2. Agree to the exact time and date the two of you will again meet to discuss her progress.
3. Let her know that you are open to hearing back from her sooner if it will assist her.

Your next meeting with the employee needs to be fairly soon. More than a month is too long. At that meeting, the actions and goal list needs to be updated and signed by the employee. Once again, the date and time of your next meeting needs to be established.

If she is not improving, the time until the next meeting needs to be shortened. If she is showing signs of progress, it may be appropriate to allow a bit more time until you meet again. This process will continue until the employee is either performing up to standards or is dismissed.

As this process continues, one of two things will happen. Either the underperforming employee's performance will improve to a reasonable level or it will not. If performance has not improved, it will be clear to you and likely the employee that she is not suited for her current position. The time you have spent on this process is well worth your while because you now know quite clearly that you need to remove her from the position. It also may have the effect of making it clear to the employee that she is not suited for her current role.

Casting the employee's potential dismissal in terms of helping her find a position for which she is better suited is how you just may get a "thank you" from her if you ultimately have to let her go. In addition, your efforts have made clear to the other members of your team that you are committed to everyone on the team being successful, if possible.

You owe it to the rest of the team members to keep them informed. And that includes telling them when they're performing well. Too many managers assume that if employees don't get bad performance reports, they know they're doing okay. This is usually not the case. Those employees tend to believe you don't give a damn.

YOU HAVE CONCLUDED THAT
THE EMPLOYEE IS NOT A FIT FOR HIS POSITION

Only after you are completely convinced that you have a below-satisfactory performer with little or no hope of bringing the performance up to proper standards should you consider termination as a possible solution.

There are alternatives to dismissing the problem employee. Here are some key questions to ask yourself before taking the final step of termination:

- Is it possible that this employee could handle some other job in your own area that is currently available?
- If an opening is coming up in another area, can the employee make a contribution there?
- Is this a situation where a person has been hired for the wrong job? Does the company gain anything by firing someone who might be useful somewhere else?
- Is your company large enough that the employee could be moved to another area with no stigma?

Former employees are part of a company's public. Can you handle the situation in such a way that you don't deplete your company's storehouse of civic goodwill?

Even though the employee won't like being fired, can you handle the procedure so that the employee will acknowledge having been given every opportunity, consequently agree that you had no choice in the matter, and possibly even thank you for helping him realize that his position was not a match for his talents?

Listen to this warning against taking the coward's way out and blaming the mysterious *they*. "As far as I'm concerned, five errors a day isn't too bad, but *they* say we have to get it down to three, or *they* will force me to let you go." That indicates you're merely a puppet. Someone else is pulling the strings and you don't have a mind of your own.

PREPARE THE GROUNDS FOR THE DIVORCE

Documentation of the underperforming employee's results is critically important. Of course, you must keep these records for all your employees. If your company has a formal performance appraisal system, then you may be adequately covered.

Records are important because being sued for dismissing an employee is becoming more common. You should ask yourself, "If I have to, can I fully justify this dismissal?" If you can answer yes, that's all you need worry about.

FLEXIBILITY AND CONSISTENCY

Some of your people will need to be dismissed because of excessive absenteeism. Companies have such a wide variety of sick-leave programs, however, that it's impossible to discuss what level of absenteeism is satisfactory. Some companies have fixed programs that allow, for example, one sick day per month or twelve per year, cumulatively. Other companies have a method that allows managerial discretion based on the individual situation. Admittedly, this kind of program is more difficult to administer than one with hard-and-fast rules to follow. In evaluating the merits of each case, you must be able to defend your decision.

One disadvantage in having no formal program is the serious risk that decisions will not be made consistently throughout the company. For example, generous managers may be inclined to excuse almost any absence and pay the absentee; other managers may be stricter and dock for days missed. Having no formal program means the communication between departments and managers has to be extremely good, ensuring that approximately the same standards apply throughout the company.

MERGERS AND BUYOUTS

Mergers and buyouts are common. Often, everyone is told that the new corporation is planning on no personnel changes, but within six months, the personnel changes begin. Reorganization takes place and some people are fired. After a corporate takeover, people are scrambling to protect their own positions. Some people survive and some don't. Those who do not survive are not necessarily inadequate. They may be filling positions that are duplicated in the parent organization. Some people are fired because they are too high in the organization or because their salary is too high.

If you become involved in one of these takeovers, you can only hope that the parent corporation is humane. If it is necessary to let some people go, it should be done in a way that acknowledges responsibility to these human beings. Continuing their salary for a reasonable length of time, providing office space and secretarial help while they look for a new position, and offering personal career counseling are some methods used to soften the blow.

It is doubtful that you as manager will have anything new to tell employees about the takeover, although you may get saddled with the job of telling some people in your area that they are being let go. It may even be possible that you have to select the people who are to be let go. You may be told to reduce staff by 10 percent or reduce salary costs by 20 percent. These are difficult decisions because they often have little to do with performance. All you can do is carry out the task in as humane a manner as possible.

When faced with this undesirable task, make all your decisions with a focus on the employees who will be retained. How you treat the departing team members will be closely observed by the team members who are staying. By being as thoughtful and humane as your organization's policies allow, you send the message that you value the contributions of the departing employees. This strongly suggests that you also value the contributions of the employees who will continue on your team and lessens the long-term negative impact of the layoffs.

In this case everyone knows the staff reduction is a result of the merger, so you might as well tie it to that; it at least allows people to save face. If they can't save their jobs, saving face is some consolation. Use whatever influence you have with the organization to generate some help for these people.

Seniority is often a poor way to pick employees to be let go, but that's how many companies operate in the interest of "fairness" (and to avoid being sued). If the last people hired are the first fired, at least none of them can complain that such a system is personal.

DOWNSIZING

Downsizing is a word that strikes fear in employee groups. We won't get into all the controversy over downsizing, except to say that it does not always achieve the desired results. We'll discuss two basic elements: your survival as an employee and the role you might be required to play as a new manager.

Your boss is going to be worried about her own survival and looking at your area of responsibility. The downsizing tremor is felt through the entire organization. Many managers and executives who thought they were immune from the downsizing virus end up being totally shocked.

The best advice is, "Don't let them see you sweat." Have confidence in your ability. Asking about your survival is just another problem piled on your manager. Instead of going into your boss's office and trying to find out what your prospects are for survival, take a different approach. Why not say, "I know that this is going to be a difficult time for you. I want you to know that I'm here to help you any way I can."

No one can guarantee your survival in a downsizing operation, but you may increase the odds if you are a part of the solution rather than whining about your own job and putting an additional burden on your manager's shoulders.

As a manager, you may end up giving some bad news to people who are losing their jobs. The comments in the previous section on mergers and buyouts also apply: It's important that you find a humane way to handle these personal contacts with a keen awareness that your actions will be closely observed by the employees who remain.

Even if you survive the downsizing, it's difficult to feel great about your good fortune when many of your friends did not fare as well. You may even feel a bit guilty about your survival, and that is a perfectly natural reaction for a humane manager.

THE DISMISSAL DRAMA

So far we've discussed events leading up to a dismissal. Now let's focus on the dismissal, the timing of which you control.

Most managers like to stage the drama late Friday afternoon. By the time it's over, all the coworkers of the person being fired have left the office. Thus, if it is necessary for the dismissed employee to vacate his workstation immediately, he won't have to endure the humiliation of "clearing out" in front of an audience. Also, the employee can use the weekend to prepare for seeking other employment, applying for unemployment compensation, or doing whatever else needs to be done.

Any money due at the time of the dismissal should be given to the dismissed employee at the end of the interview. Being fired is enough of an emotional blow; wondering when the final check will arrive can only add to the misery. Severance pay—if that's the company's policy—should be given at the same time. Unused vacation time or sick leave should also be included in the compensation.

Put yourself in the other person's position. Despite your best efforts, he may still not feel the termination was completely justified. Unless he receives every dollar coming to him, he might think, "Well, I suppose I'll have to hire an attorney to get the money they owe me!" Remove that thought from the dismissed employee's mind by taking care of all those matters in advance.

Another courtesy that is owed to the employee is to keep your intention to fire her as confidential as possible. Of course, the human resources and the payroll departments will have to know. But other than discussing it with the necessary management people, you should treat the matter confidentially.

The final scene in the dismissal drama is bound to be most uncomfortable for you, the manager. This is because in that highly charged final interview, it may be just the two of you face-to-face. If you are concerned the dismissed employee may behave poorly, you would be wise to include an additional colleague in the meeting. Someone from human resources or a fellow manager are good candidates. This way there is a third person present if the contents of the interview later become a point of contention. Whether or not you have a colleague join you, it would be wise to summarize the interview in writing as soon as it is over to assist you in recalling the details of the meeting if necessary.

A good way to start the dismissal or termination interview is to review in brief what has happened. Don't drag it out and make it a recitation of all the other person's mistakes. It should go something like this:

"As you know from our past conversations, we have standards on the position you were in that have to be met. As I've mentioned to you from time to time over the past few weeks, your work is not up to those standards. Unfortunately, our efforts to get you up to that level of performance have not been successful. I don't believe it's because of any lack of effort on your part. However, it hasn't worked out. Based on all of our conversations, I don't think that comes as any surprise to you. We're going to have to terminate your services as of today. I really regret that. I wanted it to work out just as much as you did. But it hasn't worked out, and so we have to face up to reality. Here's the final check, including one month's severance pay plus your unused vacation and sick-leave time. I am hopeful you will soon have a new position that is a better fit for your skills."

You can vary your remarks to fit the individual situation, but the above words say what needs to be said. They don't sugarcoat the bad news and they're not too blunt either. You have to come up with a statement you're comfortable with that fits the situation.

Fortunately, the days of putting a pink slip in someone's pay envelope are gone. That practice was highly inhumane. One can understand the necessity for it in a factory where thousands of people are all being temporarily laid off or where the entire business is being closed and everybody is going. Situations like that are not related to the performance of the individual. When someone is being let go because of a failure to perform or live up to company standards, the only way to handle it is on a one-on-one basis. As manager, you might prefer to avoid the direct confrontation, but it's part of your responsibilities and must be dealt with straight on. In most companies, this final interview is the last step in the disciplinary procedure and under employment law it is considered the appropriate thing to do.

LAST THOUGHTS ON FIRING

When you consider it thoughtfully, you realize that keeping an unsatisfactory employee on the job is unfair not only to the company but also to the employee. No one is comfortable in a job he is not performing well. It is also unfair to the team members who are performing at or above established standards.

There are many instances where being fired has turned out to be the biggest favor a company can do for an employee who isn't suited for his job. It may not seem that way to the employee at the time, but later on, he'll know it was the right thing and that he actually came out ahead in the long run.

Some managers feel like failures if they have to fire anyone. This statistic may help you out. Research on employee termination has shown that seven out of ten people who get dismissed do better on their next job, in both performance and salary. Their former job was a poor fit; being fired allowed them to find a better fit for themselves.

Let's end on the most important point in this chapter. You must be absolutely certain in your own mind that the dismissal is deserved. You must be sure you're being as objective as you can possibly be. If in doubt, use a more experienced manager or a human resources professional as a sounding board. Then when you know you have to fire the employee, make sure it doesn't come as a surprise, and handle it in a considerate, humane, and thoughtful manner.

17

HAVING A LEGAL AWARENESS

IT IS VERY IMPORTANT AS A FIRST-TIME manager that you know current employment laws, practices, and regulations set by federal, state, and local governments in order to avoid any legal liability. You do not need to be an expert, however, because that is the job of human resources. When in doubt about what you can and cannot do, or if you are not sure, for example, what constitutes sexual harassment in the workplace, you need to find out.

It would be to your benefit to have a brief overview of the main legal pitfalls that new managers need to avoid and what your legal responsibilities are as a manager. You need to focus on the legal issues around sexual harassment, disability, substance abuse, privacy, family and medical leave, and workplace violence. Once again, you do not have to be the legal expert here. However, under the eyes of the law, ignorance is not an acceptable excuse. Far too many companies are sued and have to pay out huge sums of money because their managers were ignorant of the laws or did nothing to enforce them.

SEXUAL HARASSMENT

Sexual harassment occurs whenever unwelcome behavior on the basis of gender impacts an individual's job. According to the Equal Employment Opportunity Commission, sexual harassment is defined as unwelcome sexual advances, requests for sexual favors, and other verbal or physical conduct of a sexual nature that interferes with an individual's work performance or creates a hostile or offensive working environment. Any organization is liable for being a hostile environment, unless the organization can show it acted to prevent and correct sexually harassing behavior. Basically, what that means is if you allow, do not recognize, or do nothing about sexual harassment in your department, the company can be legally liable. Beyond the desire to create a positive and safe work environment, putting your organization's assets and reputation at risk in this way will likely not have a positive impact on your career.

DANGER SIGNS

To help you out in preventing and being aware of sexual harassment in your work environment, you should be aware of the following danger signs:

- Telling sexual jokes
- Making kissing sounds
- Discussing sexual topics
- Referring to a work colleague by terms of endearment like "sweetie" or "hot" or "baby"
- Making derogatory comments about a particular gender
- Displaying inappropriate images, whether on computer screens or mobile phones, hanging up in the office or work space, worn on clothing, or on coffee mugs or drinking glasses
- Any form of touching that another person feels is inappropriate (even shaking someone's hand inappropriately)
- Assigning less important responsibilities to members of a particular gender
- Not giving promotional opportunities equally to all staff members
- Giving individuals preferential treatment because of their gender

As you see from this list of danger signs, sexual harassment can be obvious behavior or it can occur in more subtle ways.

Most organizations have training classes on what sexual harassment means and how to prevent it in the workplace. Many other organizations have their employees take a short online course and then have them state that they have read the information and will abide by it. They may also be given a test. Having staff take the test and sign off on it shows the government that the company has made every effort to educate its staff. As a manager, you need to do everything in your control to make sure your staff understands that sexual harassment is not tolerated in any form whatsoever. And as a manager, you must report any incidents of sexual harassment immediately. If you avoid doing so, you and your organization are at risk.

DISABILITY

The Americans with Disabilities Act (ADA) bars discrimination against the disabled. The term *disability* means having a physical or mental impairment that substantially limits one or more major life activities of an individual, having a record of such an impairment, or being regarded as having such an impairment.

You are allowed to tell a job applicant that the job she is pursuing has certain physical or mental requirements, but you must do so for all applicants for the same position. You can then ask the applicant if she is willing and able to perform those duties. Most companies today make every effort to accommodate the needs of the disabled. They consider it a vital part of their role as responsible members of the community and see disabled employees as an important source of talent.

It is imperative that your department is free of any discrimination or harassment of the disabled. The following example concerns discrimination based on disability. In a local branch of a large banking organization, two employees, both bank clerks, were candidates for promotion to branch manager. They had equivalent banking skills, tenure, performance reviews, and so forth. One of the candidates, Henry, was really great at customer service. Customers would always remark how Henry was helpful and professional. So you might be thinking that Henry got the job because he had an edge over the other candidate, Marcia. Wrong. He did not get the job because he was disabled.

The branch manager making the hiring decision used the following reasoning. She said that an important part of the job was the socializing that took place after work and on weekends with the branch manager and other staff members. Quite often, these activities were physical in nature— rafting, bike riding, volleyball, and so forth. Since Henry could not participate in these activities, the branch manager decided to promote Marcia. You won't be surprised to learn that Henry filed a lawsuit and won.

SUBSTANCE ABUSE

Most companies have employee handbooks that list behaviors that, if committed by an employee on work premises, are cause for immediate dismissal. Using drugs or alcohol is on the top of that list. However, drug and alcohol abusers are considered to be physically handicapped under the Federal Rehabilitation Act of 1973 and are thereby protected from discrimination. As a manager, you must be aware of the following.

First, you cannot accuse someone of being intoxicated or on drugs. You can ask an employee if she has been drinking or abusing drugs. If the employee denies it, you are legally required to describe the symptoms that led you to ask the question in the first place. The symptoms may be sleeping on the job, slurring words, banging into furniture or equipment, exhibiting productivity or quality issues, and so forth. Your best bet is to focus only on the employee's behavior. If the employee does not have a good reason for behaving that way, you are permitted to send the employee home for her safety and for the safety of others. If you do this, do not allow the person to drive home on her own. You and the company are legally responsible if something happens to the employee or if the person causes an accident on the way home.

Second, do not share information about employees who have suspected drug or alcohol problems. This could be the cause of a lawsuit for defaming character. The only individuals with whom you would want to share such information are your manager, human resources, and a qualified counselor.

Third, you and the organization have the responsibility under most state laws of finding avenues for an employee's rehabilitation. You must try to get the employee to an employee-assistance program professional, who can give the employee the right guidance. If the person's behavior does not improve and the person is not enrolled in a rehabilitation program, you can begin disciplinary procedures.

As a manager, it is important that you be familiar with both the policies of your organization and the laws of the state in which you are located. Make sure to get this information from your human resources organization soon after you get started in your management role.

PRIVACY

Most companies have the legal right to inspect an employee's work area, listen to voice mail, or look at email and computer files, if they feel they have just cause. Nevertheless, our society considers every person to have a right to a reasonable level of privacy. Therefore, you need to find out what information about an employee you can and cannot disclose to other parties. For example, you cannot disclose drug test results, payroll information, or credit information such as consumer loans.

FAMILY AND MEDICAL LEAVE

The Family and Medical Leave Act (FMLA) permits employees to take unpaid leave for up to twelve weeks per year. Currently, the law applies only to organizations with fifty or more employees. Under the law, an employer must grant an eligible employee unpaid leave:

- For the birth and care of a newborn child of the employee
- For placement with the employee of a son or daughter for adoption or foster care
- To care for a spouse, son, daughter, or parent with a serious health condition
- To take medical leave when the employee is unable to work because of a serious health condition
- For qualifying circumstances arising out of the fact that the employee's spouse, son, daughter, or parent is on active duty or has been called to active duty status as a member of the National Guard or Reserves

Under law, an employee's job or a similar position is guaranteed upon his return. Employees are also entitled to receive all their health benefits while on family leave. An employee must have worked for an organization for approximately twelve months before he is eligible to apply.

This is general information. It is important that you get the latest information on the Family and Medical Leave Act from your human resources team.

VIOLENCE IN THE WORKPLACE

Unfortunately, violence in the workplace is all-too-common and should be a concern for every organization and manager. Examples of workplace violence include threats, verbal abuse, bullying, shoving, pushing, passive-aggressive behavior such as accessing and damaging the computer system, and use of a dangerous or lethal weapon.

Every organization and manager needs to demonstrate that they are doing everything possible to maintain an environment free of violence. The following warning signs can indicate that your department or organization might be a candidate for violence:

- Employees have no or little opportunity for their views to be heard.
- Training is not provided to develop new skills.
- Poor supervision—studies have shown that this is the number one cause of increased levels of violence at work. The violence is often directed at the bad manager.
- Lack of respect for employees.
- Employees have a history of workplace violence.
- Employees are having severe personal problems.
- Substance abuse is present.
- Employees undergo significant changes in their appearance, interpersonal communication, and other behaviors.
- The environment encourages fierce competition between employees or groups of employees resulting in some individuals feeling like they are losers.
- The security system does not do an adequate job of screening "outsiders."

If you have to deal personally with a violent individual within your own department, try to stay calm, use nonthreatening language, try to keep the person talking, and alert company security. Do not try to handle a threatening situation alone.

THE MANAGER'S ROLE

You have a critical role in establishing and maintaining a safe and respectful workplace. It is one of your most important managerial responsibilities. It is also a legal responsibility. The example you set will significantly influence what your team members see as acceptable and unacceptable behavior. Remember, when you are not sure what to do in any of the areas discussed in this chapter, contact someone who does.

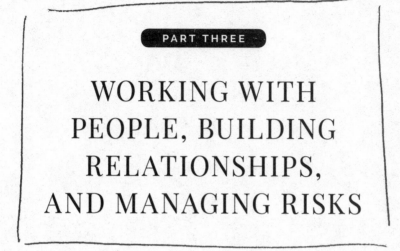

PART THREE

WORKING WITH PEOPLE, BUILDING RELATIONSHIPS, AND MANAGING RISKS

Successful management involves crafting constructive relationships and recognizing and managing opportunities.

18

NO SECRETS

TOO MANY MANAGERS, BOTH FIRST-TIME and long-time, take some private plea-sure in knowing something that others do not know. They assume that if they don't give others certain information, the others don't know about it. That is a flawed conclusion. If you do not let your people know what's going on, they will either seek out the information from other sources or simply make assumptions. This can work against you in two ways. The information your team members get from other sources may be incorrect or they may assume something that is not accurate. Even worse than that, they may act on the incorrect information or assumptions.

There are some bad managers out there who do not like to share infor-mation with their direct reports. They believe that if they keep informa-tion to themselves, they will have more control and be more powerful. They are mistaken. The most powerful managers are those who share information with their direct reports, thereby giving their team members the ability to be more self-directed.

You bolster your credibility by providing accurate information in a timely manner. Doing so will cause your people to come to see you as a reliable source of information. You also contribute to the effectiveness of your organization. By providing accurate information you make it more likely that your people can make good decisions on their own. The ability to make good decisions unassisted is the core of empowerment. Providing good information is part of the empowerment process—as is the goal clarity that we address throughout this book.

You've probably heard this before—and it's an important fact for managers to be constantly aware of: People don't act upon the facts; they act upon their perception of the facts. It is one of the manager's key duties to see that the facts and the perceptions are basically the same.

Very little that goes on in an organization needs to be secret. Often the things that are secret are merely a matter of timing: "We need to sit on this for a couple of weeks until the details are worked out."

The delight some managers feel in holding unnecessary secrets from staff is potential trouble. If people's assumptions about what was discussed at a managers' meeting are incorrect, and they act upon those false assumptions, it is very likely they will be going in the wrong direction and possibly working at cross-purposes to you and the team. It is more difficult to correct people's knowledge of what is *not* so than it is to let them know what *is* so in the first place.

To be clear, not all information should be shared with your team. There are valid reasons to withhold some information temporarily or in some cases permanently. Your judgment in determining if and when to disclose information is a vital part of your role as a manager.

A TYPICAL SITUATION

In many organizations, there is a regularly scheduled managers' meeting—for example, it's held at 8:30 a.m. each Monday. This becomes known as the Monday Morning Managers' Meeting. It's held every Monday except when a holiday is celebrated on Monday, in which case the meeting is held on Tuesday morning. (We have all seen notices saying, "The Monday morning meeting will be held on Tuesday.")

If this is commonly a one-hour meeting and you and a fellow manager stroll back together after two hours or more, some of the staff will think or make comments like, "Well, I wonder what they decided today!" Or, "They've been gone for hours; something big is going on." Perhaps what really happened was that the local United Way executive had asked for a meeting to explain some organizational changes. Since your company is an important corporate citizen, the United Way is simply building corporate support. It doesn't directly affect the company, but it's a matter of community public relations. The meeting about the United Way is fairly innocuous, but if you communicate nothing, some people are likely to assume that something big is going on.

Everyone has a desire to know what's going on. You have hopefully hired team members who are capable of taking initiative and making their own decisions. Not providing them with the information they need to do both works against you and your goals.

In employee surveys, one of the higher rankings, in terms of what information is most desired, goes to "a need to know of changes that affect me." People need to know even about things that may not affect them; if they know nothing, they assume something. Often that assumption is wrong, and too often it isn't even close.

As a manager or executive, you are better off communicating too much than too little.

Let's suppose that you have fifteen people in your department and you have three section supervisors who are each responsible for five people. The three section supervisors also have some work assignments of their own. (This arrangement is typical for the first step in management.) When you return from the weekly managers' meeting, call the three supervisors into your office and give them a brief overview of what went on at the meeting. They can then each inform their five staffers. You cannot allow these supervisors to keep it to themselves. They must communicate, too.

If you follow this approach consistently, you will build an empowered staff that will share with friends in other departments, "Our manager does a good job of letting us know what is going on." If you do otherwise, you're going to have a lot of false information floating around to correct—and that is possible only if you become aware of it.

19

THE HUMAN RESOURCES
DEPARTMENT

THE HUMAN RESOURCES DEPARTMENT (BETTER KNOWN AS HR) can be one of your biggest allies when you are beginning your management career. The department can help you out in many of the areas that new managers are not familiar with, including hiring, coaching, training and development, employee assistance programs, benefits, wage and salary administration, discipline procedures, promotions, performance appraisals, dealing with difficult bosses, termination, and all the legalities involved in managing. It is a good idea for you to familiarize yourself with what your HR department or HR person can do for you. For your own success and the success of your team, you need to build a good working relationship with HR.

A MANAGER'S INVOLVEMENT IN HIRING

How much you will interact with HR when hiring depends on how much latitude you're allowed in the selection process. In many companies, HR does the initial screening of prospective employees, but the final decision is left to the appropriate manager. The overall selection process is strengthened if the final choice is made at the departmental or operating level. If a manager had nothing to say about the person who was hired and is unhappy with the choice, the new employee is the victim of a difficult situation not of her creation. Fortunately, most companies allow the operating department to make the final selection from three to five qualified candidates.

Sometimes, their own bosses exclude first-time managers from the hiring process. While this exclusion may be well intentioned, it is a serious mistake. As we will address, hiring is one the most important responsibilities of a manager. The sooner a new manager can start to develop their hiring skills the better. The experienced manager should, at a very minimum, include the new manager in the process. And with some seasoning, he should allow that manager to select the people for whom she will be held accountable.

Managers have a far greater commitment to the success of selections they've made than they do to those who were selected for them and then assigned. The manager should not be able to think, "I never would have hired this dud." There will be a temptation to think in those terms when the manager has been cut out of the process.

Although people working in HR consider themselves experts on selecting employees, it doesn't matter who they think is the best qualified if the person is someone you don't want. How you react to the recommendations of HR people is important. You must take their recommendations seriously. This assumes that through talks with you they fully understand what the job requires. If they don't, it's because you haven't given them the information they need. They can't be experts on every job in the company, even with access to all the job descriptions. You're the expert on the jobs in your area of responsibility, and you ought to know what is required.

PROMOTION AND OTHER EMPLOYEE MATTERS

You'll also become involved with the HR department in promotions. There will be a natural inclination to promote people from within your organization, for good reason. You are most familiar with them and their performances and they are most familiar with your operation.

When you need to look to other areas of the company for the staff you need, the people in HR will be in a position to help you. For example, they can show you the original data collected when the person was hired and most information acquired since. In most cases, they'll consult with the department that employs the person you want to promote and get important information you might not have gotten on your own. Also, in some companies, the HR department administers employee benefit programs, so you might be going to HR on behalf of direct reports who are having difficulties with some aspect of the program.

If you haven't managed people before, HR can be a strong resource for you. You can usually go there for advice and counsel on supervisory problems you have not encountered before. The HR department is also the usual repository for books and articles on the management of people.

In many companies, the HR department oversees the training program. It will serve you well to quickly get familiar with training options for both you and your people. Quality training can be a great advantage but only if you are aware of the options.

Since HR serves the entire company, you can often talk with someone there about "people problems" that you might be reluctant to discuss with your own superior. So, you can look to HR for assistance not only in selecting people but also in training and managing them.

As a resource for your own career development, the HR department can suggest courses and programs you can take to improve your managerial and technical skills. HR can also be consulted about promotional opportunities, and can help develop action plans with you for how you can achieve those promotions. Keep in mind that just as HR helps you identify candidates for promotions, it also does the same for other managers who may be interested in you.

Many organizations use the HR department as a place where employees can go with any problems they don't wish to discuss with their own bosses. This can be a valuable service both to the employees and to the company. Hopefully, your HR department has been properly trained and educated in its function.

If at times you sense your HR department is not serving you well you will need to be cautious, diplomatic, and thorough. If you need to take issue with them tread lightly and make sure you have your facts straight. They will not like the suggestion that they are not doing an excellent job. You will need to have a well-prepared and tight case if you want to challenge them. By all means approach them with a collaborative as opposed to a confrontational tone.

If that approach does not work you will have to make a thoughtful assessment about the value of confronting them directly or escalating the issue. Be cautious and certain that the tension you will be creating is worth it to you in the long run. They can make your life difficult if they choose.

In short, HR will be able to assist you in your overall management job and with your personal agenda as well. To be highly regarded by a competent HR department is a great asset, so don't be a stranger to that part of your organization.

20

THE CURRENT STATE OF LOYALTY

IF THERE IS ONE SUBJECT THAT has fallen into disrepute in recent years, it is loyalty. While it still exists, it tends to be granted more sparingly and only when it is seen as having been earned. Changing employers is common. The more transient nature of today's workforce contributes to decreased loyalty.

There is a prevailing attitude that loyalty should be withheld until it is clearly proven that it is deserved: The manager shouldn't receive loyalty until she has earned it. The employee shouldn't receive it until he has demonstrated it is deserved. Lastly, the company doesn't receive loyalty until everyone—management and staff—feels it is justified. So, in many organizations, the lack of loyalty means less teamwork because no one trusts or is loyal to anyone else.

LOYALTY IS OUT OF FASHION

Unfortunately, loyalty in business is rare. Almost everyone feels that if one company acquires another, and the announcement is made that "we plan no personnel changes in the acquired company," it is a statement with no validity. The statement itself is perceived as the first step in a major reorganization and the subsequent loss of jobs. This perception is based on many examples of wholesale layoffs just a few months after reassurances to the contrary.

There have been many greedy, ruthless, and shortsighted acts. There also have been some reorganizations and mergers that were a matter of survival for the companies involved. People see friends in other companies being reorganized right out of their jobs. So, there are some cynical boards, some greedy manipulators, and some concerned owners trying to save a company. At the same time, there are managers and employees who trust no one. What to do?

Showing loyalty is often seen as a sign of naiveté. In many cases that may be valid, but if loyalty gets a bad rap, then it also follows that there may be times when it is withheld and it ought to be granted.

Do we become cynical and never show loyalty? Or do we give our loyalty until it is proven that it is not deserved? There is much to recommend the second option. Being cynical not only hurts the organization but also hurts you personally. If you have a cynical, nontrusting attitude, you become a cynic. A comedian who is a cynic can be a brilliant performer. A manager who is a cynic is a poor role model and will not be inspiring to his team.

So it's in your best interest to be reasonably loyal, not only to the organization but also to your manager and your team members. This means not criticizing your company in the community. You may be the only person associated with your organization that many of your friends and acquaintances know—your comments and observations will be the sum total of what those people know about your company. If you are negative and critical, that impression will be passed on not only to the people you know but likely others as well. Such an outcome does not serve you well.

A reasonable level of loyalty also means not trashing the people you lead. Even if there are times when you feel completely justified, avoid the temptation. Disparaging remarks say more about you than they do the object of your scorn. Give the organization and its people the benefit of the doubt. If you have come to the conclusion that your organization absolutely does not deserve your loyalty, it is time for you to move on.

21

————

IS THERE SUCH A THING AS MOTIVATION?

SOME MANAGERS' DEFINITION OF MOTIVATION IS "do what I want you to do, with a minimum of trouble." That is authority, pure and simple. It is definitely not motivation. It is using your positional power to get people to do things not because they want to but because they have no choice.

Motivation is getting people to want to do what needs to be done, willingly and not by force. The best managers spend time finding out what motivates their employees, blend those motivations with the needs of the organization, then create an environment in which their employees can be successful. There are many ways to find out what motivates your employees. You can observe their behavior, get to know them after a few months, or have them fill out a survey or questionnaire. There is one other method: Ask them!

SELF-MOTIVATION

The only motivation that really works is self-motivation. While your people may genuinely want to see the organization succeed, they are primarily motivated by their own interests. The most successful managers artfully align the self-interests of their team members with the goals of the organization.

When you do a job because it aligns with your self-interest, your motivation is self-perpetuating. You don't have to be forced into doing it. One of the primary responsibilities of a manager is to change the feelings of team members from "have to" to "want to."

Also, a good manager gets the job done by finding out how different people respond. If they are self-motivated, then they might be self-motivated either to get the job done or to just get by. They react in different ways, and you need to understand them well enough to know how they react and to what.

Some people are self-motivated by the possibility of a promotion. As soon as they see a relationship between their current performance and a promotion, they'll strive to perform at the top of their ability. Others seek their manager's approval. Since satisfactory performance is how they receive approval, they follow that path. Still others like to compete in a friendly way with their peers. This type of person wants to be the best performer in the area and so will work hard at achieving that objective.

Many people are working simply for the dollar, and the way to get more dollars is to perform well to maximize the next salary increase. Many others take great personal pride in doing whatever they do well. Depending on the condition of the labor market, a number of people will be working hard to keep from being unemployed.

Some team members bring their feelings for family into their attitude toward the job, but that is often tied into one of the other reasons mentioned—pursuing the dollar. They want to be able to provide more for their family, which requires more dollars.

You can increase the likelihood that your team members will tap into their self-motivation by making sure you provide them with the goal clarity discussed in Chapter 9. When they have a clear understanding of what needs to be accomplished and are allowed, within the boundaries you provide, to proceed as they see fit they are likely to be more engaged.

THE APPEAL OF A BARN RAISING

Most of us are motivated, whether we realize it or not, by the opportunity to be part of something greater than ourselves. It is likely that some of your most joyous memories involved working with others to achieve something you could not have done by yourself.

Think of an old-fashioned barn raising in which many members of a community joined forces for a few days to build a barn for a neighbor. The important element is that they worked together to do something none of them could do on their own, at least not in the same amount of time. Similar experiences for you could be a community fundraiser for a family in significant need, a team that created an app or worked on a new piece of software, a project team that developed a new product, serving in a military role where joint effort was critical, or a sporting team that did particularly well when each team member's talents were effectively applied.

When you create a setting where your people see that their efforts are contributing to a positive outcome well beyond what they could achieve individually, they will be more motivated and find greater meaning in what they do.

THE MANAGER'S ROLE

Learning how to maximize the performance of staff is a vital and permanent part of your daily work life. You'll have varying levels of turnover, which brings in new people. You need to get to know and understand them. Your obligation in this matter deserves particular emphasis. Employees want to be understood. They want to feel that their tasks lead to meaningful outcomes. They want to feel important as people, not as pieces of production to get the job done. Your genuine concern for them will shine through in all you do. To understand and appreciate them doesn't mean you need to be a parental figure. Nor do you need to compromise your principles as far as quality of work is concerned.

Concern for and understanding of your staff are signs of management strength, not weakness. The so-called tough, autocratic boss may achieve satisfactory results for a while, but over the long haul, this strategy will work against him. The performance he receives is driven in large part by fear, and his people will be inclined to give only the minimum they can get away with.

Many managers believe that if you are fair, concerned, and understanding, you can't be tough when the situation demands or requires it. Nothing is further from the truth. It actually makes the show of authority much more effective because it is rarely displayed.

There is one area in particular that you must handle with skill and diplomacy. Remember that some of your staff might be self-motivated in order to provide for their families. Of this group, some employees will respond favorably to your interest in their families, but others will consider personal inquiries an invasion of their privacy. So how does a manager handle these contradictory positions? If an employee on her own offers information about her family, you can then inquire about the family. In conversation, you'll learn about spouse, children, hobbies, and other interests. With this type of employee, you can make an inquiry such as, "How did Jeff and his team do in Little League last night?" This is a prime example of getting to know your employees—with their permission—and it fits into the concept that everyone is not motivated by the same things.

On the other hand, if you have an employee who never volunteers anything about her personal life, leave it alone and don't violate the obvious preference for privacy. In getting to know your employees, there is a tendency to work with the new people and ignore the seasoned employees who do an outstanding job. Of course, it's important to bring the new people up to speed, but you must never take the outstanding employees for granted. The outstanding achievers need to know how much their quality performance is noticed and appreciated.

DOVETAILING

If you are familiar with carpentry, you know what a dovetail joint is. It is one of the strongest ways to join two pieces of wood, for example for the corner of a drawer. The name comes from the shape of the interlocking "teeth" in the joint that get wider as they get longer, similar to the shape of a dove's tail. In this joint two different pieces of wood are joined together to create a strong connection.

There is a powerful management technique that takes this same approach, joining two different elements to create a strong connection. The two elements are the aspirations of your individual team members and the needs of your organization. When you can align the professional and personal goals of a team member with the needs of your organization, you have a committed and engaged employee.

Dovetailing involves two simple steps. First, get to know the members of your team. Let them tell you about their professional and personal goals and interests. This is not something that can be rushed. You will need to build some healthy and deserved trust with team members before you ask them about these types of interests. Often you will be able to discern them by just being a good listener. As your rapport develops, employees will often tell you about their non-work activities. Be attentive to what they share.

A good question to get this kind of discussion started is, "What are your professional goals? What do you want to be doing three years from now?" Most employees will be pleased that you are interested. Be fully open about why you are asking, to help put them at ease. Tell them that you are always looking for ways to blend the interests and aspirations of your team members with the needs of the organization.

The second step is to be attentive for opportunities to align these personal aspirations with what your organization needs to accomplish. This concept is illustrated in Figure 21-1.

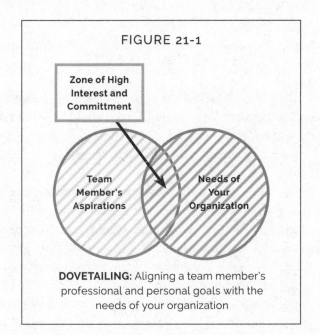

FIGURE 21-1

Zone of High Interest and Committment

Team Member's Aspirations

Needs of Your Organization

DOVETAILING: Aligning a team member's professional and personal goals with the needs of your organization

For example, let's say you learn that one of your employees is learning to speak and write Spanish. A few weeks later, you are sitting in a staff meeting led by your boss when she mentions that the company is close to creating a formal strategic alliance with a company in Central America. Perfect. There may be a way to get your team member involved with that initiative to everyone's benefit. Your team member will be able to improve and utilize his Spanish. The company will have an improved ability to communicate with the strategic partner. And you will be a part of an exciting new initiative.

Or let's say you are running a marketing operation and one of your team members who does market data collection and analysis tells you that she hopes to transition into information technology someday. When there is a need for staff-level interaction with the information technology department, that employee is the obvious choice. She is excited about the exposure to an area of interest and you get an employee who will be extra engaged. Will you lose her ultimately to an IT role? Probably. But you would lose her anyway sooner or later and in the meantime you have a team member who is involved and enthusiastic.

The more you can employ dovetailing, the more dedicated your team will be. You will also be addressing one of your primary responsibilities as a manager and a leader—developing your people.

THE ROLE PLAYED BY TITLES

The value of titles is underestimated in far too many organizations.

Titles don't cost a company anything, so you ought to be liberal in using them as long as you maintain equity within the organization. For example, you can't have one department that's liberal in the use of titles and another that is conservative.

The banking industry is well known for this practice, and although some executives in other businesses put them down for it, I think the banks know exactly what they're doing. A customer of a bank dealing with the vice president of consumer loans will feel much more gratified than dealing with a loan clerk. The spouse of the vice president of consumer loans is surely a greater booster of the bank than the spouse of the loan clerk. The bank's standing in the community is elevated by its liberal use of titles. The vice president in this instance may have the same duties as a loan clerk, but which one has the more positive self-image and the stronger self-motivation? The answer is obvious.

As you move up the corporate ladder, you may have an opportunity to influence your company's policy regarding the use of titles. There must be an orderly manner in their use. You don't start a new employee with a super title for a routine clerical position. An impressive title should serve as recognition for superior performance.

A company's morale can be increased dramatically by a more enlightened use of titles. Titles can go a long way toward giving an employee a sense of self-esteem and of being appreciated. The next time your company has a salary freeze, consider giving a key employee a new title. You may be surprised by the positive response. If you would like to give her a raise but can't due to the freeze acknowledge as much. Be clear that you realize that a new title is not a substitute for a raise but for now it is all you have the ability to do. She already knows she won't be getting a raise, but the new title shows that you appreciate her work.

We all want to feel important, and so do our employees. You will be well served by helping them experience that feeling.

THE STATUS SYMBOL

Another matter that falls in the motivation area is the status symbol. Obviously, status symbols work or they wouldn't find such widespread application in the business world.

The key to the executive washroom has almost become a joke, but it is still an effective perk. The size of an office or workspace, the quality of furniture, preferred parking, company-paid club memberships, company-leased automobiles for executive use, corporate aircraft—the proliferation of status symbols is limited only by the human imagination.

All could be considered as attempts to inspire people to raise their aspirations. These things are not important in themselves, but indicate that the employee is recognized as having arrived at a certain level in the organization. They're a lot more important to those who don't have them than to those who do. There is an old saying that goes: "Why is it that most of the people who say money isn't important are the ones who have plenty of it?" The same goes for status symbols.

A company should not become overly concerned about status symbols, but if it makes them available to its employees, it should not then criticize those same employees for longing after these methods of "keeping score." Actually, for most people, it's not the acquisition of the symbols that is important; it's what they signify to other people. Many status symbols would fall by the wayside if no one else knew you had achieved them. It's fine for you to want to attain certain status symbols, but it's important that you keep them in proper perspective. Don't let them become so critical to you that it'll tear you up if you don't attain them as quickly as you think you should.

You cannot substitute status symbols for a satisfactory salary program or a good management approach. Unfortunately, some managers and even some companies think otherwise. They treat people badly or pay them below the competition and then figure they can make up for it with status symbols. This attitude is an insult to the intelligence of their employees.

Status symbols are the icing on the cake; they are not the cake itself. When used with intelligence and some insight into human behavior, status symbols can be a valuable tool.

NEED FOR ACHIEVEMENT

Some employees have a need for achievement. Usually, they are employees whose needs for security, salary, working conditions, status, rewards, and so forth have been met. Employees who have this need usually want to be involved in decisionmaking, want to further develop their skills and talents, find new projects and tasks challenging, and want to advance in the organization. If you can satisfy these needs, you will not only have a self-motivated employee working with you but a highly productive one as well.

SUBJECTIVITY OF MOTIVATION

Many new managers are highly motivated, and that's great. But they make the mistake of believing that their employees will be motivated by what motivates the manager. That is likely not the case. Keep in mind that very different things may motivate your direct reports. This is not a problem—just be sure not to impose your beliefs or value system onto others. Also remember what motivates someone today may not motivate the same person in a few months. For example, today you may be motivated by achievement. Next month, you go out and buy a new house with a bigger mortgage. Now having job security—a steady job with a good salary—will motivate you. Try not to make assumptions about what motivates your team members. You need to find out and then act upon it.

22

UNDERSTANDING RISK INCLINATION

RESEARCH HAS BEEN DONE ON INDIVIDUAL and organizational risk inclination that broadens our understanding of the subject. The research provides a way for people to quantify their risk inclination and determine their risk quotient (or RQ). This research is presented in my book *The Power of Risk—How Intelligent Choices Will Make You More Successful, A Step-by-Step Guide*. You will learn how to determine your RQ in this chapter, but first let's discuss risk inclination.

STYLES OF RISK TAKING

By accepting your new management position, you decided to take some risks. Foremost, you moved from a position where you were likely performing well to take on a new challenge with no guarantee of success. This suggests that you have some willingness to take a career-related risk, at least when familiar with the people and organization offering you the promotion and when given the opportunity to fully assess it. The amount of time you took to decide whether to accept the promotion to your new position likely provides you with some insights into your risk-taking style. If you accepted the position immediately, you are probably a bit bolder, or you knew the offer was coming and had plenty of time to assess the pros and cons in advance. If you took a good deal of time to consider it, you likely have a more cautious style of risk taking.

DETERMINING RQS

The Power of Risk presents a risk-assessment tool that was completed by hundreds of people as a part of the research done for the book. It is a simple process. To determine your RQ, rate yourself on a scale of 1 to 10 with 1 being very risk averse and 10 being very risk inclined in the following areas of risk. Your ratings do not need to be whole numbers—4.6 or 5.7 are fine, just as are 4 and 6.

- ✍ **Physical Risks.** Activities that involve some risk of injury. Riding a motorcycle, river rafting, rock climbing, or skydiving are some examples.

- ✍ **Career Risks.** Risks such as job changes, taking on new responsibilities, or seeking promotions.

- ✍ **Financial Risks.** Your risk tolerance in investing, borrowing, and lending money.

- ✍ **Social Risks.** Risks like introducing yourself to someone you don't know or putting yourself in an unfamiliar social situation even at the risk of possible embarrassment.

- ✍ **Intellectual Risks.** Things like your willingness to study a difficult topic, pursue information that challenges your convictions, or read an intellectually challenging book.

- ✍ **Creative Risks.** Risks such as painting, drawing, taking on a writing challenge, or pursuing an unconventional design.

- ✍ **Relationship Risks.** Risks such as a willingness to pursue a new relationship, spend time with someone despite an uncertain outcome, or make a relationship commitment.

- ✍ **Emotional Risks.** Willingness to be emotionally vulnerable.

- ✍ **Spiritual Risks.** Willingness to place your trust in concepts that may be impossible to prove or that you do not fully understand.

Now total your ratings for the nine different types of risk and divide them by nine to get the average. That number is your RQ.

HOW DO YOU COMPARE TO OTHERS?

You now have your RQ but no real sense of what it means. The research showed that the average RQ of over three hundred people who completed the risk profile is 6.5. For men it is a bit higher at 6.7. The average for women is 6.3. Comparing your RQ to these results gives you a sense of how your risk inclination compares to others. This awareness will help you be more effective in interacting with others. If your RQ is well above the 6.5 average you need to know that you see the world differently than most people. You are more comfortable with risk and uncertainty. Though these can be valuable traits they can also be frightening to people who are risk averse. It is important that you have that awareness.

On the other hand, if your RQ is well below the 6.5 average you also have a different perspective than most. You are likely more cautious and deliberative than many. You take more convincing before making a decision and may see those with a bias for action as careless at times.

YOUR TEAM MEMBERS' RQS

You may want to give the members of your team the opportunity to determine their RQs. Make it into an interesting self-awareness exercise then let them share their RQs with their colleagues, if they are comfortable doing so. This can be constructive in a number of ways. First, it raises the topic of risk inclination as an important element of everyone's personal traits. It will also allow them to better understand how they may see a situation differently than their colleagues.

PUTTING YOUR AWARENESS OF RISK INCLINATION TO WORK

Your awareness of the risk inclination of various members of your team can help you be a better manager in a variety of ways. When assigning tasks add the risk inclination of the candidates to the factors you consider. If the task requires a lot of analysis and data gathering, you may find that someone who is less risk inclined would be a better choice.

If the task is on a tight timeline that will demand an accelerated pace you may find that a team member who is more risk inclined would be a better fit. Most of all, keep each team member's level of risk inclination in mind when making assignments and structuring project teams and departments.

GROUP SOCIALIZATION

From the field of sociology comes an important concept that can assist you as a manager. The concept of group socialization tells us that various traits—including risk inclination—are magnified when a high or low level is dominant within a group, team, department, or company. This means that if you create a project team that consists solely of people with higher-than-average risk inclination the aggregate risk inclination of the team will be even higher than that of the individuals. This is basically because they have an encouraging effect on one another.

You may want to create such an effect because the team's responsibilities will require them to very bold and aggressive. Putting together a team that consists solely of people who are more risk inclined will have just such a magnifying effect.

Similarly, you can create a team that is less risk inclined than all of its members if they are all have a below-average risk inclination. This could be exactly what you want based on the challenges the team faces.

Group socialization also tells you that by staffing a team or department with some people with risk inclinations above average and some who are below average, they will tend to have a moderating effect on one another. This means that the magnification effect that is present when the risk inclination of the group is uniformly high or low will be avoided.

This could be exactly what you want. It may be that you will be well served to intentionally create some healthy tension by putting together some people with above-average risk inclinations and some with below-average risk inclinations. The check they will naturally place on one another may be best for the task. This could be because you need the group to be thorough and methodical but also not get caught up in excessive analysis that results in an unacceptably slow pace or a hesitance to make decisions or recommendations.

RQS ARE SITUATIONAL

Be mindful that RQs change. They are affected by successes, setbacks, and other events in a person's professional and personal life. As an example, you may have observed someone becoming more comfortable with risk at a midpoint in her life once her children have become adults and are no longer reliant on her. It is not uncommon to see people redirect their careers at this point. So, if you have a team member with a 4.5 RQ today, do not necessarily assume it will be the same a year from now. It may go up, down, or stay the same.

AWARENESS OF RISK INCLINATION

You probably have already done a mental inventory of the attributes and traits of your individual team members, perhaps without really thinking of it. If asked, you could probably even assign each team member an approximate RQ that may not be far off from the RQ they would determine by going through the process presented earlier in this chapter. This increased awareness will serve you well as a manager.

When utilizing this awareness keep in mind that there is no ideal or even preferred level of risk inclination. People who are less risk inclined can make a valuable contribution if they assess opportunities cautiously in ways that more risk-inclined people may not. They are often more careful and methodical. Being more reluctant to take a risk they may also be more likely to require a higher level of research and data. While a person who has a bias toward action my find this frustrating, the less risk-inclined person is making a valuable contribution through their requirements.

On the other hand, more risk-inclined people often have a bias for action that can be vital to getting an initiative started. The goal is not to change a team member's risk inclination, but to be aware of it so you have a fuller understanding of how to motivate her and utilize her talents.

Let's say that you have not really thought about your team members' individual levels of risk inclination, which could lead to the flawed assumption that they are all pretty much the same. Now think about offering the opportunity to two team members to take a temporary assignment out of town to set up a new operation. Assume that one team member is quite risk inclined and the other is not. This opportunity may be beyond exciting to the team member who is more comfortable with risk. He may be thinking immediately about the excitement of getting to know a new setting, meeting new people, visiting new restaurants, discovering new cultural offerings, and even finding new recreational opportunities.

The less risk-inclined person may be thinking about all the hassles of living away from home, not knowing the area, having to find new service providers, not knowing which neighborhoods to avoid, and more.

Needless to say, the level of enthusiasm you receive from each team member is likely to vary significantly. This may seem perplexing if you have not taken their individual RQs into account. You may be able to convince both team members to take the temporary assignment, but you need to take a different approach based on their RQs.

RISK AWARENESS IN PERSUASION AND COMMUNICATION

Keep a person's risk inclination in mind when assessing how best to communicate with and motivate him. An awareness of individual risk inclination is also important when you are working with members of your organization beyond your team. Think about the level of risk inclination of the various senior executives in your organization. Rate each on a scale of 1 to 10 with 1 being very risk averse and 10 being very risk inclined.

What does this tell you about how you would sell them on an idea? You would want to explain to the executives with lower risk inclinations all the steps that can be taken to lessen the risks involved. For the executives who are more risk inclined, you would want to focus on the opportunities presented by the idea. Spending a lot of time telling more risk-inclined executives about the risk reduction steps you presented to their less risk-inclined peers may not interest them.

For all these reasons, it is valuable for you to have an awareness of your RQ, the RQs of others, and how they compare.

GAINING INSIGHTS

Now, you do not know the specific RQ of any given individual unless they have gone through the process of determining it and then shared the results with you. While you probably have a general idea, making a hard-and-fast assumption can be dangerous. A few probing questions can help you clarify your assessment, such as asking, "What information is going to be most important to you when I present you with a new opportunity? I don't have anything specific in mind. I just want to be prepared in case something comes along." There is nothing deceptive in your question. You are just trying to better understand your colleague so you can work more effectively with her.

Have fun with your increased awareness of individual risk inclination. It is a powerful awareness that can help you be more successful.

23

ENCOURAGING INITIATIVE
AND INNOVATION

THE PACE OF BUSINESS CONTINUES TO accelerate. Technology has made the faster pace possible while intense domestic and global competition has made it necessary. Amazingly, it was not that long ago that email, mobile phones, text messaging, video conferencing, and even overnight delivery did not exist. These are just some examples of tools that have quickened the speed at which business is conducted. It is only in the last few decades that companies have had to learn to compete effectively with foreign competitors.

Older, more layered, and gradual management structures and methods worked fine when all organizations used them. But as technology and communications tools have supported faster decisionmaking, the old methods have had to be updated. As you continue in your career as a manager, you will see the pace at which decisions are made and actions are taken continue to quicken. It is important that your leadership style keeps pace as things move faster.

A structure and culture that requires centralized decisionmaking is no longer sustainable. To be responsive to the challenges of the ever faster pace of business, good decisions need to be made at lower levels. Your organization needs to be agile. Stated simply, you and your team will not be successful if you create a structure in which you make all the decisions.

RESPONDING TO FLAWED DECISIONS
OR ACTIONS

When you establish clear organizational goal clarity, it will improve the quality of the decisions your people make. Even with that done, will your people always make the same decision you would? No. Will your people at times make inferior decisions? Yes. Will they at times also make superior decisions? Yes.

So, here is the question: Assume you are on a plane with no Wi-Fi, on vacation on a scuba boat, or cannot be interrupted in a meeting with a client. The specifics are not important. The point is that you are not available. Better yet, you are available but one of your team members is doing exactly what you have encouraged him to do and taking initiative. He makes a decision that seems to be a good one at the time based on the available information. Soon after, circumstances change and it turns out to be a bad decision. Not only is it a bad decision, it is going to be a costly decision that reflects poorly on you. The question is, how will you respond?

Will you call the person into your office and tell him that he really messed up? Will you suggest that he was off base by even trying to make the decision? Will you tell him to make sure he comes to you next time so you can make the decision?

If you do any of these things, how do you think he will respond the next time he is presented with an opportunity to take initiative? Almost certainly, he will not take action or make a decision on his own. Is that really your intent? Do you want to discourage him from taking initiative for a long time to come?

If your response to what turns out to be a flawed decision is to chastise, berate, or criticize, you are undercutting yourself. All the encouragement you give your team to take initiative, be resourceful, think like business owners, and be entrepreneurial will be wasted. Not only will your encouragement be wasted on the team member who made the flawed decision, but every other team member who becomes aware of the situation will also be more reluctant to take initiative.

When this happens, as it inevitably will, you need to bite your tongue and keep the long-term view in mind. To continue to encourage initiative-taking and the decentralized decisionmaking that will make your team more agile and effective, you need to take these steps:

1. Review the circumstances of the situation with the team member(s) involved.
2. Do not be critical.
3. Explain that your goal is to make sure everyone learns from the experience and that the mistake is not repeated.
4. Drive the conversation toward what can be done differently next time to get a better outcome.
5. Make it clear that while the team members cannot afford to make the same mistake again, you appreciate their willingness to take initiative and want to encourage them to continue to do so.

When you follow these steps, you will send the clear message that you are serious about empowering your people. You will benefit from your ability to restrain any anger that may have surfaced when you first learned of the flawed outcome.

You may be wise to explain the situation to your supervisor so she understands the bigger picture behind the flawed outcome. Emphasize that the team member did what they were asked to do and the training value that you have gained from the situation. While the less-than-ideal outcome is undesirable, it was created by an uncommon situation and is part of helping a team member grow.

PROMOTING INNOVATION

In addition to the ability to be agile and able to move quickly, intense competition requires organizations to be innovative, such as by devising new products, services, or methods that allow a company to be more successful. Innovation can be dramatic, as in the introduction of new products like smart speakers or self-driving cars. These are certainly innovations, but they are the exception. Most innovation is much more gradual and incremental. Every time you find a better way to do something, you are being innovative.

At its core, innovation is important because very few organizations can continue to exist, let alone be successful, if they are not continually improving. Look back at how your company's methods, services, and product offerings have changed in just the last five years. All of these changes were a form of innovation, necessary to preserve or increase your company's ability to compete successfully.

Innovation involves risk. By definition, risk means uncertain outcomes. Put another way, if the outcomes were certain, it would not be a risk. So, how do you encourage your team members to be innovative knowing that their ideas will not all be successful? The answer is by rewarding the effort as much as the outcome. If you reward only successful outcomes, you will get very little, if any, innovative effort from your team. When the outcome is disappointing, you need to follow steps similar to those used to handle flawed decisions or action:

1. Review the circumstances of the innovative effort with the team member(s) involved.
2. Do not be critical.
3. Explain that your goal is to make sure everyone learns from the experience and that the outcome is better next time.
4. Drive the conversation toward what can be done differently next time to get a better outcome.
5. Make it clear that while the effort was not as successful as desired this time, you appreciate their willingness to be innovative and creative and want to encourage them to continue to do so.

Why the focus on negative outcomes? Because responding to the positive outcome is easy. All involved will be congratulated and rewarded. It is how you respond to the negative or less-successful outcome that will determine the climate for innovation in your organization.

REWARD INITIATIVE THE SAME AS OUTCOME

The challenge with any form of incentive is that you will get what you incentivize. Ask any sales manager what happens when you pay extra commissions on a certain product. The sales team will sell more of them. It is the same with innovation. The problem is that the process of innovating is inherently imperfect. If you reward only success, you will get a lot less initiative because of the fear of failed outcomes.

The solution is to have a system of rewards and awards that recognizes initiative whatever the outcome. This may sound odd and even a bit disquieting. The whole idea of business is to reward the winners. That's true, but creating a culture that yields innovation requires a different and perhaps even counterintuitive approach. You have to recognize and reward a well-founded and executed effort that for some reason did not achieve the desired outcome in the same way you reward the innovations that did.

If this idea is making you feel uncomfortable, think about this. How many times have you seen a person or team succeed in large part due to luck while a person or team that actually did a better job was not successful due primarily to circumstances beyond their control such as changes in market conditions or the competitive environment? Almost certainly examples come to mind. Can you see how rewarding only the person or team that was successful this time will discourage innovation next time? It will.

In practice this means you have to treat a well-conceived and executed effort that was not fully successful the same as a successful effort in terms of performance appraisals, bonuses, rewards, and awards. If you have an award program for innovation, you need to have two tracks of awards. Those involved in the successful efforts may receive something you call the Innovators Award. Those who are a part of the well-conceived and executed effort that was not fully successful may receive something such as the Strivers Award.

This does not mean that you treat poorly conceived and executed efforts the same as successes. If the effort was unsuccessful due to poor decisions or performance, it should be treated as such. It is the efforts at innovation and initiative that were unsuccessful due to factors largely beyond the control of the team that deserve recognition equal to successes. Examples of such circumstances would be funding canceled midway through a project or sudden, unexpected external changes.

Will this approach upset the members of teams that have been successful when they are treated the same as less successful teams? Perhaps. Should that occur, simply remind them that they may be on one of the teams that is less successful next time through no fault of their own.

Encouraging initiative and innovation requires you to send the clear message that you value both even though they do not always yield the desired outcome. Done well, you will enjoy a lot more progress than setbacks and your team will have more fun and be more engaged in its work.

24

IMPROVING OUTCOMES

A BIG PART OF YOUR RESPONSIBILITY as a manager is to find ways to do things better—faster, cheaper, and more efficiently. And you need to be successful much more often than you are not. This means you have to always be mindful of opportunities for improvement. It also means you need to be able to execute well.

To use a shooting metaphor, you will not be successful if you shoot before you aim nor if you aim forever and never pull the trigger. You need to aim well, then shoot. Now think about how many more times you would hit the target if you could improve your aim even after you've pulled the trigger—the entire time the bullet is traveling from the gun to the target. This is the purpose of intelligent risk taking.

INTELLIGENT RISK TAKING

Risk taking suffers from a spotty reputation because it can lead to bad outcomes. There is a big difference between risk taking done well and risk taking done poorly. Since the goal is to be successful as often as possible, you need to risk *intelligently*. This is the idea behind the concept of intelligent risk taking, which is also drawn from the book *The Power of Risk*.

Since a risk is any action with an uncertain outcome, that means most of what you do in your work involves risk. The secret is to steer the risk skillfully—the effort, the initiative, the idea, the process—to a successful outcome.

Intelligent risk taking centers around increasing the chances of a positive outcome and decreasing the chances of a negative outcome. It involves six steps:

1. Identifying the risk
2. Assessing the likely outcomes
3. Improving the chances of success
4. Updating the assessment of likely outcomes
5. Conducting a disaster check
6. Deciding and proceeding

IDENTIFYING THE RISK

As simple as it sounds, this is a critical step. Before you can thoughtfully determine what action you want to take, you have to identify exactly what risk you are taking. You need to commit it to writing and keep it as succinct as possible.

A good example of identifying a risk is: "Commit $250,000 to an effort to expand international sales by 40 percent in eighteen months that includes hiring or transferring two employees." A poor example is: "Increase international sales." The difference is that the good example is much clearer on what is being risked, the action that is being considered, and the goal of the effort.

Another good example is: "Invest $185,000 in an automated inventory control system that will reduce spoilage and inventory loss by 8 percent." A bad example of the same idea is: "Buy an inventory control system that will decrease inventory losses."

You see the point. You want to be as specific as possible based on the information available to you.

ASSESSING THE OUTCOMES

Next determine the range of outcomes and the chances of each. Do not make this step too complex unless you are considering a very expensive or involved initiative. Identifying a best case outcome, a midcase outcome, and a worst case outcome is likely to be enough in most situations.

Using the risk identified above related to increasing international sales, your possible outcomes could be something like these.

- **Best Case Outcome.** International sales increase 40 percent.
- **Middle Case Outcome.** International sales increase 20 percent.
- **Worst Case Outcome.** International sales do not increase.

Now, based on thoughtfully assessing the state of the market, economic vitality, competition, the quality of the people you think you can find for the initiative, and any other factors you choose to consider, assign a likelihood to each outcome as a percentage. This may be as follows.

- **Best Case Outcome.** International sales increase 40 percent. Chance of this outcome is 30 percent.
- **Middle Case Outcome.** International sales increase 20 percent. Chance of this outcome is 50 percent.
- **Worst Case Outcome.** International sales do not increase. Chance of this outcome is 20 percent.

As you can see, the total of the possible outcomes is 100 percent. Yours need to total to 100 percent, also.

Let's take a look at what you have gained so far from this process. You have clearly stated exactly what risk, effort, idea, or initiative you are considering. That in itself is valuable because it will help you keep focused on exactly what you are assessing and not get distracted by what you are not assessing. You have also identified the likely outcomes of the effort and the estimated chances of each. By doing this, you are practicing a good deal of mental discipline. Even without the rest of the steps, you are already getting value from the process because you are being thoughtful about what you are considering and what you hope to gain from it.

IMPROVING THE CHANCES OF SUCCESS

This is the most important and valuable step of the intelligent risk-taking process. The most significant way you improve the chances is by identifying success enhancement measures. Success enhancement centers on developing "possibility of success enhancement measures"—POSEMs for short—pronounced like the animals known for being able to fool you into thinking they are sleeping when they're not: opossums.

A POSEM is any effort that can improve the chances of a desirable outcome or reduce the chances of an undesirable outcome for the initiative you are considering. Some POSEMs for this example include:

✍ Hiring people who have been successful in pursuing a similar effort. In this case, that may mean finding people with experience in international sales. It would be even better if they have experience with the product or service they will be selling. Better yet if they have experience in the same foreign markets they will be approaching. The point is to reap the benefit of the experience of the people you select.

✍ Investing in market research to get a more authoritative assessment of the potential and competition in each of the countries the team will be pursuing.

✍ Partnering with local distributors or providers in the markets you will be pursuing to get the benefit of their local knowledge and connections.

Identifying and implementing POSEMs is not an original idea. It is the role of all managers to identify ways to reduce risks that are part of nearly every day's work. POSEMs are your opportunity to be creative, to think expansively. When coming up with POSEMs, give yourself permission to think outside the box. You will not use every idea that surfaces, but you will miss some good ideas if you do not allow yourself to think broadly. Ask yourself, "What if . . ." questions. "What if we had the best people?" "What if we had unique insights?" "What if we could create a distinct advantage over our competition?" Then ask yourself how you can do these things.

Many POSEMs involve doing some research. Think about all the assumptions you are making in assessing the outcomes. Now think about all of the assumptions that you would be wise to validate. Being better informed will help you make a better decision. Just don't fall into the trap of waiting until you have an answer to every possible question before you make a decision. By then the opportunity will likely have passed you by.

UPDATING THE ASSESSMENT
OF LIKELY OUTCOMES

If you identified some powerful POSEMs and have a plan to implement them, they will have a positive impact on the likely outcomes. For this reason, the chances of each likely outcome need to be updated. For purposes of illustration, let's assume you proceed with the three POSEMs listed above and they affect the likely outcomes in this way:

- **Best Case Outcome**. International sales increase 40 percent. Chance of this outcome increases from 30 percent to 50 percent.
- **Middle Case Outcome**. International sales increase 20 percent. Chance of this outcome decreases from 50 percent to 40 percent.
- **Worst Case Outcome**. International sales do not increase. Chance of this outcome decreases from 20 percent to 10 percent.

As you can see, the total of the chances is still 100 percent.

The POSEMs have had a profound impact. They have significantly improved the chances of increasing international sales by the target margin. This is the power of the intelligent risk-taking process.

CONDUCTING A DISASTER CHECK

Before making a decision on whether to proceed with the risk, effort, idea, or initiative you are considering, you need to conduct a disaster check. A disaster check just means asking yourself if you can live with the worst possible outcome. What is the worst thing that can happen, and is it survivable?

With the example we are using as an illustration, it appears the worst case is investing $250,000 and getting no increase in international sales. The question is whether this is a survivable outcome. If it would destroy the organization or your career, the answer is probably not. If you can live with it even though you will be very disappointed, then the idea has passed the disaster check. You are now ready to move to the final step of intelligent risk taking.

DECIDING AND PROCEEDING

You have now identified the exact risk, effort, idea, or initiative you are considering and ways to improve the chances of a good outcome. You have also quantified the chances of various outcomes and subjected the idea to a disaster check. It is now time for you or those involved in the decisionmaking process to make a decision. Before you do, consider one more important element—you never stop identifying and implementing more POSEMs. We started this discussion of intelligent risk taking by equating the decisionmaking process to the ability to steer the bullet toward the target even after it has left the gun. This is exactly what continuing to identify and implement POSEMs does for you. If you are creative and diligent, you should be able to continue to improve the chances of a desirable outcome.

It is now time to decide. You may choose to go forward or you may not. Deciding not to proceed may be the best decision. Regardless of what you decide, you can make your decision confidently knowing that you made a very well-informed and thoughtfully considered decision. That is what managers are paid to do.

25

THE GENERATION GAP

FIRST-TIME MANAGERS CAN BE ALL AGES. There are new managers who are in their twenties, others in their thirties and forties, and some in their fifties and sixties. Three situations exist with regard to age differences between managers and the people reporting to them:

1. The mature manager supervises people who are younger.
2. The young manager supervises people who are older.
3. The mature or young manager leads a group of varied ages, some younger, some older, and some of the same generation.

Conflicts sometimes occur when a young manager supervises older workers. In some cases, mature people may resent working for a young manager. A large part of this problem can be the attitude of the older employee and the possible impetuousness of the younger manager. Therefore, we will first address the problems encountered by a young manager supervising a workforce predominately older than herself.

If you are the younger manager, you want your approach to be a little more gradual than may be your inclination. You want the staff to think of you as mature beyond your years. If your actions create that impression, sooner or later it becomes a fact in everyone's mind.

Take time making changes; go a touch slower. Don't throw your weight around by making decisions right and left, and too quickly. Many older employees will read quick decisions as being impulsive. Know that you may be subject to a double standard. The same actions that can be seen as impulsive when you take them could be seen as appropriate if taken by an older manager. It is just the price of your early success. Quick action by an older manager can be seen as decisive. The same action by a young manager can earn him the label "impetuous." What you need to do is give people time to get used to you being there. So don't build barriers that you later have to dismantle.

MISTAKES TO AVOID

Often, new managers makes changes right away, avoid the rule of incremental change, and use all their newfound authority. That approach upsets everyone, but it can be particularly bothersome to employees who have been around a while.

You don't have to know the answer to every question brought to you. Faking an answer when you don't know it is a mistake, and experienced employees will likely see through it instantly. If you can't answer a question say, "Good question. I don't know the answer, but I'll find out and get back to you." This candor avoids the image of being a know-it-all kid. In the minds of some older employees—and some not so old—you haven't lived long enough to have all the answers.

Demonstrate early and often that, like all good managers, you are concerned about the well-being of every person reporting to you. As a manager, you need to be a salesperson. Your job is to sell your employees on the concept that they are all fortunate to have you.

STRATEGIES FOR THE YOUNG MANAGER

Make your older employees more comfortable with your supervision by delaying some of the commonsense and fairly obvious decisions you have to make as manager. You know that you can make them almost immediately, but when you are new on a job, occasionally postpone your decision when possible to show that you are giving the matter thought.

For example, if an older employee brings you a problem that he considers serious, but about which you feel you can make an immediate decision, consider saying, "Let me think about that for a while and I'll get back to you tomorrow morning." That way you indicate that you are thoughtful and want to get all the facts, thus dispelling the young, know-it-all image. You also show that you are *not* impetuous, which is a frequent complaint about young managers.

Or, in the same situation, you might consider asking, "Do you have a recommendation?" or "What do you think ought to be done?" If the person bringing the problem strikes you as having common sense, give it a try. But if the person is someone whose judgment you have not had a chance to assess or who tells you how to build a clock when you ask the time, you may be better off passing on this idea.

GENERATIONAL INSIGHTS

Each generation has unique characteristics. In most workplaces you will have colleagues in at least three distinctive generations. Those are Baby Boomers (born 1946–1964), Gen Xers (born 1965–1976) and Millennials who are also known as Gen Y (born 1977–1995). It is important that you appreciate the differing traits and motivators that are common in each generation. While there are always exceptions to broad generalizations, there are some commonalities that often surface in these generations that can prove helpful to you. Figure 25-1 presents many of them.

✍ Motivating **Baby Boomers** requires that you value their expertise and provide them with traditional incentives such as compensation and promotions. They will take a fair amount of initiative consistent with being ambitious and goal-oriented. When successful they appreciate understated recognition, commensurate authority which they see as needed to achieve more, and perks such as reserved parking and a nice office in addition to their compensation.

✍ **Gen Xers** are also ambitious but prefer more autonomy. They place great value on flexibility, the ability to work independently, and not being micro-managed. Professional improvement is important to them, which leads them to value training and tuition reimbursement. They are incentivized by their compensation, a flexible work schedule, and independence in the form of telecommuting.

✍ **Millennials** are optimistic, very tech savvy, and expect flexibility. They are motivated by their contributions and opinions being valued. Their idealism surfaces in their need for a sense of regular progress, being a part of something they believe is important, and liking their work. Being members of a generation that has always had constant communication facilitated by technology, they value being well-informed, receiving feedback often, and interacting with senior leaders. Like Gen Xers, they consider flexibility important.

You will find that both Millennials and Gen Xers want broad discretion in how and when they work. Their approach can be, "Tell me what I need to get done then leave me alone to do it." Managing them closely can cause them to react negatively. You will also find that employees from these generations often value their personal time more than older team members. When given the opportunity to take on more responsibility and receive increased compensation at the expense of their personal time, they may not be interested.

FIGURE 25-1. TALENT MANAGEMENT MATRIX

	YEARS BORN	TRAITS	MOTIVATORS	THEY VALUE	INCENTIVES AND REWARDS
MILLENNIALS (aka Gen Y)	1977–1995	optimistic multi-taskers expect flexibility	being valued a sense of progress opinion valued a mission they believe in	liking their work being well-informed interaction w/ senior leaders skills training opportunities to grow & advance feedback	compensation and benefits personal time flexibility
GEN X	1965–1976	drive ambition prefer autonomy	bonuses/ stock flexibility	flexibility working independently self-improvement regular and public recognition	compensation flexibility telecommuting tuition reimbursement
BABY BOOMERS	1946–1964	ambitious goal-oriented identities drawn from work	compensation promotions recognition retirement funding	expertise being recognized and valued titles	compensation occasional feedback authority perks

THE MANAGER AS A MENTOR

High-performing employees almost by definition desire to grow professionally. This may mean expanding their skillset, advancement, or both. Casting yourself as a mentor can help you keep such high performers engaged. The more they see you as facilitating their professional goals, the more engaged they will be.

Being a mentor simply means that you take the professional growth of employees into account as you lead them and do all you can to facilitate that growth, consistent with the needs of the organization. If you are seen in your organization as a person who helps people grow and advance, you will never have any problems recruiting internally. Ambitious people will seek you out.

While it is not only younger employees who value a mentor relationship, they are more inclined to value such a dynamic. Some younger employees have been raised to chafe at direct authority and do not respond well to being told what to do. Structuring your relationship with them as having a mentor dynamic can allow you to get the same results using a different method. By allowing them to see how your insights and directions will assist their growth, in addition to allowing the organization to achieve its goals, you will be able to manage them in a way that works for both of you.

You might be thinking, "Why do I need to deal with a younger employee differently? They need to buck up and accept the ways of the world." You may be able to take that approach for a while, but you'll be swimming upstream. The first reason this attitude will work against you is that part of being an effective manager is being aware that one style of leadership does not work for everyone. An effective leader knows that she needs to be aware of and responsive to each follower's unique traits if she is going to evoke the best performance. An example is how a talented coach of an athletic team uses different methods to coach different athletes. The second reason this will work against you is that each day, more young employees enter the workforce. If you do not know how to adapt your style to lead them, you will make yourself obsolete.

Be careful in your mentor's role that you do not mistake it for being a best friend. While it is certainly good to have a positive relationship with the people you lead, you are not their best buddy.

ADDITIONAL INSIGHTS

There is some advantage in reviewing the past performance appraisals of your direct reports when you take on a managerial job, but remember to keep an open mind. The appraisals may be generally correct, but we've all known managers with blind spots about certain staff members. We have all heard about managers who inherit an employee who supposedly never had an original idea, but by using a different approach, the manager is able to receive some good ideas from this person. So don't give up on people too soon; you may find you have the ability to reach them.

26

MANAGING REMOTE EMPLOYEES

SOME OF YOUR TEAM MAY BE located offsite. Others may occasionally or regularly telecommute. If either is the case you will need to manage the situation.

There are valid reasons for employees to be located remotely. Lower labor costs may create a significant incentive for a company. There may also be a need for the person to be closer to customers or suppliers. Time zones may be a factor. Some information technology operations intentionally have teams spread around the world to better facilitate twenty-four hour support.

The merits of telecommuting can be hotly debated. Some well-known companies have decided to eliminate telecommuting or work-from-home as an option. If your organization allows it you need to manage telecommuting team members effectively.

REMOTELY LOCATED EMPLOYEES

It is important that as much as possible you treat members of your team who are offsite the same as onsite members. You need to be similarly accessible and communicate with them at least as much. You will want to use all the communication tools available to you including email, text, phone, and video with a bias toward video. Video calls or video conferences afford richer communication than the other modes.

You will want to have weekly one-on-one meetings as with your onsite direct reports. Create regular opportunities to meet with your remote employees in person. There is value in both visiting their worksite and in their coming to the location of the onsite team. Depending on how far away they are located you may want to meet with them at their location at least annually and also bring them to your location at least once a year. This in-person contact is vital in a variety of ways. Of course there is no better way to get to know someone. In addition, by bringing them to your location they will be able to get to know their fellow team members better.

EXPECTATIONS

You will need to have clear written expectations so your remote team members know what is expected of them. Subjects addressed may include:

- Performance goals
- Reporting requirements
- Availability—theirs and yours
- Response times—theirs and yours
- Work hours per week

The methods for delegating effectively that you will find in Chapter 36 apply with remote employees. At the core of effective management of offsite employees is the need to have absolute clarity of outcomes and schedules—meaning what they need to deliver and when they need to deliver it by.

TELECOMMUTING EMPLOYEES

Team members who work from home full time should be handled similarly to remotely located employees. Employees who telecommute occasionally are a simpler matter.

Employees who work from home a few days a week will still be in the office regularly. This will give you opportunities for the all-important in-person communication that helps you be effective. If you have telecommuters, you need to have written expectations similar to those you have for team members that are remotely located. All the same issues apply including accessibility, response times, and working hours. With occasional telecommuters your weekly one-on-one meetings with each of your direct reports can be in person, which is far preferable. Most of all you will need to again have a clear understanding of outcomes and schedules for which they will be held accountable.

27

SOCIAL MEDIA IN THE WORKPLACE

SOCIAL MEDIA SUCH AS FACEBOOK, LINKEDIN, Twitter, and Instagram are an everyday part of life. Your team members are likely active in some or all of them. As a manager you need to proactively address the implications of their possible presence in the workplace.

There are at least four different aspects to work-related use of social media. These are:

1. *Official use.* Official statements on behalf of the company to the public using social media platforms.
2. *Professional use at work.* Use of social media as a part of pursuing the organization's mission. Examples are research, recruiting, or promoting the company's products or services.
3. *Personal use at work.* Accessing personal social media accounts during work hours or on employer-owned devices.
4. *Personal use on personal time and personal devices.* Use of a personal nature that does not take place during work hours or on employer-owned devices.

Official use is specifically for those responsible for public relations, investor relations, public information, and similar roles. Unless your team is responsible for some of these areas it does not affect you.

Professional use at work is an appropriate tool. If your people use social media as a work-related tool you need to have clear written guidelines on what is and is not allowed in their posts.

Personal use at work needs to be addressed intentionally. Ignoring it can easily cause you problems. Many companies have outright prohibitions on personal use of social media during work hours or on employer-owned devices. These policies often prohibit using company email addresses for personal social media accounts. Reasons often cited for such policies are loss of productivity and potential liability. If this is your organization's policy it needs to be clearly communicated.

As with any other workplace issue, you will need to address noncompliance. Monitoring your employees' possible violations of the policy by following their accounts is precarious. You will definitely want to get guidance from your human resources or your legal departments before doing so.

Your policy or your company's policy may be a bit more lenient as it relates to personal use. It may allow use of personal media during breaks on personal devices. It may even allow any reasonable use. The most important point is that the policy needs to be clear and fully communicated.

Personal use of social media by employees on personal time and personal devices should generally not be something that involves an employer. The exception is when an employee posts confidential or proprietary company information or makes statements that are critical of the company or colleagues. These situations are an absolute minefield of potential liability and legal issues that should be addressed very cautiously under the guidance of your human resources or legal departments.

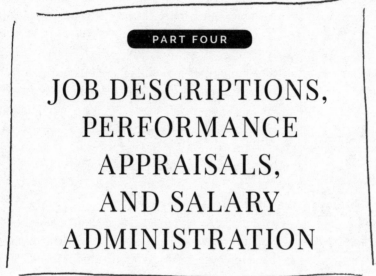

PART FOUR

JOB DESCRIPTIONS, PERFORMANCE APPRAISALS, AND SALARY ADMINISTRATION

Your ability to effectively handle the administrative side of people management will significantly influence your success.

28

WRITING JOB DESCRIPTIONS

JOB DESCRIPTIONS, PERFORMANCE APPRAISALS, and salary administration are important management tools and valuable functions that every company performs, either formally or informally. But if the people administering them are not properly instructed in the purpose and use of these tools, they can be seriously mismanaged.

We need to speak of these functions from a conceptual viewpoint. Discussion of precise details (such as the forms used) is not feasible because of the great variety in approaches that exists between industries, and even between companies within individual industries.

Even companies without a formal program use these techniques—although sometimes poorly. Informality is more likely to occur in smaller companies that are controlled by family members or by one or two people at the top. These individuals may feel they're being equitable and that all their employees are satisfied with the fair treatment they're receiving. That may indeed be the case, but the chances of it are remote. Even without a formal program, someone in charge decides which jobs are most important (job evaluation), makes a judgment on how well people are doing (performance appraisal), and decides how much each employee is going to be paid (salary administration). So even if the motto is "We're all like one happy family, and as the parent I make all the decisions on the basis of what's fair," the company does have a program—with all the idiosyncratic biases of the "parent" thrown in.

JOB DESCRIPTION BASICS

Most companies use job descriptions, although they may range from very informal to highly structured descriptions. A job description describes *what* is done in varying detail, and it usually includes hierarchical relationships.

Some companies write their own job descriptions; others use a system designed by a management consulting service whereby some company people are trained to write the descriptions and others are taught how to score the jobs to rank them within the organization.

A job description typically tells what is done, the educational background required, how much experience is needed to perform the work competently, what the specific accountability of the job is, and the extent of supervisory or management responsibility. The description may also spell out short-term and long-term objectives and detail the relationships of people involved, including what position each job reports to. It will often mention the personal contacts the job requires, such as interactions with the public or governmental agencies.

THE THREE-TIER APPROACH

When writing job descriptions, you'll find it helpful to use the "three-tier approach." The three tiers are:

1. Technical skills and knowledge
2. Behaviors
3. Interpersonal skills

In tier one, you specify what the person will need to do—the technical skills and knowledge required.

Then you add a behavior-based tier to the description. This tier describes the way the person will need to act or behave while performing the job duties. For example, the behaviors needed in tier two might include having good follow-through, being innovative and creative, or showing a commitment to quality.

The third tier is the interpersonal skills tier. Here the requirements for a particular job might include being a good listener, being a team player, or accepting criticism from others.

Many job descriptions focus only on the technical aspects of the job, which is tier one. However, the behavioral and interpersonal ones are just as important. In fact, most experienced managers say that behavioral and interpersonal competencies are greater predictors of an individual's success on the job. When writing job descriptions, make sure that each of the three tiers is addressed.

JOB SCORES

At some point, you'll write a job description, either for yourself or for some of the people reporting to you. Some companies allow the description to be written by the employee and then reviewed and modified as necessary by the manager. It is best if the description is a joint effort by the employee and the manager so that there is agreement as to what the job includes. This will help reduce disagreements down the road.

A committee specifically trained for that purpose usually does the scoring of the job. Often, the HR department does it. (We will not discuss how, because that varies by company.) The points arrived at in the ratings process will usually determine a salary range for each job, and the range may go from new and inexperienced to a fully seasoned professional on the job. If the midpoint salary of a job is considered 100 percent, then the bottom of the range could be 75 or 80 percent of that and the maximum for the outstanding performance would be 120 to 125 percent of that midpoint.

Since everyone knows that the score determines salary range, the score becomes crucial in many people's minds. As a result, there is a tendency for people to overwrite job descriptions in order to enhance the salary range. Filling a job description with such boilerplate copy usually works to a disadvantage. If a description is puffed up, it forces the committee to wade through the hyperbole to get to the facts. Job evaluation committees know exactly what the writers are doing, so the puffing up has the opposite effect. On the other hand, job descriptions that are lean, accurate, and to the point aid the committee in doing its work. So, if you write a job description, avoid the temptation to load it up. It is highly unlikely you will fool or impress the scoring committee.

29

DOING PERFORMANCE APPRAISALS

PERFORMANCE APPRAISALS CAN BE AS INFORMAL as telling someone "You're doing a nice job," or as elaborate as a full written report and a formal meeting with the employee.

Clearly, all of us like to know how we're doing. A formal system of performance appraisal—for example, one or two planned reviews with the employee each year for the specific purpose of discussing how she's doing—is preferable to the informal method, which is too often equivalent to doing nothing.

Some managers are convinced that they communicate effectively with their employees and that their employees know exactly where they stand. An interview with the employees, however, will often indicate that they feel the need for greater communication.

Many managers still approach their supervisory role with the motto, "If I don't hear anything, I know I'm doing okay." That doesn't cut it. Top-echelon managers often avoid discussing all performances except those that require emergency action. They feel that performance appraisals are necessary for the rank and file but members of the executive team are above such things. The rationale is that these officials are clearly in control of the situation and of themselves and don't need to be told how they're doing. Just the opposite is true. Members of the executive team often have an even greater need to be told how their superiors view their performance.

Performance appraisals are a powerful management tool that are often underutilized or neglected. Let's be honest—lots of managers really dislike conducting performance appraisals. This often results in them being done poorly and leading to a negative experience for the employee. Done well, performance appraisals will help you be more successful as a leader. Done poorly or not at all, they are a missed opportunity and can expose you and your organization to unnecessary liability. It is in your best interest to commit to doing them well and on schedule. Doing so will not only make you a much more effective manager it will also distinguish you among your peers.

LEGAL REQUIREMENT

In organizations with fifty or more regular employees (this may vary by state and by the nature of your business), it is a legal requirement to keep accurate and up-to-date records on every employee's performance, no matter what level the employee is. It is also a legal requirement that a formal interview take place at least once a year. The performance appraisal form is considered to be a legal document. Often in employment cases that go to court, the first thing the judge or referee will ask for is the history of performance appraisals. Performance appraisals are a great liability when they are not done, when they are done inaccurately, or when they are done with bias.

If an employee ever tells you, "I don't think so" during an appraisal meeting or after having reviewed his appraisal form or received his rating, you have not done your job well. There should never be any surprises at performance appraisal time. If you have done your job of communicating throughout the year and have continually told your employees how they are doing, you will never get that surprised response.

There are no specific rules for how often to review performance. Many managers have informal performance review meetings throughout the year just to ensure that there are no surprises. This is called *performance coaching*. Performance coaching is a regularly scheduled discussion between the manager and the employee to review the level of performance being met. Performance coaching is informal, can be documented if the employee wants it to be, and uses no forms. This type of coaching allows you to modify goals or set new ones, and to add or eliminate tasks or assignments.

Some companies require their managers to have quarterly sessions to avoid any surprises managers may get from their employees. A synonym for performance appraisal is *performance review.* If you think about it, this means that the once-a-year session is just a review of what has already been communicated throughout the year.

A MANAGER'S RESPONSIBILITIES

As a manager, you have a responsibility to follow some basic guidelines when writing and conducting performance appraisals. Here are the seven tenets of performance appraisal:

1. Set goals and objectives so employees know what is expected of them.
2. Provide training and coaching to help employees succeed.
3. Provide ongoing feedback on performance.
4. Prepare the paperwork for the review.
5. Conduct the review in a timely manner.
6. Understand and communicate the review's importance.
7. Be thorough and base the review on the employee's performance, not on your own attitude.

THE APPRAISAL FORM

A formal system should be designed in such a way that it considers as many elements of the job as possible. The manager should be forced to make some judgment about each of the important factors. This means, first of all, that the manager must be knowledgeable about the job and the employee's performance. That is why the appraisal should be done at the level closest to the job being reviewed. A manager three levels above the position in question can't handle the judgments as well as the manager in daily contact with the employee being appraised. It can be reviewed by higher-level management, but the appraisal will be more accurate when done by someone in daily contact with the job.

Here are some items that appear on a typical performance appraisal form. There may be anywhere from three to ten degrees of performance effectiveness for each category, the extremes being "outstanding" on the one end and "unsatisfactory" on the other:

- Volumes or production levels
- Thoroughness
- Accuracy (may be identified as error rate)
- Initiative/self-starting
- Attitude
- Ability to learn
- Cooperation/ability to work effectively with others
- Attendance and punctuality

You can probably think of other factors applying to your own business that ought to be included. Some systems may use a numeric weighting for each of the factors, arriving at a final rating that will be given to the employee. The entire form becomes a part of the employee's personnel file. The ranking scheme might be something like this:

- 80 to 100 points: *Outstanding*
- 60 to 80 points: *Commendable*
- 50 to 60 points: *Satisfactory*
- 40 to 50 points: *Needs improvement*
- Less than 40 points: *Unsatisfactory*

The ranges can be narrower or broader if your system requires it. You'll note that in this example, 50 to 60 points generates a performance description of "satisfactory." In some companies, this would be entitled "average performance." *Satisfactory* is the better word. Most people resent being called average—they consider it demeaning. The words *satisfactory* and *needs improvement* are more useful than *average* and *below average*. There are millions of average people in this world, but it is probably rare to find a satisfactory employee who thought she was just average.

Let's make another point about performance appraisals. Some managers have a rating in their mind, and they work backward to get it. You're "gaming the system" if you do that. It's usually done because the manager doesn't want to tell an employee that he needs improvement. But when you delay a tough decision, you're setting yourself up for much greater problems down the road.

THE INTERVIEW

The performance appraisal interview with the employee is crucial. You should plan to hold it at a time when you'll be unhurried. Allow yourself as much time as is needed to cover all facets of the job. Answer all questions. Listen to everything the employee has to say. Your willingness to hear your subordinate out may be as important as the discussion itself. Employees are so used to dealing with managers who behave as though everything is an emergency that, when given time to talk to their superior about their own dreams and aspirations, they may feel uncomfortable.

The conversation with your direct report is so important that you should avoid being interrupted. This should even include calls from the president of the company. The president should be informed that you are in the middle of a performance appraisal interview; she can decide if she still needs to talk to you at that time. This may include turning off or silencing your mobile phone. You may want to do this at the beginning of the interview and ask the employee to do the same. A comment like, "I want to make sure we can both fully focus on this conversation" shows that you place a high value on the review and the employee.

Of course, anyone in any organization can be interrupted for emergencies, and if that is the case, let your employee know what is happening and why you need to interrupt the appraisal meeting. It is quite disconcerting to be telling another person about your ambitions and feelings only to have the other break the spell by taking telephone calls or looking at incoming emails or text messages.

During the performance appraisal interview, you should direct the tone of the discussion but not dominate it. While you have a message to convey, the session will be more constructive and less threatening if it is more of a discussion. Do not hesitate to say things like, "I get the sense that you would be more effective if you took more initiative. What are your thoughts on that?" You'll be surprised how often an employee actually assesses her performance more harshly than you. Many studies have shown that managers rate their direct reports higher than the direct reports rate themselves. By engaging employees in the assessment, you are likely to get more buy-in to the process and reduce any air of defensiveness.

Eventually you will have an employee tell you he is strong in an area you know to be a weakness. This is inevitable. When this happens, you have an opportunity to use your coaching skills to help him see where he is coming up short. Do not get defensive or raise your voice. Comments like, "Well, let me tell you how I arrive at that conclusion" will serve you much better than, "You're way off and I am going to tell you why."

Keep in mind that the goal of a performance appraisal is twofold. First, its purpose is to give the employee an accurate assessment of how she is doing. Second, and more important, is to inspire her to improve her performance. This needs to be foremost in your mind as you are preparing for and going through the assessment process.

You need to go over each performance appraisal factor with your employee. You want to make known what you consider to be your employee's strengths on the job and what areas require some improvement. You'll seldom get disagreement on the areas you designate as strengths, but you're likely to encounter disagreement when you start discussing weaknesses. This is where you have to allow employees to express their own feelings.

Some people will never hear anything positive if it follows something they consider negative, such as an area that needs improvement. As a result, never start off a performance appraisal meeting with anything that might be construed by the team member as negative. Start with a couple of positives.

Do you have documentation that indicates where the employee is weak and where improvement is needed? Your case is much stronger if buttressed by hard evidence. Production or quality records are much more convincing than a manager's intuition. When you come up against the team member's disagreement, that difference of opinion is important and should be discussed. The employee may have some valuable input that might cause you to revisit your assessment. Be open to it. It's possible that you're wrong. Documented facts, if available, will help clarify disputed assessments.

Here is another way to engage your staff in performance appraisals. Before sitting down to share your observations, give all the members of your staff a blank evaluation form and ask them to evaluate their own performance. When you sit down to meet with the team member, compare their appraisals with yours. Again, you will often find that their ratings are lower than yours. This is another method that will allow you and your team members to discuss both of your views of each factor rated and keep the process more conversational. You will find that your staff will learn a great deal about performance appraisal from the method, and you will learn a great deal more about the people you manage.

Be cautious about pointing out the areas in which employees should show improvement and not going far enough. If you're going to tell employees where their job performance is not up to expectations, then you must also tell *how* it can be improved. This needs to be thought through in great detail before the interview is conducted. Keep in mind that your goal is to inspire and facilitate performance improvement.

THE AGENDA

This brings us to the preparation time that is essential to a successful performance appraisal interview. You should sit down and decide what points you want to cover in the conversation. You might even prepare a brief outline of what you want to discuss. It's possible that the performance appraisal form your company uses may trigger all the proper thoughts in your mind. However, you must anticipate that it will not. You'll look foolish if you fail to cover all the bases and have to ask the employee to come back into your office a day later to review some important point that you forgot.

Make an outline of the significant items you should cover. Here are some questions you might ask as you prepare the outline:

- What areas of this employee's performance or attitude should you mention?
- What areas not covered in the performance appraisal do you need to mention?
- What are some of the items of personal interest about this employee that you should bring up?
- What questions should you ask that are likely to generate some conversation and opinions about the work?
- How can you help this employee do a better job? What are the areas in which this employee will be self-motivated?
- How can you let this employee know he is important to you personally, not just for the work performed?
- How does this employee fit into the company's future plans? Is this person promotable? What can you do to help her advance?

This is the type of self-examination you should go through before beginning the session with the employee. A few minutes spent preparing for the conversation will greatly increase the positive impact of your performance appraisal interviews.

THE SATISFACTORY EMPLOYEE

Many managers prepare thoroughly for interviews with problem employees. They know those interviews might get difficult and they'd better see to it that they are ready to support their assessments. You should be just as thorough in preparing for an interview with a satisfactory employee. Occasionally, you'll be surprised by an outstanding staff member who'll turn a conversation you thought was going to be all sweetness and light into a real disaster.

As you spend more years in management, you'll find that the satisfactory employee sometimes uses this interview to unload some of the problems that have been festering. The problems vary with the situation. Here are some examples:

- "I'm not advancing fast enough."
- "My salary is not fair for the work I do."
- "You keep telling me that I am doing a great job, but my pay doesn't reflect it."
- "My coworkers are not performing up to standards."
- "As manager, you don't pay enough attention to subordinates who are getting the job done."
- "Good performance is not appreciated or recognized."

You should welcome such input from your satisfactory employees, even though you risk hearing what you don't want to hear. Let's face it, many employees will tell you only what they think you want to hear; but a rare and precious few will tell the truth, and these you must listen to carefully. What this team member has to say may be valuable to you and help fill in some gaps in your awareness. Don't fall into the "shoot the messenger" syndrome. Although the news a messenger brings you makes you unhappy, the fault is not with the messenger; punishing the carrier won't change the truth of the message carried. Ignorance may be bliss, but it can be fatal in a managerial career.

Of course, the information you're receiving may not exactly reflect the facts. You're receiving it through one team member's filters. That doesn't make it any less valuable. You may not have been around long enough to know how to sort out what is important and what is window dressing. If the satisfactory employee believes it's important enough to bring to your attention, then you ought to listen to it. Besides, this employee surely knows you prefer a trouble-free interview to one filled with problems, so you know the matter would not have come up unless the employee felt strongly about it.

It's possible that you may occasionally have a troublemaker on your hands who just enjoys stirring things up, but these people are usually not your satisfactory employees.

APPRAISAL INFLATION

One of the biggest flaws with the performance appraisal process is managers who rate nearly every employee satisfactory or better, even though some are not. This seems to be driven by a desire to avoid conflict. Don't fall into this trap. By not addressing areas where the employee needs to improve you are not doing her or yourself any favors. You are instead undermining the value of an honest appraisal and creating the misimpression in the employee's mind that she is doing just fine. If you take this path, you can be assured that you will not get performance improvement from the employee. You just told her she is doing fine.

In addition, it is highly likely that at some point she will share the results of her assessment with her colleagues. What effect do you think it will have on your top performers' motivation when they learn that a team member who is clearly weaker was assessed the same as or close to them?

Finally, by not addressing the areas the employee needs to improve you are setting yourself up for future problems. What happens when you have to reduce the size of your staff? Presumably, you will want to let your weaker performers go. You could now be faced with a situation where the employees you plan to lay off have a legitimate complaint. They have received nothing but positive performance appraisals. You are now on thin legal ice and open to accusations of favoritism or worse.

FOR LESS FORMAL INTERIM APPRAISALS

Keep in mind that all performance appraisals do not need to be as formal as we have discussed so far in this chapter. In Chapter 14 we talked about an improvement plan that can help you assist an underperforming employee. This tool is not just for problem employees. The simple page divided into thirds with the categories *strengths*, *areas for improvement*, and *goals* can serve you well in many employee management situations.

You may have a solid team member who comes to you to ask how she can improve her chances of being promoted. The one-page improvement plan works great in this situation. It also works for a team member who was not selected for a position he pursued. As a manager, you will at times have the joy of working with employees who are serious and focused on being the best they can be. This type of contributor is a pleasure to have on your team but can also be demanding. Again, the one-page improvement plan is a great way for you to keep him engaged and assist him with the improvement goals that will facilitate his professional growth.

AN OPEN-DOOR POLICY

"My door is always open." How many times have you said it yourself? It doesn't take the employees long to find out what the statement really means.

"My door is always open, as long as you don't come in here to tell me about any new problems." That's one possible meaning. "My door is always open, but don't come in to talk about money or a better job." That's another. "My door is always open, but I don't want to hear about your personal problems." Your employees know what you really mean or they soon figure it out.

Then there are the managers who are likely to say, or think, "I don't want my people to like me. I just want them to respect me." Don't you find it easier to respect people you like?

Your performance appraisal interviews should encourage your employees to say whatever they have in mind. The more open the communication between both parties, the better chance that you'll have a satisfactory working relationship.

SUBJECTIVITY FACTORS

Even though we need to be as objective as we possibly can and treat our employees fairly, we are still human. Being human, we allow biases to creep into our evaluations of others. It is very likely that you will like some employees more than others. That is only normal. But you need to filter your personal likes and dislikes when conducting performance appraisals. Also, be careful about overcorrecting by being particularly harsh with an employee you find enjoyable or pleasant. Hard data will help you be more objective.

Some managers are guilty of the "halo effect." Consider that you are evaluating an employee on five different goals that she is supposed to accomplish. Let's say one of the goals is reducing the department's error rate by 5 percent. This goal means more to you than anything else. If the employee accomplishes this goal, you may find you give her a figurative halo, like an angel's halo. In your mind, the employee can do no wrong. You are blinded by the halo. When the halo effect occurs, it is easy to overrate everything else that the employee does. Halo effects occur everywhere in life. Let's use a school example. If a teacher's favorite subject is science and a child is great in science, the teacher puts a halo on that child's head and gives him a higher rating in math and history because she was biased by his science aptitude.

The opposite of the halo effect is called the "horns effect." If the employee does not reduce the error rate, she gets horns over her head instead. Everything she does, even if it is great, can be diminished in the eyes of the manager because the employee has the horns.

Then there is the "recentness effect." As managers—and as human beings—we tend to remember what has happened more recently. So, if employees really care about their appraisal and they know it is coming up on June 1, they will do great work during April and May. This is not unlike the child who behaves better as the holidays approach hoping to receive more gifts as a result. In order to avoid this effect, you need to document and keep thorough records throughout the rating period.

Another managerial subjectivity factor is the "strictness effect." Many managers believe that an employee can always improve and that no employee is perfect. Most people would agree with that attitude. But many of those same managers would never rate anyone in the highest category (for example, "exceeds expectations"). This makes no sense and can be demoralizing. If team members have exceeded their goals and performed at an incredibly high level, why not give them the top rating? These managers would probably not even give the top rating to Babe Ruth if he were an employee of theirs. You've probably seen or heard of cases where a child will get a top grade, say 99 percent, on a test and a parent will ask, "What happened?" instead of praising the accomplishment. These parents obviously believe in the strictness effect. They think they are pushing their children on to greater achievement by insisting on perfection, but can you imagine what a demoralizing impact this has on a child?

There is one more subjectivity factor or bias that can creep into performance appraisals. Many new managers—or managers in general who are not familiar with their employees—are guilty of "central tendency." Let's say your review system has five rating categories—1 through 5, with 5 being the highest. If a manager is not sure which category to put an employee in because he has not done his homework of setting goals, doing quarterly reviews, documenting performance, and so forth, the manager dumps the employee into the middle category. This is not fair because that employee may belong in a different rating category. Falling victim to the "central tendency" will also undermine your credibility as a manager and send the message that you do not value your team members enough to do the research necessary to provide a valid performance appraisal.

THE USE OF BEHAVIORAL COMMENTS

When you write comments on the appraisal form, try to use behavioral examples that demonstrate why you rated someone as you did. For example, do not say, "Jason doesn't care about his work." Instead say, on January 8, February 4, and so forth, "Jason handed in reports after the deadline to which he committed."

Also, be very careful about the comments you use. Remember that this is a legal document and you do not want to be open to a lawsuit. There are many documented incidents of incredibly tasteless and legally troublesome comments written by managers on appraisal forms. Make sure you never write a comment like any of the following examples:

- "The wheel is turning but the hamster is dead."
- "One neuron short of a synapse."
- "The gates are down, the lights are working, but the train is nowhere to be found."
- "She has a full six-pack, but she does not have that plastic thing to hold it all together."
- "Bright as Alaska in December."

POST APPRAISAL

When you have completed the appraisal interview, it is a good idea to review how you did so you can improve and do better on the next interview. Here is a checklist that will help you out. Ask yourself if you:

- Explained the purpose of the interview
- Found out the employee's views and feelings on her performance
- Allowed the employee to do the majority of the talking
- Pointed out where the employee is doing well
- Offered suggestions for improving performance and asked the employee for suggestions (if necessary)
- Put the employee at ease by creating a relaxed environment
- Agreed on action plans for improving performance (if necessary)
- Set a time frame for improving performance (if necessary)

ONLINE PERFORMANCE APPRAISALS

Online performance appraisal systems are readily available and worth investigating. They have many desirable attributes that may appeal to you. In addition to allowing authorized people to access the appraisals from any location some offer writing assistance and scan for language that has the potential to cause legal issues. Some also have a goal management function that facilitates follow-up and accountability for goals set during the interview.

CLOSING THOUGHT

Performance appraisals are hard work. You need to keep accurate documentation, communicate constantly throughout the year, follow legal guidelines, fill out the forms correctly, conduct an effective interview, and then examine how the entire process went. The appraisal process is also quite time-consuming. You cannot do well by scrambling at the last minute to cobble together the information you need. But if you do an excellent job here, you will have employees who know what is expected of them and who trust that you will be working with them to help them succeed. Performance appraisals—if they are done well, are taken seriously by you, and are fair—can be a very effective management tool and a great motivator for each of your employees.

30

SALARY ADMINISTRATION

IT SHOULD BE OBVIOUS THAT JOB descriptions, performance appraisals, and salary administration all fit together in one overall plan. They are designed to provide accurate descriptions of what people do, give fair evaluations of their performance, and pay them a salary that is reasonable for their efforts. All these factors must bear a proper relationship to one another and make a contribution to the organization's overall goals.

If you have a job evaluation program, you probably also have salary ranges for each position in the organization. As a manager, you work within that scale.

It makes sense to have a minimum and a maximum salary for each position. You can't allow a situation to develop in which an individual could stay on the same job for years and receive a salary out of all proportion to what the task is worth. It's important to make certain that long-term employees are aware of this situation, especially as they get close to the salary cap on the job. For most well-qualified people this is not a problem, because they'll usually be promoted to another job with a larger salary range. However, in your managerial career, you will encounter long-term employees who remain in the same jobs. Perhaps they don't want to be promoted. Perhaps they are at their level of competence and cannot handle the next position up the ladder.

These people need to know that there is a limit to what the job is worth to the organization. You have to tell these individuals that once they are at the maximum, the only way they can receive more money is if the top end of the salary range for their type of position is increased. This may happen, for example, through a cost-of-living increase that raises the ranges on all jobs by a certain percent. Should that occur, you would have a little room for awarding salary increases.

Nonetheless, long-term employees who stay in the same job for an extended period of time and who are at maximum salary level need to have continued incentives. They are capable and should be kept on the job. Many companies have solved this problem by instituting annual financial awards related to years of service. Another approach is an annual discretionary performance bonus.

The salary administration program for all other employees usually includes a salary recommendation within a range of pay increases, based on the kind of performance appraisal the employee has received. Since the two procedures have such an impact on each other, some companies separate the salary recommendation from the performance appraisal rating. In that way, a manager's idea of what a salary increase ought to be is not allowed to determine the performance appraisal given. If as manager you make both determinations at the same time, you'll be tempted to take the answer you want and work backward to justify it. It remains difficult to separate salary consideration from the performance appraisal, but completing the procedures several weeks or months apart may help.

Let's assume your company does have salary ranges for each job and there is some limitation on what you can recommend. No doubt the salary ranges overlap. For example, a veteran employee on a lower-level job could be paid more than a newer employee on a higher-level job. An outstanding performer at one level could be paid more than a mediocre worker one level up.

EQUITY

As the manager, you're concerned with equity. You should review the salaries of all the people who report to you. You might begin by listing all the jobs in your department, from top to bottom. You might then write the monthly salary next to each name. Based on what you know about the job performances, do the salaries look reasonable? Is there any salary that looks out of line?

Another method you can use is to rank the jobs in the order of importance to the department, as you perceive the situation. How does that compare with top management's evaluation of the importance of the jobs? If there are differences you can't reconcile or accept, then it would be wise to schedule a meeting with your supervisor to see what can be done about it.

In this matter of rankings, appraisals, and salaries, it is important once again to emphasize a critical point. As mentioned in Chapter 29, recognize—and be willing to admit to yourself—that you like some employees more than others. You're fooling yourself if you think you like them all equally. Certain personality types are more agreeable to you than others. It is vital that you keep these personality preferences from unduly influencing the decisions you make about appraisals, salaries, and promotions.

In recommending a salary increase for several employees, you'll have some tricky decisions to make. If the company makes all its salary adjustments at the same time each year, then it's fairly easy to compare one recommendation against another. You can make all your decisions at one time and see how they stack up with one another. But if salary decisions occur throughout the year—for example, if they are tied to the worker's employment anniversary—it's more difficult to have all the decisions spread out in front of you.

Although maintaining equity in this type of situation is difficult, it is possible if you keep adequate records. Retain copies of all your job descriptions, performance appraisals, and salary recommendations. Some companies encourage supervisors not to keep such records and to depend on the human resources department's records. Maintaining your own set is worth the effort, however; you'll then have the records when you want them. Keep these records in a file that is locked or password protected, and do not allow any employee access to the file—not even a secretary or assistant who works closely with you. This kind of information has a way of getting shared if it becomes known.

THE SALARY RECOMMENDATION

In making a salary recommendation, be as sure as you possibly can that it's a reasonable amount. It should be neither too low nor too high and at the same time it must fit within the framework of the performance the employee gives the company. An increase that is too high, for example, could create an "encore" problem. Anything less than the same amount offered the next time around may be considered an insult or an indication of inferior performance by the employee. However, an unusually large increase coming at the time of a promotion doesn't run that same encore danger because it can be tied to a specific, non-recurring event. In that case, you must explain to the employee why the increase is so large and why it doesn't create a precedent for future increases.

Since a small increase can be considered an insult, you'd perhaps do better to recommend no increase at all rather than a pittance. Sometimes a small increase is a dodge, and is given because the supervisor lacks the courage to recommend no increase. But this only postpones the inevitable reckoning; you are better off confronting the situation immediately and honestly.

When considering the amount of the raise, it's essential that you not allow the employee's need to be an important factor. This may seem inhumane, but consider these points. If you based salary increases on need, the employee in the most desperate state of need would be the highest paid. If that person were also the best performer, you'd have no problem. But what if the employee's performance was merely average?

This does not mean you should be insensitive to the personal challenges of your team members. There are valuable nonmonetary things you can offer to assist them based on their circumstances. It may be that an employee has become a caretaker for a parent or is having challenges with childcare. Allowing him to telecommute or participate in meetings through teleconferencing may significantly assist him. Flexible work hours are another nonmonetary means you can consider that may be very helpful to the team member while not compromising the integrity of your compensation structure.

The common thread that must run through salary administration is merit. Basing your salary recommendations on who has been with the company the longest, who has the greatest number of children, or whose mother is ill moves you away from your responsibilities as a salary administrator and puts you in the charity business. If you have direct reports with financial problems, you can be helpful as a friend, a good listener, or a source of information about where to go for professional assistance, but you can't use the salary dollars you're charged with as a method of solving the social problems of your direct reports.

When you're making a salary adjustment for an employee who's having difficulty, there is a great temptation to add a few more dollars than you would otherwise. You must resist that temptation and base your decision strictly on the performance of the individual employee.

TALENT MANAGEMENT

Because part of a manager's job is anticipating challenges and requirements before they arrive you need to be thinking ahead regarding the skills and capabilities your people need. Start by asking yourself how the tasks your team needs to accomplish will be different in the future. What do you see ahead that will cause your team's mission to change? If you are not sure, talk to your supervisor and some of your peers. Ask them, "What changes do you see coming that will cause my team's role to evolve?"

An example could be an increased capability to do more of your tasks online. There may be possible acquisitions that could cause your team to have to do things differently. An example could be future dealings with colleagues or customers who do not speak the same native language as your team.

Another issue could be the natural advancement of some of your team members. Some of your people may be obvious candidates for promotion or near retirement. You need to be ready for either so your team is not suddenly much less capable because you did not plan ahead.

Planning ahead means looking at each of your team member's capabilities with future challenges or personnel changes in mind. This process is not as challenging as you may think. The Talent Management Matrix, shown again here in Figure 30-1 will make it straightforward.

Here is the process:

1. First identify what time horizon you are planning for. That is the projected date near the top of the matrix. It may only be six months from now or as far as two years out. Planning more than two years ahead is tough because there are so many variables.
2. List each member of your team in the first column.
3. In the second column titled *Current Capabilities* list that person's primary capabilities that they use to do their job.
4. This step is the one that requires the most thought. With the responsibilities you see in the future for your team as influenced by changes in the organization or personnel list the capabilities they will need to have in the future in the column titled *Required Future Capabilities*. Some of these will likely be the same as the capabilities they currently need to be successful. It may be that for some of your

FIGURE 30-1. TALENT MANAGEMENT MATRIX

TEAM MEMBER	CURRENT CAPABILITIES	REQUIRED FUTURE CAPABILITIES	MISSING CAPABILITIES	MEANS FOR DEVELOPING MISSING CAPABILITIES	TO BE PROVIDED BY OTHERS
NAME	1. _____ 2. _____ 3. _____ 4. _____	1. _____ 2. _____ 3. _____ 4. _____	1. _____ 2. _____ 3. _____ 4. _____	1. _____ 2. _____ 3. _____ 4. _____	❑ ❑ ❑ ❑
NAME	1. _____ 2. _____ 3. _____ 4. _____	1. _____ 2. _____ 3. _____ 4. _____	1. _____ 2. _____ 3. _____ 4. _____	1. _____ 2. _____ 3. _____ 4. _____	❑ ❑ ❑ ❑
NAME	1. _____ 2. _____ 3. _____ 4. _____	1. _____ 2. _____ 3. _____ 4. _____	1. _____ 2. _____ 3. _____ 4. _____	1. _____ 2. _____ 3. _____ 4. _____	❑ ❑ ❑ ❑

team members nothing will change. That is fine. Determining that is valuable. For others there may be a need for them to add capabilities they do not currently have. List those.

5. Now look at the capabilities that each team member will need that they currently do not have. Those go into the column titled *Missing Capabilities*.

6. Next you need to determine how the team member is going to gain those capabilities. Examples may be internal training, external training, online courses, shadowing someone who has that capability, on-the-job training, cross training or whatever method you see as appropriate. These go into the column titled *Means for Developing Missing Capabilities*.

7. Your final task in this assessment is to determine if it is not realistic for a certain team member to acquire any of the capabilities that will be needed. If that is the case, put a checkmark in the final column indicating that capability will need to be provided by someone else— either another team member, someone new, or an external resource.

Here is an example. Let's say that your organization is moving into a market that will require some on your team to have the ability to communicate in a language they do not currently speak. This will then be one of the items listed in both the Required Future Capabilities column and the Missing Capabilities column.

The first obvious thing to do is determine if anyone on your team already has that ability. Assuming they do not you need to determine how this talent is going to be acquired. It may be that an online language training course is appropriate. Or evening language classes if available may be appropriate. Part of the training process may be having the person travel to a setting where the language they need to learn is spoken.

Alternatively, you may determine that there are other ways to address this need. Let's say you determine that all that is needed is the occasional translation of some forms. That is something that you can pay an outside source to handle, or perhaps there is someone in your organization who is not on your team who can to that. It may be that only occasional translation is needed and an outside real-time translation service is available.

The important part is that you are planning ahead so you will not be caught by surprise. That is your job as a manager. The second part is that a thoughtfully completed Talent Management Matrix is a powerful tool when working with your supervisor. Think about how much better it makes your case for adding a member to your team if you place it in front of your supervisor to explain your reasoning.

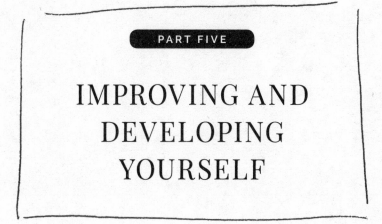

PART FIVE

IMPROVING AND DEVELOPING YOURSELF

In addition to using your abilities to help others improve, make sure to work on yourself as well.

31

HAVING EMOTIONAL INTELLIGENCE

EMOTIONAL INTELLIGENCE IS A MANAGEMENT concept with which you need to be familiar. Social scientists and psychologists have found that managers and leaders who have high levels of emotional intelligence, or a high emotional quotient (EQ), seem to do much better in their managerial and leadership roles than their counterparts who have average or low EQs. These experts have also found that individuals high in EQ experience more career success, build stronger personal relationships, enjoy better health due to better stress management techniques, motivate themselves and others to achieve greater accomplishments, and have the capacity to trust others and be trusted. According to these same experts, intelligence as measured by a traditional IQ test seems to have no bearing on managerial success.

HISTORY OF EQ

The concept of emotional intelligence was made popular in the 1995 book *Emotional Intelligence: Why It Can Matter More Than IQ*, written by Dr. Daniel Goleman. Since the book's publication, there have been many articles and books written on the topic. In addition, practically every well-respected management-training program now has a module or two on how to be emotionally intelligent.

IQ

IQ, or intelligence quotient, comprises competencies quite different from those of EQ. People high in IQ have great mathematical abilities. They also have extensive understanding of vocabulary and language, test high in abstract reasoning and spatial abilities, and have excellent comprehension skills. For the most part, IQ level is determined at birth. That is, there is a large genetic predisposition to what one's IQ will be. Over the years, IQ scores can change, but probably not more than fifteen points on the average. On the other hand, emotional intelligence is a learned behavior. An EQ score can change dramatically over the years.

EQ

Having emotional intelligence basically means that you have emotional smarts. If you can answer yes to the following questions, you probably have high levels of emotional intelligence:

- Can you walk into a room and sense the mood?
- Can you recognize the emotional states of others?
- Do you know when you are becoming emotional and can you control it if you want to?
- Under stressful and chaotic situations, can you evoke positive emotions in others?
- Can you and do you express to others how you are feeling and what your emotions are?

These EQ abilities seem to be very close to the supportive behaviors we mentioned earlier. EQ is a combination of having people skills and knowing a lot about yourself.

THE EQ TEST

Let's have a little fun now. Below are ten items that determine EQ levels. For each item, rate your own ability on a scale of 1 to 10, with 10 being the highest. If you want to get an accurate score you will need to be honest.

1. When in stressful situations, I find ways to relax.
2. I can stay calm when others verbally attack me.
3. I can easily identify my own mood shifts.
4. It is easy to "come back" after a major setback.
5. I have effective interpersonal skills like listening, giving feedback, and motivating others.
6. It is easy for me to show empathy to others.
7. I know when others are distressed or upset.
8. Even when working on a boring project, I can show high levels of energy.
9. I just seem to know what others are thinking.
10. I use positive, instead of negative "self-talk."

A score above 85 means you are already emotionally intelligent. A score above 75 means you are well on your way to becoming emotionally intelligent.

EQ AND MANAGING

No doubt you can see the connection between EQ and being a successful manager. Managing people is very different from managing tasks and projects. The EQ skills of recognizing your own feelings and the feeling of others; being able to express your emotions appropriately; being self-motivated and getting others to be; and being able to deal with stress, tension, and chaos and helping others do the same mark the excellent manager of today's workplace.

32

DEVELOPING A POSITIVE
SELF-IMAGE

HAVING A POSITIVE OPINION OF YOUR own ability is not an ego problem if it's a realistic assessment.

People can get awfully mixed up in dealing with this ego thing. There are always people who want you to feel guilty if you have a healthy opinion of yourself. But as the old saying goes, "love your neighbor as yourself." This implies that your capacity to love your neighbor is determined by your capacity to love yourself. This principle applies to management, too.

Many excellent books have been written on the subject of self-image, and they have important concepts in them for the manager. Here are a few basics that will help you in your managerial career.

The fact is, we fall or rise by our self-image. If we have a low opinion of ourselves and believe we're going to fail, our subconscious will try to deliver that result. Conversely, if we have a high opinion of ourselves and think we're going to succeed, our chances for success are greatly increased. That is an oversimplification, but it conveys the thought. If you think success, if you look successful, if you're confident of being successful, you greatly increase your chances of being successful. It's primarily a matter of attitude. If you believe you are a failure that is what you're likely to be.

Closely related to this is the concept of the *self-fulfilling prophecy*. Basically, the prophecy states that we treat people the way we are told they behave or the way we think they will behave.

To reinforce a successful attitude, you need some success along the way. Now that you've moved into your first managerial position, every success you have will serve as a building block to further achievements.

It should be obvious that you can't substitute feelings of success for actual accomplishments. You can't have the appearance without any substance. That would be a sham. You'll soon be found out, and to your disadvantage.

AN IMPRESSION OF ARROGANCE

One of the most serious problems observed in newly appointed young managers is the impression they can give of arrogance. Be careful that you don't mishandle your feelings of success so that you are seen as being arrogant. A manager can feel pride in having been elevated into the managerial ranks without appearing cocky. Rather, the impression conveyed should be one of quiet confidence.

Do you suspect there are people in your organization who don't believe you were the right selection and who'd delight in your failure? That is not only possible; it's likely. An attitude that can be construed as arrogant is going to make these people more likely to conclude that they're correct in their assessment of you.

STRATEGIES FOR IMPROVING SELF-IMAGE

Anyone can work on improving her self-image. Here are three methods that have proven successful. The first method is called *visualization*. You try to visualize a specific outcome that is important to you. Visualization is a tool commonly used by successful athletes. Competitive skiers are not allowed to do practice runs on a course before a competition. When they make their competitive run they will ski the course for the first time. You may have seen Olympic skiers spend hours on a course before they run it, visualizing how they want to take each turn. Lots of competitive athletes do the same, including gymnasts, kayakers, snowboarders, skydivers, and many others.

The same tool can serve you well in nonathletic pursuits. Just like a competitive athlete, you can visualize a specific outcome. It may be closing a big contract, getting a round of applause for conducting a seminar, or getting that smile of affection from a loved one for showing support. You may want to visualize getting your point across with your CEO, or disciplining an employee, or doing a presentation in front of the board of directors.

What happens in visualization, after periods of practice, is that these visual images become part of how we view our actions and ourselves. The brain records these pictures for later use. Visualization is not wishful thinking. It is programming your mind for the outcome you desire.

The next method is called *win-win*. In this method, you give people a lot of positive feedback and work hard to help others succeed. This makes you feel better about their work as well as your abilities as a manager. Helping others succeed is not only a way to improve your self-image; it also makes managing more fulfilling.

The last technique is *positive self-talk*. It is estimated that we send ourselves more than a thousand messages a day. If you want to build up your self-image, make sure that these messages are positive ones. The more you do this, the more the brain builds a positive sense of self. Examples of positive self-talk include the following:

- "I am improving my management skills each day."
- "I can handle this."
- "I made a mistake but I will do better next time."

Positive self-talk is like having an MP3 player in your mind that sends you only positive messages.

BEING SKITTISH ABOUT MISTAKES

In carrying out your duties as a manager, you'll make an occasional mistake. You'll exercise bad judgment. It happens to all of us. How you view and handle these mistakes is important not only to your own development, but also in how others perceive you. Your credibility is at stake. Be completely honest with yourself and everyone you associate with. Don't try to cover up a mistake, rationalize it or—worse—imply that it might be someone else's fault. Many managers have trouble getting the following two statements out of their mouths: "I made a mistake" and "I'm sorry." It's as though the words are stuck in their throats. These statements are not signs of weakness. They are signs of confidence and an acknowledgment that you are human.

New managers often have difficulty accepting responsibility for the mistakes of people who report to them. So skittish are these managers about mistakes that they avoid criticism by handling the more complex work themselves. When they do this, they create two destructive outcomes: They make themselves much less promotable and they kill themselves with extra work. These are the costs of their insecurities.

The way to solve this problem is to build your entire managerial role. You select better trainers; you become a better selector of people; you develop better internal controls that minimize mistakes and their impact. And when mistakes happen and you're the culprit, you admit it, correct it, learn from it, and—above all—don't agonize over it. Then you and the staff move on.

SELF-INFATUATION AND SELF-CONTRADICTION

You have to put forth your best image, but don't be so successful at it that, like the movie star, you fall for your own publicity. Be willing to admit to yourself what your shortcomings are. You'd be surprised at how many managers can't do that. They, of course, have shortcomings. They can't be experts at everything. But in ascending to their position, they find that many people start catering to them. It takes an unusual manager to realize that all the honoring treatment doesn't increase intelligence or boost knowledge. It's easy and pleasant to sit back and accept all that bowing and scraping. The manager is soon convinced that the adoration is deserved. Perhaps the charisma you think is personal is merely created by the position you hold.

When I was at the corporate headquarters of a large technology company in Silicon Valley I heard a cautionary tale about people catering to a new manager. Soon after a new CEO was selected he was walking to a meeting with some subordinates when he commented that the hallway they were passing through would look better if it was painted light green. A few days later when he passed through the same hallway he was surprised and embarrassed to see that the hallway was now light green. He never intended for it to actually be repainted. His was just a passing comment. This experience taught him an important lesson quickly—be careful with your offhand remarks. The desire of your subordinates to please may yield unintended and undesirable results.

The *infallibility syndrome* becomes most noticeable at the level of chief executive officer. Between the beginning manager and the top post are varying degrees of infallibility that seem to go with the job. You have to keep an honest perspective about who you are. Yet some CEOs fall into the infallibility trap. This may explain in part why the average tenure of chief executive officers of Fortune 500 companies is just over four and a half years.

If you were named CEO, you wouldn't automatically become smarter than you were the day before. But people would start listening to you as though you were dispensing pearls of great wisdom. You didn't get smarter; you just gained more power. Don't confuse the two!

Pay little attention to what executives say in this regard. Pay more attention to what they do. If an executive says, "I hire people who are smarter than I am," think about what he does. Do all the people he hires seem to be clones of him? If an executive says, "I encourage my people to disagree with me. I don't want to be surrounded by yes men," remember what happened last week when the executive snapped off the head of a subordinate who expressed a different point of view. If an executive says, "My door is always open," and then looks visibly upset when you walk in saying, "Do you have a moment?" the words ring hollow, indeed. The words are contradicted by actions and attitude.

Throughout your business life, you'll encounter executives who espouse impressive management philosophies. The main problem is if they wield their authority using other, less desirable concepts.

SHORTCOMINGS AND PREJUDICIAL MINDSETS

You don't need to advertise your weaknesses. That's foolish; just be willing to admit them to yourself and do all you can to correct them. For example, the things you probably don't do well are also the things that you don't enjoy. That's hardly a coincidence. Exercise some self-discipline and get the chores you don't like out of the way. Remember that in your performance appraisal, the quality of your work will not excuse errors in the tasks you don't like. So, even the tasks you don't care for demand quality performance. Every job has aspects to it that you're not going to like; get them done well, so they are out of the way and you can get to the parts you enjoy.

Be willing to admit that you may have mindsets or attitudes that are a problem. You can't take the edge off them if you do not acknowledge them. For example, think of the manager who has a prejudice against other managers who leave the office at five. He believes that when people become managers, their work comes first and social and family obligations have to wait. He also believes that any manager who leaves so early could not possibly have gotten all her work done, or done it well. His attitude probably derives from an inability to get his own work done if he leaves the office at five.

That's his prejudice; it's his mindset. It's not provable; it's an emotional feeling he has. In dealing with managers who have a life outside of work, this type of manager must be aware of his mindset and make every effort to overcome it—but without overcompensating for it. It's a tough situation, but we must first be willing to admit a fault or a strongly held belief before we can deal with it.

An ability to identify and acknowledge any deeply held beliefs or biases is a core element of emotional maturity. You do not have to set them aside, only understand how they impact your perception of, and dealings with, others. You do not want to be like the person you have almost certainly experienced who overwhelms the room with her excessively stated beliefs. This might be fine when the person is spending social time with like-minded friends, but it does not work in a business setting.

Most people's inclination when confronted by such a person is to minimize their connection and the sharing of information for fear of not aligning with his mindset. The person who chooses to "wear his beliefs on his sleeve" suffers for that style.

YOUR OBJECTIVITY

Through the years we have all come across managers who tell us they're looking at a problem objectively, and then proceed to explain their attitudes or solutions in a clearly subjective way. When a manager starts off by claiming to be completely objective, you must wonder why she says this. When you hear such a statement it is wise to be extra aware of exactly the opposite—a lack of objectivity.

It's unlikely that you will ever be able to be completely objective. We are the sum of all our experiences. We like some of our staff better than others, and may not even be able to explain why; it could be personal chemistry. As long as you recognize this, you can compensate by dealing fairly with those who are less liked.

It seems better for the manager not to bring up the subject of objectivity or subjectivity. How about being as honest as you can be in your dealings with people, and not get into all the shadings of objectivity and

subjectivity? The recognition of how difficult it is to be completely objective is a good place to begin.

When your manager asks you, "Are you being objective?" your answer
ought to be, "I try to be." No one can guarantee that he is completely objective, but an effort in that direction is admirable.

QUIET CONFIDENCE

Develop quiet confidence in your decisionmaking ability. As you make
more and more decisions, you will get better at it. Most management decisions do not require extraordinary wisdom; they require your ability to
acquire the facts and know when you have enough information to make
the decision.

Don't make emotional decisions and rationalize them afterward. When
you do, you will find yourself defending a decision that you wish you hadn't
made. A bad decision is not worth defending, even if you're the person who
made it. Once you rationalize a bad decision, you're trapped.

Too many new managers believe that they have to be fast decisionmakers in order to be successful. This creates an image of shooting from
the hip, which is not a desirable image to foster. The other extreme is
taking a great deal of time to make decisions.

Balance and moderation are the keys. You don't want to make decisions
so quickly that they are poor decisions, or take forever to make decisions.
Assemble the information you need knowing that you will often not have
complete or perfect information, assess the situation, and decide. Don't be
rash but also do not set unachievable requirements for information. If you
do, the opportunity will likely have passed you by before you decide.

DECISIONMAKING

It is important for your confidence to be able to use a variety of decisionmaking methods. There are four: solo, participative, delegated, and
elevated.

✍ **Solo decisionmaking** is when you make the decision yourself. This is
   the method you will likely use when you are the expert, time is short,
   or involving members of your team would not be appropriate because

of the nature of the decision. A personnel decision is an example of a matter you may need to handle without involving members of your team. This does not mean you shouldn't seek advice from people whom you do not supervise. You may be well-served to seek input from colleagues outside your organization, your supervisor, or even people who are not with your company before making a solo decision.

✍ **Participative decisionmaking** involves getting input from your staff members and making them a part of the process. The participative method can assist you with getting buy-in on the decision, help you make a better decision by getting those who will be a part of implementing the decision involved, and also may have some training value. Involving team members in making a decision can help them better understand the process and allow them to improve their skills.

✍ **A delegated decision** is one you allow the team to make for you. You would use this decisionmaking method when the team is more knowledgeable than you are or you are comfortable with any of the possible outcomes. As with the participative method, delegating the decision has training value and sends a clear message to the team members involved that you trust their judgment.

✍ **An elevated decision** is one you decide should be made by someone above you in the organization. This could be because you are not qualified to make the decision. A decision that will impact people beyond your team may also be appropriate for you to elevate. Elevate decisions reluctantly. You do not want to be seen as someone who is not willing or able to make decisions, but there may be times when you should legitimately remove yourself from the process.

Don't be the type of manager who uses only one method of making decisions. Be flexible in your approach. When you are able to select the correct decision method for the situation, your confidence and self-image will soar.

AUTHENTIC LEADERSHIP

No doubt you have been advised to lead by example. It's excellent advice. There is, however, another level beyond leading by example—authentic leadership. Authentic leadership is about gaining the regard of your team by being real and genuine. There are two inseparable elements of authentic leadership—exhibiting the behavior you seek and matching your actions with your statements.

Your team members observe you closely. They give you some regard and even deference because you are the boss. When you lead authentically, you will receive the genuine regard and respect of your team by choice instead of by necessity. That is true leadership.

Because you're the boss, your people will likely be responsive and respectful enough not to create problems for themselves. When you are an authentic leader, the dynamic changes; your people will move from being responsive out of necessity to being inspired and engaged. It's powerful.

If you exhibit high personal standards, you will inspire the same in your team members. If you are thoughtful and ethical in your decision-making, you will inspire the same. If you are respectful of your colleagues even when you disagree with them, you will inspire respectful behavior. If you conduct yourself with class, you will set a higher standard for your team.

So be honest with yourself; recognize who you are and the example you want to set. Then do it. It will make you both an inspiring leader and a better person.

OFFICE POLITICS: PLAYING THE GAME

As we already mentioned, you're judged by the performance of your area of responsibility. The people who report to you are as important to your future as are the people to whom you report. That leads directly to the matter of office politics. It exists everywhere. People recoil at the idea of office politics, and that is because not all people hold politics and politicians in high regard. The reality is that whenever more than two people are involved, there will be an element of politics.

Consider this rather positive definition of politics: the total complex of relations between people in society. From this perspective, you can see that politics are present in all settings that involve people. The game of office politics exists, and nearly everyone plays it. You're either a participant or a spectator. Most managers are participants.

Some people are viewed as "cold turkeys" by those who report to them but as "warm, generous human beings" by their superiors. This may be because these people are really playing the game, but in the long run they're working against themselves. However much they may succeed in fulfilling their ambitions at the office, they'll fail as human beings.

If getting promoted is more important to you than your integrity, than being your own person, then you'd better skip the rest of this chapter because you won't like much of what it says.

Almost anyone can succeed temporarily by being an opportunist, but consider the price paid in getting there. Granted, many of the decisions made about promotions will not seem fair to you, and they won't all be made on the basis of ability. Life is not fair, so don't expect it to be.

Often, individuals feel that many promotions are made on the basis of something other than fairness and ability. But even though most companies try to make these decisions fairly, it doesn't always come off that way. Besides, a decision that seems perfectly rational to the executive who is making it may not seem rational to you, especially if you thought you were the likely candidate for the promotion.

In spite of that, you still have to prepare yourself if you want to get promoted. If you depend on luck or serendipity, your chances are greatly diminished. You have everything to gain and nothing to lose by being prepared. Who knows, your opportunity for promotion may come from outside your company. You want to be prepared for that possibility, too.

PREPARING YOUR UNDERSTUDY

As soon as you've mastered your job, you must start looking for an understudy. The reason for this is clear. Decisionmakers are going to be less likely to promote you if doing so will create an operational void. By having an understudy who is prepared to take your position, you make yourself a better candidate for promotion.

Finding the appropriate understudy can be a delicate matter. You should not select your potential replacement too early. If the candidate doesn't develop properly and fails to demonstrate the skills needed to move into your job, you could have a serious problem. Changing your mind about a successor you've already selected is likely to create all sorts of problems.

How you go about preparing for your own replacement is of critical importance. If you already have a team member who is perfectly capable in the job, it's merely a matter of helping that person develop as thoroughly and as rapidly as possible.

Give the candidate bits and pieces of your job to perform. Under no circumstance should you delegate your entire job to the person and then sit back and read newspapers and business magazines. The company obviously didn't put you in the position for that purpose.

Allow your understudy to do more and more aspects of your job until he has learned most of it. Make sure the understudy does each section of the job frequently enough that it won't be forgotten. Occasionally, invite the understudy to participate in the interviewing process when you're hiring new employees.

Assuming the understudy is performing satisfactorily, start your political campaign for your prospective replacement. Make sure your boss knows how well the person is developing. On performance appraisals, use terms and phrases such as "promotable" and "is developing into an outstanding management prospect." Of course, never say these things if they're untrue; that would probably work to the disadvantage of both you and your understudy. But if the understudy is developing well, communicate it up to the next level without being blatant about it.

You run the risk that the understudy might get promoted out from under you. It's still a risk worth taking. Even if this happens to you several times, you'll get the reputation of being an outstanding developer of people. That will add to your own promotability. Besides, you'll find that developing employees can be a highly satisfying experience. And while you're worrying about preparing your people for promotion, perhaps your own boss is just as concerned about you and your future.

USING MULTIPLE CHOICES

If you don't have an understudy already in place, you should assign parts of your job to several people and see how they run with the added responsibility and the new opportunity. This is indeed to your advantage, since training several replacements at once makes it unlikely that all the candidates will be promoted out from under you. This in-depth backstopping will serve you well in emergencies.

Don't be in too big a hurry to move a single candidate into the position of understudy. The moment you name a person as your deputy, others stop striving for the job. That is the trouble with any promotion. Those who don't get it may stop aspiring to it, which usually has an adverse effect on their performance, even though it may be temporary.

The following management concept may be of value to you: Always hold something out for your team members to aspire to. If you get to the point where you have to select a single team member as your heir apparent, then let the other candidates know that opportunities still exist for them in other departments, and that you'll help them toward their goals of promotion.

As long as you continue to have several prospects vying for the position, however, you must treat them as equals. Rotate the assignments among them. Make sure that all of them are exposed to all aspects of your job. If you're gone from the office occasionally, take turns putting each of them in charge of the operation. Give them all a chance at managing the personnel aspects of the job, too.

On a regular basis, meet with all the candidates at once and discuss your job with them. Don't say, "Let's discuss my job." Rather, talk about some specific problems they've encountered. All of them will benefit from the discussion. If one of them had to face an unusual management problem in your absence, why shouldn't all of them profit from the experience?

AVOIDING THE PERILS OF INDISPENSABILITY

Once again, it is important not to allow yourself to become indispensable. Some managers trap themselves into this kind of situation. In their effort to ensure the quality of work, they request that all difficult questions and decisions be referred to them. It doesn't take long for employees to figure out that anything out of the ordinary will soon be going to the boss. The time taken from your day is not the only problem. The more fundamental trouble is that your people soon stop trying to work out more complex problems by themselves.

It's important that your people be encouraged to find answers on their own. They'll be better employees for it. There are limits, of course, to the areas of responsibility that can be delegated to them. It's good management to allow staff members some responsibility while still assuring them that the executive is accountable for their performance.

You've heard people worrying about whether the company would get along without them while they're on vacation. They have it backward: Their real worry is that the company *will* get along just fine without them. The manager who is doing the right kind of job in developing employees and backup management can leave with the assurance that the department will function smoothly in her absence. The truly efficient and dedicated executive, indeed, has progressed to the point where she can even be gone permanently—to a promotion or to another company. There are managers who, in a misguided view of what their job requires, make themselves indispensable and spend the rest of their business careers proving it—by never being moved from that position.

The main problem with such people is that they don't understand what the job of management is about. Management isn't doing—it's seeing that it gets done.

FOLLOWING YOUR PREDECESSOR

It helps a great deal if your predecessor in the job was a real disaster who left the place in a shambles. Unless you're a complete loser, you'll look like a champion by comparison. Sadly, that is preferable to stepping into a smooth-running operation. Following a company hero who is retiring or was promoted to a higher level position at another organization is difficult because no matter how well you perform, it's tough to be compared with a hero and the legend that time bestows upon him.

So if you ever have a choice between moving into an area of chaos or assuming a nice, clean operation, go with the disaster. It could be a great opportunity to establish a reputation that will stay with you your entire career. You'll not regret it and you will likely learn more from the experience.

CONTINUING YOUR EDUCATION

In preparing yourself for promotion, consider expanding your knowledge of the business you're in. It's not enough to become expert in just your area of responsibility. You must understand more about your company's entire operation.

You can acquire this additional knowledge in several ways. For instance, you can broaden your knowledge through selected readings. Your own boss may be able to recommend reading material that fits closely into your company's operation and philosophy. No boss is ever insulted when asked for advice. However, a word of caution: Don't ask for advice too often, because your boss will either suspect you can't make up your mind about too many things or figure you're seeking a favor. Neither of these impressions will help your cause.

If your company offers education programs, sign up for them. Even if you can't see any immediate benefit from them, they'll serve you well over the long haul. In addition, you're displaying an eagerness to learn. Make sure the classes and training you take are related to your current role and aspirations. You do not want to be perceived as someone who signs up for every class offered, regardless of its relevance. Also be reasonable in how much time you take away from your primary tasks for the education. The best way to increase the chances of being promoted is by doing an excellent job.

DRESSING FOR SUCCESS

Styles come and go, so what is inappropriate for business today may seem satisfactory in a couple of years, or even months, down the road. As a manager, you should not try to be a trendsetter by wearing far-out, extreme, avant-garde clothing. You might not think it fair, but you will not advance your career if some executive refers to you, in conversations, as "that kooky dresser down on the first floor."

What is acceptable or extreme may vary by the kind of business you are in or the area of the country. For instance, what might work in a fashion magazine's office would seem inappropriate in a tradition-bound life insurance company. What may be acceptable in the Southwest may not sit well in the East. Obviously, what you wear as a manager in a factory is altogether different from what you wear in an office. The point is that if you are going to be successful, it helps if you look successful—but not extreme. Your appearance should make a quiet statement, not shout.

The following story points out how dress can differ from company to company. Several years ago, a young man had an interview scheduled at one of the more creative departments within a motion picture studio in Hollywood. He called up his contact there and asked her what the dress was. She replied, "casual." So, the young man arrived in slacks and a nice pressed shirt. He walked into the room and everyone was dressed in tank tops and shorts! The word casual obviously meant different things to the interviewee and to his contact. Despite being on a different wavelength, however, the young man still landed the job.

This story not only proves that companies have different ideas on style and dress; it also shows that you'll make fewer fashion mistakes as a businessperson by being a bit overdressed than by being underdressed. If you go to an event wearing a suit and tie, and you find it's casual when you arrive, you can always take off the jacket and tie. If you dress casually and find that everyone is in a suit and tie, you cannot easily add apparel to get in sync.

A rule of thumb is this: If you're not sure what to wear, you're better to go more formal than casual. A second rule of thumb is that when you are in doubt, be attentive to how the senior leaders in your organization present themselves.

TOOTING YOUR OWN HORN, BUT SOFTLY

You can be the greatest thing since sliced bread, but if you're the only one who knows it, you won't go anywhere with your many talents. You need to get the word to the decisionmakers in your organization in the most effective way possible.

If you're obviously tooting your own horn, people are going to react negatively. You may come off as a blowhard—a reputation that will not serve you well. There are people with a great deal of ability who are too blatant in their self-promotion. It turns people off and has the opposite effect from the intended result.

You must be subtle. You want to be regarded as someone who is communicating effectively.

The following example shows how a situation might be handled so as not to be offensive to others and generate a negative reaction: Let's say the local community college is offering courses that you think might help you do your job better, and thereby make you more promotable. Here are some ways to make sure your boss and the company are aware of your educational efforts. (Anything that gets the job done without overkill is the goal.)

Send a note to the human resources department, with a copy to your boss, asking that your personnel records show that you're taking the course. That puts the information in your file, where anyone examining your record and looking at candidates for promotion will see it. Upon completing the course, again notify HR of the successful conclusion. If a certificate of completion is provided, send a copy to HR for your file.

Engage in casual conversation with your boss (if she hasn't acknowledged the copy of the note to HR), and mention something along the lines of, "The instructor in my accounting class made an interesting point last night. . . ." The boss may ask, "What accounting class?"

Place the textbooks on your desk. Eventually you will get the desired question.

Ask your boss for clarification of a class discussion item that you did not fully understand.

If you have a classmate meet you at the office for lunch, introduce her to your boss. "Mr. Jones, I'd like you to meet someone I met in my accounting class, Liz Smith."

You get the idea. The subtler you are, the less likely your efforts will come off as excessive. Your boss, who knows something about self-promotion, recognizes that you are communicating about your accomplishments. If you do it well, she may even admire your style.

Being the most qualified new manager in your organization is great, but you will not be serving yourself well if no one knows it. Very few bosses will approach you and say, "Tell me—what are you doing to prepare yourself for promotion?" So you have to help them.

Some executives espouse the philosophy that if you do a great job, the promotions and raises will take care of themselves. This is a risky strategy, and you can't afford to take such chances. If your superiors don't know what you're doing, how can they take your accomplishments into consideration? Develop a style of communicating the important aspects of your development, but do it with a degree of understatement so that others do not become offended or see you as too pushy.

AWARENESS THROUGH PRESENTING

One of the best ways to make your colleagues aware of your abilities is to develop your presentation skills. When you become comfortable presenting, you can pursue opportunities to illustrate your talents and knowledge. You will set yourself apart from the majority of people, who seek to avoid presenting. Most important, everyone in the audience will become more aware of you, your position, and your capabilities.

If you are like most people, you are not very excited by the thought of public speaking. Your reluctance is likely related to limited or even negative experiences. Chapter 39 will give you specific suggestions for moving past these limitations and improving your presentation skills.

BUT IS THE GAME WORTH THE PRIZE?

Being an outstanding manager and concurrently working up to the next rung on the ladder is a constant in almost every manager's career—unless he loses interest in moving higher. There is nothing wrong with not wanting to pay the price of moving to the next level. That is healthy if it's what you feel, because it means you're in touch with yourself. We all may reach a point where we are no longer considered promotable. Conversely, we may still be considered promotable, but we are comfortable where we are and don't want the aggravation that goes with the next promotion. Besides, the promotion pyramid gets much narrower the closer it gets to the top. Remember, the chair of the board of directors and CEO are no longer promotable—at least in the present company.

In earlier editions of this book, we mentioned that you have a right to know where you stand as far as promotability is concerned. We even suggested that there was nothing wrong with *pressing* for that information. Let's rethink this. If you don't care to be promoted, why ask? If you are offered a promotion, however, that's flattering and you might even change your mind.

If you want to be promoted and you think a promotion is long overdue, why ask and have some boss say, "No, I don't believe you are promotable," or have your boss dodge the question and leave you dissatisfied? What if you ask, and your boss puts a note in your file that says, "Manager Jones pressed me about promotion. Told him he's topped out." Now, let's say your boss leaves and goes to another company, and you're getting along famously with the new executive. You'd rather not have that "he's topped out" comment in your file. Why trigger that possible response—which may be faulty—and have it carved in stone?

If you desire additional promotions, it helps to keep your eye on the ball and not be distracted by some future possibility. While there is nothing wrong with letting a decisionmaker know you would welcome a new challenge, the greatest favor you can do for your career is to be outstanding at the job you hold right now. Mastering your current job is your first priority. Every other ambition must be secondary to that objective.

ACQUIRING A SPONSOR

It helps to have a boss who sings your praise at the executive level. Develop good relationships with all the executives with whom you come in contact, who know the quality of your performance, and who recognize your healthy, upbeat attitude. If the only one who thinks highly of you is your boss, and she leaves the company, you've lost your advocate—unless your boss offers you a great job in her new company. It helps if many executives in the organization know your name in positive terms. Being sponsored by several star executives is a great thing. Gladly accept committee assignments that put you in contact with managers and executives beyond your own department, consistent with your other commitments.

HAVING STYLE AND MERIT

Achieving the objectives discussed in this chapter requires excellent performance and self-confidence on your part. Often, the difference between a satisfactory job and a great job is image or style. Your style colors a superior's perception of your performance, especially if the style is one to which your superior reacts positively. But a bad or offensive style is similarly critical in evoking a negative response.

Doing a great job and maximizing the mileage you get out of that is one thing; conning people into thinking you're doing an outstanding job when you're not is quite another and will create problems. The message and the performance must be in sync.

33

MANAGING YOUR OWN TIME

HAVE YOU EVER COME HOME FROM the office with the feeling that you didn't accomplish any of the things you wanted to get done that day? We all have days like that, spent entirely in putting out brushfires. Sometimes it can't be helped, but if it's happening to you regularly, part of the problem may be your own lack of time-management.

SMALLER SEGMENTS

The following approach to time-management has worked wonders for a successful nonfiction author. Let's hear it in his own words:

"When I first started writing seriously about ten years ago, I'd set a goal of writing a full chapter every week, yet the entire week would go by without my having written a single line. The reason was my perception of needing to block out many hours for a chapter. Nothing was happening. Then I decided to break my goal down into smaller segments. The goal became to write two pages each day. Occasionally, I'd miss a day; then I'd set a goal of four pages for the next day. If for some unforeseen reason I missed more than two days, I did not make the goal a cumulative one, or I'd be right back to the block I had with the entire chapter.

"As a result of setting more reasonable goals, I started getting material written, even though other demands on my time remained unchanged. The only change was my attitude toward, and approach to, the problem. Sometimes I would sit down to write my two pages and ended up writing much more, ten or fifteen. If I had established a goal for that day of fifteen pages, I would not have begun to write."

The message is that you can overwhelm yourself into inaction by thinking that you need to be able to complete an entire project all at one time before you get started. Accept that you will likely need to break the project down into smaller segments that can be completed in smaller time periods.

THE LIST

You've probably heard of the late U.S. industrialist Henry Kaiser. Among his many achievements was establishing a company that built cargo vessels called Liberty ships during World War II. These ships were fully constructed in a matter of days—truly a spectacular accomplishment.

The first thing Kaiser did on entering the office in the morning was to sit at his desk with a legal-size pad on which he listed the items he wished to accomplish that day, with the items in priority order. During the day, the list remained on top of his desk. As a goal was accomplished, he drew a line through it. Goals that didn't get accomplished that day would be put on the next day's list. Kaiser always tried to work on his priority items first.

Try this simple approach to organizing your day and you will be pleasantly surprised at how much more you are able to accomplish. You're forced to plan the day's activities as you write down the day's objectives. That's probably the greatest value of the technique.

There are many tools we have today that were not available to Mr. Kaiser that make keeping your to-do list even easier. You may choose to keep your list on your phone, tablet, or computer and there are applications for this purpose. A web search for "goal management software" shows pages of results. Perhaps a simple document in your word processing application that you update regularly is sufficient. As computer screens keep getting larger and cheaper, you may choose to keep your list always posted in the corner of one of your screens.

Smartphones have lots of list-keeping capability and specific goal and task listing applications. A search for "goal list" in the Apple app store or on an Android smartphone yields dozens of apps.

You may prefer to use a simple small notepad you can keep in your pocket and always have with you. Use the tool that works best for you, but use one.

TIMING THE TASK

There is one modification you might make in your task list system that may make it even more useful. You know your own body better than anyone else. If you're at the peak of your energy levels early in the day, you should do the tasks that require high energy the first thing each day. On the other hand, if you don't hit your stride until later in the day, try to match the tasks to your different energy levels. It also helps to discipline yourself to do the things you don't care for when you are at your higher energy times, but still focus on getting the high-priority items done first. The less-important ones can wait.

There is another factor to consider as you plan your day. Some tasks on your list require you to be more creative and others more logical or sequential in addressing the task. A creative task may be writing a project proposal or crafting a presentation. Preparing a production report or doing budget calculations are examples of logical or sequential tasks.

Dividing tasks in this way correlates to what are commonly referred to as right-brain and left-brain activities. Right-brain tasks are the creative ones and left-brain tasks are the logic-based ones. The side of your brain you're using is not as important as remembering that there are different types of tasks. Another way to think of the process you use to address tasks is either *circular*, for the creative ones, or *linear*, for the logic-based ones.

Some people find they perform creative tasks better at certain times of the day, such as early in the morning or later in the evening. In turn, they may be more efficient performing logical tasks during certain periods of the day. Keep this in mind as you observe when you are most productive. Is there a task you have been trying to accomplish for a while that actually went quite well when you finally got to it? Make note of the time of day and whether it was a creative or logical task. Multiple observations of this type can give you insights that will help you be more productive.

Some people are more productive when they group creative tasks and logical tasks. The idea is that addressing different types of tasks requires a different thought process. You may benefit by trying to do creative tasks before lunch and logical tasks after lunch, or the other way around. I know of people who find it very difficult to return to creative tasks after they have taken up logical tasks so they try to schedule the creative tasks first.

THE FLAMMABLE TASK LIST

Everyone reading this is probably thinking that task and goal lists are great, but my days are so crazy sometimes I cannot get to a single planned task regardless of what method I use to keep my list. True. Some days it just seems like your task list is flammable—as soon as the day starts it goes up in flames. This is reality, but it is not a valid reason to not subject yourself to the discipline of planning your day.

Part of the reason you have been selected to be a manager is that you have illustrated that you have judgment. One of the ways you will need to use your judgment is to know when to stick to your task list, when to set it aside, and when to revise it. You will likely have to revise it during the day—and often many times in the same day. Your ability to do this well significantly influences your level of success. Many accomplished senior executives seem to have an innate ability to reprioritize based on changes in circumstances. Observe the leaders in your organization who do this well and learn from them.

PRIORITIZING THE TASK

Some managers divide their task list into three categories: A, B, and C. The A items are the crucial ones that must get done first. If you have several A items, you need to prioritize the tasks within that category. The B items can wait until you have the time. The C items are not urgent. Then there are those managers who like to do their C items first because they get a sense of accomplishment. Do not fall into that trap. When you do this, you are not only accomplishing very little, you run a serious risk of leaving some critical items in your A category undone and creating significant problems.

Keep in mind that circumstances can change and result in an A-category task changing in priority to become a B-category task. A few minutes taken throughout the day to validate and refresh your task list will pay you back many times over in increased productivity.

If an A item is too big, complex, or overwhelming, break it down into a few parts, just as the author in the example did with his writing. Instead of being one task in your list, it will be a few. An example would be developing your operating budget for the coming year. This is a big task. If seeing, "Create budget for next year" on your task list seems so overwhelming that you are not getting started, you may want to break it down into a few smaller tasks such as:

- Create quarterly revenue projections for next year.
- Determine tentative staffing levels for next year.
- Get projected materials costs for next year from purchasing.

Many people get a psychological lift by drawing a line through the tasks that have been completed. If you are using a goal-tracking program or application, you may want to give yourself a sense of accomplishment by moving them onto a list of completed items instead of deleting them. Some people use a big marking pen to cross out completed items. It's great to sit there at the end of the day's activities and see those big marks across so many tasks.

If you handwrite your list, don't throw the list away when you leave the office. The next morning, yesterday's list will serve two purposes. It will remind you of all you accomplished the day before—there's nothing wrong with that—and will inform you of what remains unaccomplished. These items then go on the new list. That's especially important for long-range projects that might get accidentally dropped from the list. Too many creative ideas and projects get away from us because we didn't write them down.

Have you ever gone to bed with an office problem on your mind, only to wake up in the middle of the night with a solution? Then you wake in the morning and it's gone—you can't retrieve the idea from your memory. A paper and pen on your nightstand for jotting such thoughts down during the night solves these retrieval problems.

THE TYRANNY OF THE IMMEDIATE

One of the biggest challenges to being efficient and productive is interruptions. Some interruptions are legitimate and need to be addressed right away. This requires the artful reprioritizing mentioned above.

Most interruptions do not need to be addressed immediately if at all. Technology has presented us with infinite opportunities for being interrupted. Emails, text messages, mobile phone calls, instant messages, tweets, and meeting requests are just some examples of interruptions facilitated by technology with which previous generations were not challenged.

What all of these have in common is the appearance, at least initially, that they are urgent. While some may indeed be urgent, it is very likely that most are not. When something appears to be urgent, it is tempting to give it priority. Suddenly, it will effectively rocket to the top of your task or goal list even though it may not really belong there. In a matter of moments, it has undermined all your careful planning and prioritizing. This is the tyranny of the immediate—the perceived immediate rules.

To be successful and stay on task, do not fall victim to the tyranny of the immediate. Be very discerning before you let a text message suddenly commandeer your afternoon. Before you let that happen, ask yourself. "Where does this issue belong on my task list—category A, B, C, or not at all?" It is tempting to respond like an ambulance driver to a new challenge. It can be exciting. But before you do, make sure it is what you really need to be doing. Don't fall victim to the tyranny of the *perceived* immediate.

THE CLOSED PERIOD

Some organizations follow a closed-office procedure you may want to use in mapping out your own day to accomplish more. For example, an office will have a two-hour closed period, where it's business as usual except that no one in the office goes to see anyone else. No one makes interoffice phone calls and no company meetings are ever scheduled during this closed period. Genuine emergencies are handled expeditiously; calls from clients, customers, or other outsiders are accepted.

This idea has a great deal of merit. It means you'll have two hours each day when no one from within the company is going to call you on the phone or come into your office. It gives you an opportunity to control what you do during the specified period. If respected, it should also reduce the impact of technology-facilitated interruptions from internal sources that can lead to the tyranny of the immediate.

Perhaps some person got the idea while working in the office on a weekend and noticing how much more she accomplished than in the same period of time during the week. But the idea is feasible only if you don't shut off your customers or clients during the closed period. It's an idea an entire organization can use to advantage.

THE NEED FOR REFLECTING

Plan to have a quiet period each day. You may not get it every day, but it's important that you set aside some time for daydreaming and reflection. It's vital to the inner person. Also, problems that seem insurmountable often ease into proper perspective during these quiet times.

There is a level beyond setting aside some quiet time for reflection: a powerful concept called "idea liberation" from *Business Lessons from the Edge: Learn How Extreme Athletes Use Intelligent Risk Taking to Succeed in Business*, by McCormick and Karinch. Idea liberation is a creativity strategy used by many of the successful athletes and executives referenced in the book and involves two simple steps. The first is to make note of when ideas commonly come to mind for you. It is probably a time when you have fewer distractions and likely not when you are at work. Activities that often allow ideas to surface include walking, biking, hiking, exercising in nearly any way, showering, meditating, driving, sitting on a park bench, or looking out over a lake or the ocean. You get the idea. There are activities in your life during which new ideas are more likely to come to mind. Identify yours.

The second step of idea liberation is to consciously put yourself in these settings on a regular basis and be prepared to note the ideas that surface. This will likely require you to leave behind or turn off your phone and stop texting or checking emails.

The premise is that ideas are always bouncing around in your head. Much of creative thinking is about harvesting them. When we are constantly intensely engaged, we rarely notice them.

So the action step here is to observe when new ideas surface for you, then put yourself in that setting often while being aware of the ideas that come to mind. You will be pleased with the creative ideas that you harvest.

OTHER TIME-MANAGEMENT TIPS

Here are some tips recommended by managers from a variety of fields. You may find them helpful as well:

✍ Recognize that we all have the same amount of time—168 hours per week. No one has more time than you do. What you do with this time makes the difference.

✍ Set deadlines for your projects. This especially helps if you're the procrastinator type. Avoid last-minute rush jobs. Some people say they work better under stress and tight deadlines. Perhaps they could work even better if they were not under stress. They need to give it a try.

✍ Remember the difference between something being urgent vs. being important. We all have urgent things to do, but always ask how important they are. Your ability to differentiate between urgent and important is critical to your success. It is best to focus on what is important. This tracks with the earlier discussion about the tyranny of the immediate.

✍ Try keeping a record for a week or two on how you spend your time. Keep a time log and write everything down. You may be very surprised to see where a lot of your time is going. If we do not analyze our use of time, we will not be able to manage it better. Or ask others for feedback on how you use your time. They can often see what you cannot.

✍ Plan your day. Doing this in the evening before is even better than doing it each morning. This way you already know what you are going to be focusing on at the beginning of the next day. If you wait until the morning to do this planning, you may get sidetracked. But whether it is the night before or in the morning, do it.

✍ Plan your week. Even if you work on weekends, it is well worth taking a few minutes sometime on Saturday or Sunday to plan your week. Having your plan for the week before you get to work Monday will serve you well and keep you on track when the nearly inevitable emergencies pop up, whether that happens Monday morning or later in the week.

✍ Follow the 70/30 rule: Schedule no more than 70 percent of your day. Leave the rest of your time for unplanned assignments, the urgencies of others, or emergencies. If you plan every minute of your day, you will be frustrated when you do not accomplish all of your plan.

✍ Schedule set times for sending and returning telephone calls, reading and sending emails, office hours, and so forth. This does two things for you. You save time by doing similar items together and others will eventually learn your schedule.

✍ Don't wait for that perfect time for you to be in the right mood to work on a high-priority item. The time or mood may never come.

✍ Reward yourself when you get one of those A-priority items completed. Take yourself out to lunch, leave a little earlier that day, or call a friend with whom you have been meaning to reconnect.

✍ Develop the on-time habit. Show up on time, hand in things when they are due, and encourage your employees to do the same. Be the model for time mastery in your department.

✍ Consider working from home, in a remote office, in a seldom used conference room or a vacant office—somewhere people will not expect to find you when you have to work on a task that requires total focus and a minimum of interruptions. As an example, a task that may take you a few days at the office amid all your other responsibilities can often be completed in half a day working at home.

34

THE WRITTEN WORD

IT'S A SOURCE OF AMAZEMENT AND some amusement that many articulate people are reduced to blubbering incompetents when required to put their thoughts down in written form.

Some people are intimidated by a blank piece of paper or computer screen. Let's examine why this feeling of panic overtakes individuals who otherwise appear to be competent and confident.

First, we have the *test syndrome.* Some people panic when taking examinations. All they have is that blank sheet of paper and the material inside their head. Now they must translate that information onto paper. Their "test score" depends on what is on that piece of paper when it rolls out of the printer.

A second reason people may not feel confident about using the written word is that they do not read much themselves. They get through what they consider required reading for work, but they don't read for pleasure or for personal or professional development. Instead, they watch too much television or spend a lot of time online, both of which are more passive than reading. You don't learn much about good writing by watching television or websurfing. You learn about good writing by reading. Television and the internet are not to be blamed for all the social ills attributed to them, but both have lessened the time many people spend reading, which in turn has had an adverse effect on their writing skills. For the most part, email and text messaging have not helped. Much of the writing in those modalities is choppy and filled with incomplete sentences and abbreviations.

In addition, because people don't write much today—except when they are sending emails and text messages—they are intimidated when they need to write a lengthy document or even send someone a handwritten letter. An analogy to public speaking might make the point. If you seldom give a speech in public, you are probably intimidated by the situation. And when you are intimidated, you are not relaxed; you are uptight and nervous. Your manner of speaking is stiff and uncomfortable. You communicate your apprehension to the audience; people may even feel uncomfortable for you. Your manner destroys their confidence in you and in the message you are trying to deliver.

The same thing happens with written communication. If you are intimidated by the situation, your writing will be stiff and stilted. Under such circumstances, you may try to cover the situation by writing in a more formal manner, using words you would never use in conversation with a friend.

Books and courses will tell you how to write business letters and interoffice memos. They can be a big help. If writing is a challenge for you or if you'd just like to do it better, definitely seek out training or books to assist you. You are much more likely to be successful and continue to advance in your career if you express your thoughts well and persuasively in writing.

HARNESS THE POWER OF STORIES

When you are trying to make a point always consider using a story. Stories are more powerful than even a well-reasoned argument. Using a story will also make your assertions more memorable. As humans, we connect with stories. That is why talented speakers and orators will almost always use stories to make their points. You may have noticed that some of the points in this book are reinforced by examples that are in essence stories. It is very likely that you remember those points better than others. The hotel in Singapore, the team member who is studying Spanish, and the dovetail carpentry joint are all examples of using a story element to make a point.

MENTAL IMAGERY HELPS

One of the best methods for improving your writing skills is to use mental imagery. Instead of being intimidated by the blank screen or piece of paper, get a mental image of the person you are writing to. See that person in your mind. You might even go so far as to imagine the person seated in a comfortable chair at the office drinking a cup of coffee and reading your note. Or you could visualize yourself sitting in a coffeehouse telling the person the message you want to convey.

Imagine that you are having a conversation with the person in a friendly environment. Now speak. Use words you'd use in conversation. If you don't use four-syllable words in your conversations, don't use them in your written communication. Psychologists tell us that people who use certain words, these fancy types of words, only when they want to impress others in their writing are actually showing signs of having an inferiority complex. Even if you do feel uncomfortable with your writing, don't advertise it—keep it to yourself.

When conjuring up the mental picture of the person you're writing to, always imagine a friendly face. Even if you are, for example, sending an email to someone you can't stand, imagine that you're writing to a friend. *Never* conjure up hostile feelings because they may come through in your writing. Imagining a friendly face will bring a friendly, warm tone to your communication.

Now let's take a broader situation: sending an email to all the people in your department or division. You don't want to imagine forty-five people sitting in an auditorium waiting for you to speak. That is too formal a situation, and unless you're an outstanding and relaxed public speaker, the image is going to make your writing formal and uptight.

Instead, get a mental picture of two or three of the friendliest employees you have reporting to you. Imagine that you are on a coffee break or lunch break with them. Now say to them what you have to say. That is what you write. If you're writing to fellow managers in other departments, you can use similar mental images.

Now let's assume you have to write an update report to the president of the company, and let's assume she is a bit unapproachable and intimidating. Getting a mental image of the president is only going to make the situation worse. Think instead of someone who does not intimidate you. Imagine that person as the president. Now write the report. The tone will be altogether different.

Writing informally does not mean using incomplete sentences or faulty grammar. Some emails sent by educated businesspeople would make their eighth-grade English teachers cringe. Many companies offer in-house training courses specifically on how to write proper emails. When writing an email, you need to make certain your grammar and spelling are correct. Some emails can be brief and not particularly well written. But that does not mean sending them with misspellings and poorly structured or incomplete sentences. Doing so makes you look like you are unprofessional and take a haphazard approach.

There are also times when an email needs to very well written. This would be when you are seeking to persuade and the email is likely to be read by many. Always keep in mind that not only does an email represent you to others, but it is likely to be permanently archived. Emails can be forwarded countless times. Something poorly stated can find its way to colleagues you have never met. You do not want to start at a deficit in their minds when you meet them because they have read a poorly written email you sent. On the positive side, a well-written email speaks well of you and burnishes your reputation for being thoughtful, professional, and persuasive.

If you are uncomfortable about your use of grammar, vocabulary, or word choice in written communications, learn the basics. They are not that difficult and are certainly not cumbersome. Reading an inexpensive book on grammar or taking a course at a local college or high school will help you in that regard. Thesaurus or synonym websites can really help you with finding the right words when you are writing. Don't rely on an assistant or colleague to backstop you in this area. That is the easy way out and may cause you to put off achieving competence in these important skills.

There is an additional reason you should be sure that your grammar and spelling are correct in your writing. If they aren't, there's a chance that they're also incorrect in your formal speaking and even in informal conversations. If that is the case, it will have an adverse impact on future success and promotion possibilities.

So do your best to write and speak your language correctly, give it the dignity it deserves, and represent yourself well. Above all, remember—write to that friendly mental image.

35

THE GRAPEVINE

THIS CHAPTER COULD BE SUBTITLED, "The Most Effective Communication." Any organization with more than five people has a grapevine. Grapevines come about because people communicate with each other, and people have a great need to know what is going on. If they don't know, they'll speculate about what is going on. You will never put an end to the grapevine, so you might as well accept its existence and the fact that its branches reach into all corners of the organization. There is no value in assessing the grapevine as good or bad; it just is. The important thing is to understand how it works so you do not fall victim to it.

Think of the grapevine as a second—and in many cases a more efficient—communication network in your organization. If the formal communication structure of authorized memos, emails, or posts on the company intranet is the equivalent of a major highway, the grapevine is the frontage road that runs alongside it. Both roads go to the same place and sometimes the cars on the frontage road get there sooner. There are times when you sit in traffic on the highway while you watch cars fly by you on the frontage road. Similarly, sometimes the grapevine gets information distributed sooner than the formal communication structure.

One way a manager can avoid falling victim to the grapevine is to do a good job of communicating. Getting information out clearly and effectively will reduce the opportunities for the grapevine to distribute inaccurate information about your operation. There will always be speculation and gossip. But by being an effective communicator, you can reduce the *incorrect* speculation. You'll never stop it completely and need to accept that fact.

The grapevine even takes place after hours by phone or email. An example of an email in the evening might go like this: "You didn't get to hear the latest of what's happening now. I heard you were at the dentist. You won't believe this but. . . ." And so it goes on and on.

As a new manager you can probably relate to this story: A few first-time managers working in a commercial bank were wondering how quickly and efficiently the grapevine could handle a rumor. They knew that one of the principal participants was on the fifth floor. They assigned one manager from the group to go to the fifth floor and tell this person an outrageous rumor that could be remotely possible. Then the manager walked back downstairs to the first floor where his work area was. He was not gone ten minutes. When he got back to his desk, the secretary said, "You'll never believe what I just heard." She repeated the rumor the manager had delivered upstairs, with the addition of a few creative modifications.

USE THE GRAPEVINE SOMETIMES

As a manager you can tap into the grapevine for both sending and receiving. If you develop good relationships with your people, they'll tell you what is going on. In fact, some of them will vie for the opportunity to be the first to bring you the latest scoop.

You can send messages via the grapevine, too. There will be times you want to exploit its efficiency. Keep in mind that when you do, you will not be able to control the accuracy of the message as it circulates. For this reason, the emphasis should be on direct communication with your staff so you can avoid the embellishments that are commonly added by the grapevine.

If you want to put something into the grapevine as a test, first identify who you are going to use to access the network. Ask yourself, "Who in the organization would I tell if I wanted my information to be distributed as soon as possible?" The answer to your question will lead you to one of the "head grapes." Entrusting him with information will guarantee it gets into the grapevine—and likely as soon as you walk away from his workstation.

The perfect way to get the information started is to preface your statement with "Keep this under your hat, but . . ." or "This is highly confidential, but . . .". That will ensure its rapid movement through the system. Remember, the only time an item is completely confidential is when you tell no one.

36

YOUR BEST FRIEND: DELEGATION

WE CANNOT STRESS ENOUGH HOW IMPORTANT it is for a manager to know how to delegate and utilize this indispensable tool. When you delegate properly, you can focus less on performing tasks and more on managing and leading. Delegating is not *doling out*. Delegation is taking something that you currently do and giving it to one of your employees for the purpose of developing her skills and making your organization more effective. Doling out is saying to an employee, "I am too busy; you have to take some of the workload." Never try to pass off a doling out as a delegation.

BENEFITS OF DELEGATING

There are many benefits to delegating. You get employees who are more involved and motivated because they are acquiring new skills, developing themselves, and being more involved in the success of the organization. Delegation is cost effective for the organization. The company now has someone in-house who can do work that only you were able to do previously. And it frees you up to do other things that are a better use of your time and talents.

Delegating also can help you broaden your perspective. Being a successful manager requires you to be able to see challenges and opportunities as they are approaching and before they arrive. Delegating has the potential to free you up to see further into the distance. Think of it this way—your distance vision is quite limited when you are in the trenches. Delegating helps you get out of the figurative trenches of performing recurring tasks that are not the best use of your abilities.

Finally, delegating is one of the most powerful training tools at your disposal. Sending a team member to a class to expand his skills is great, but actually giving him the opportunity to take on a real task with all the challenges it presents will result in a lot more learning and professional development than any class.

WHY NEW MANAGERS DON'T DELEGATE

If delegation is so great, why don't managers do it more often? The first reason is that they do not know how; it is a skill that needs to be practiced. Then there are the insecure managers. They are afraid that the employee will do it better than they can or they think that their staff will say, "If he is delegating to us, what does he do all day?" And of course, there are those who just love the job so much that they do not want to give it up. Far and away the most common reason managers don't delegate is because they are not confident of the outcome. When they perform the task, they know exactly how it is going to be done and what the final product will look like. When they have someone else handle it, the outcome will not be exactly as if they had done it themselves.

None of these are good reasons for not delegating. The only time you should not delegate to others is if someone above you tells you not to or if you have someone who is not ready or is too busy to take on the delegation.

WHAT SHOULD NEVER BE DELEGATED

The things that should never be delegated even if you are the CEO are all your personnel responsibilities. You always keep performance appraisals, salary reviews, giving positive feedback, coaching, discipline, termination, and so forth for yourself. Interviews are an exception. As mentioned earlier, including a team member in an interview for a job candidate can be a good learning opportunity for the team member. In addition, if something were of a sensitive or secretive nature like a company downsizing, you would not delegate that task. Have a delegator's consciousness. Try to delegate 100 percent of what you can *possibly* delegate.

TO WHOM TO DELEGATE

You can potentially delegate to all your employees. But you have to handle it a little differently depending on who will be taking on the task. And remember, once again, you do not want to overload your best employees because you know they can do it. If you keep overloading them, they will burn out and you will lose your better performers. When delegating to your less-experienced or less-skilled members, make sure you clearly explain what has to be done and monitor their progress much more than you would one of your more experienced or skilled employees. You can also delegate to an employee who has failed on a previous delegation. When given another opportunity, this employee can regain lost confidence. Try delegating to your problem employees as well. A new challenge or project may cause them to change their outlook on things.

THE DELEGATION STEPS

The following is a particular sequence you may find helpful when you delegate—see if this process works for you:

1. Start off by analyzing which of your current tasks, projects, or jobs you could possibly delegate. Think about what goes into getting the job done, how long it takes, what resources are needed, and so forth.
2. Decide to whom you can delegate the task. Consider who would be most motivated by the opportunity, who has the time, who either has the skill level or could acquire the skills, and who has asked for additional responsibilities.
3. Once you make up your mind, sit down with the employee and describe as many of the details of the task as possible. Also point out the benefits of taking on the delegation. Obviously, if the person is new or inexperienced, you must spend more time with her and provide more details.
4. Come to agreement on the goal of the task and the timeline to be followed. This is vital and should be in writing. A follow-up email that states the specific outcome that was agreed to and the completion date will cover this. You may want to have the team member who is taking on the task compose the email so you can verify that he is

clear on the understanding. A complex task may involve multiple review dates and interim outcomes. The importance of this step cannot be stressed enough. Delegating successfully requires absolute goal clarity.

5. Finally, discuss how you are going to monitor the employee's progress.

THE PERFECTIONISM TRAP

Since the most common reason managers do not delegate is their uncertainty of the outcome, the issue of perfectionism needs to be addressed further. Many people mistakenly think perfectionism is a positive attribute. It is not. High personal standards are a positive attribute. That is not the same as perfectionism.

A common definition of perfectionism is seeing anything short of perfection as unacceptable. Consider this. First, perfection almost never exists. Flaws can nearly always be found in any product or outcome. Second, insisting on an outcome that you see as perfect, even though it is not, means the person you are delegating to has no discretion in how she goes about the task.

If you start the delegation process by telling the person being assigned the task exactly what she has to deliver down to the finest detail, she is not likely to be very excited about taking on the task. You are effectively making her into a robot and in the process demotivating her. You are also forgoing the benefit of her experience, perspective, and creativity—which are all different from yours.

Being a successful delegator requires you to accept and value the fact that the person taking on the task will do it differently than you will. Think of it as agreeing on the date and time the person will arrive at a distant destination, but allowing her to select her own course. Now obviously, if based on your experience, you are aware of routes to the destination that are troublesome, let her know. But trust her judgment to select a course that will work and is likely different from the one you would choose. If you do not trust her judgment on this, she is the wrong person for the task.

When it comes to your desire to achieve a perfect outcome on your own tasks there are some important factors to consider. Some tasks truly require a near perfect outcome. Many do not. The secret to managing an inclination to pursue perfection and in the process increase your efficiency is to be discerning as to which tasks require near perfection and which do not.

Here is an example. Let's say you have to make a presentation to the board of directors of your company in order to get funding for a new initiative. Such a high profile and important task genuinely requires your best efforts. While perfection cannot be achieved, in this case aiming for it is a good idea. You will likely be justified putting in a great deal of time into preparing, rehearsing, and role-playing how to respond to the questions you are likely to be asked.

By comparison, let's say that you are going to do a presentation to your team on a new process. While important, a near perfect outcome is not vital. This means that the same level of preparation you put into your presentation to the board of directors is not justified. If you find you are tempted to put forth the same level of effort you need to honestly assess your personal issues with perfectionism.

The core strategy is that you expend only the level of effort honestly required to achieve an acceptable outcome. When determining that level it is important that you are fully acknowledging that a near perfect outcome is likely to take two to three times as much of your time. Your time is finite and valuable. Use it wisely. Do not squander it by pursuing a near perfect outcome unnecessarily.

AVOID UPWARD DELEGATION

Resist taking on delegations from your direct reports. They will come to you and say they are too busy or the work is too hard or you can do it better than they can. If this happens to you, help them with the project or get a subject matter expert to help them; do not take it over. As manager, you want to be in the business of developing others, not rescuing them.

IN THE FUTURE

Delegation can be a great friend to you, your team, and the organization. It is vital to your development as a manager. Not delegating well will significantly hamper your advancement. Start thinking about what you can delegate today, tomorrow, or sometime in the future. Learn to delegate and then do it. Both you and your team members will benefit from it.

37

A SENSE OF HUMOR

MANY NEW MANAGERS TAKE THEMSELVES way too seriously. Life is challenging and can be grim. Without a sense of humor, it can be deadly. New managers need to learn not to take themselves too seriously and to develop a sense of humor.

One reason many of us take ourselves so seriously is because of the immediacy of the world in which we move. Our daily activities are important to us because they're the ones we know most intimately. Therefore, everything that happens at the office looms large in our lives. We should try to do our jobs to the best of our ability, but once we're sure in our own minds that we have done so, we shouldn't worry about it. The key phrase is *once we're sure in our own minds*. Most of us are our own worst critics.

Of course, the work we do is important. If it were not, no one would part with cold cash in return for our efforts. But we must keep what we do in perspective. It may be important in our office, and it may be important to the people who deal with our office, but it may not seem terribly significant when measured against the history of humankind. When you've had a bad day and all seems lost, remember that a hundred years from now no one will care; so why should you let it ruin your year, month, week—or evening, for that matter? Our jobs are important, but let's keep what we do in perspective.

The English author Horace Walpole (1717–1797) said, "The world is a tragedy to those who feel, but a comedy to those who think."

It's much easier not to take yourself too seriously if you have a sense of humor. Nearly everyone has some sort of sense of humor, but it is more keenly developed in some people than in others. Even if you feel your sense of humor is weak, you can improve it.

DEVELOPING A SENSE OF HUMOR

Here's a news flash that provides some hope: Many people who have a reputation for being funny, clever, and humorously creative don't really have any of these characteristics. What they have is a terrific memory and a good sense of recall. They can reach back into their memories quickly and find a humorous line they've heard or read that is appropriate to the situation at hand. They get a reputation for having a sense of humor, and they do have one, but they're not necessarily creative. It's much like the difference between perfect pitch, which some feel a person is born with, and relative pitch, which can be developed and practiced.

So you can develop a sense of humor by reading, by seeing the right kind of humorous movies, and by studying comedy. Watch television personalities who have a reputation for being funny. Watch people who are "ear funny." A cream pie in the face or a pratfall might be "sight funny," but you can't use these gags at the office, and seldom in your social life.

ENCOURAGING LAUGHTER

In addition to developing a sense of humor yourself, as a manager you also need to build a work environment that is fun and where laughter is welcome. If the workplace is a fun and enjoyable place to be, your employees will show up more, work harder, and be more productive. There are many different ways to encourage laughter in your department. Here are a few ideas:

✍ Start off each meeting with a joke or have one of your employees tell the joke.

✍ Have a bulletin board devoted to laughter. People can place cartoons, comic strips, or jokes on it for their colleagues to look at and read.

✍ A California manager turned a storeroom into a laugh room. He put a DVD player in the room and stocked it with tapes of sitcoms and comedians. When he or one of his staff members needed a laugh, they would go into the room, put in a DVD for a few minutes, and come out laughing.

You might want to try these methods or find some of your own.

HUMOR—NOT SARCASM

Achieving a reputation for having a dry sense of humor is acceptable. Acquiring a reputation as the office clown is not. Most people can appreciate the difference. Being witty is one thing; being a buffoon is quite another. But one warning: If you have never said anything funny at the office, break into humor on a gradual basis; otherwise someone will want to check the water supply.

Many people mistake sarcasm for wit. Some sarcasm can be funny, but there's a twofold problem with being sarcastic. First, you achieve a reputation for being a cynic, which is not a welcome trait in the executive suite. Second, sarcasm is often funny at someone else's expense. You don't want people to think you prey on the weaknesses or idiosyncrasies of others. Also you don't want to offend someone and make an enemy. As a rule, avoid *expense humor*, meaning humor of any kind that is at another person's expense. Doing otherwise will make you look petty and insecure.

It's best if your humorous remarks point inward or are neutral in nature. Making fun of yourself or your own foibles makes you a self-deprecating wit, which offends no one. Trading insults with another person can be fun, but it's not a practice for beginners and should be avoided.

HUMOR, THE TENSION RELIEVER

A sense of humor is most valuable when things become hectic and tense. A well-placed humorous remark can lighten the mood and relieve the tension. It's like opening a steam valve so the pressure can escape. It's healthy to see humor in tense situations. Even when it seems inappropriate to make your humorous remark aloud, thinking about it may put a smile on your face and keep you from getting a migraine.

We are surrounded by funny situations every day, but we need to notice them. As with the beauty all around us, if you don't make a point of looking for it, you'll likely miss it. With practice, however, you'll begin to see the humor in what goes on all around you.

Finally, there's a compelling reason for not taking this life and ourselves too seriously: None of us is going to get out of it alive anyway. Keep in mind that there has never been a report of a headstone engraved with the words, "I wish I'd spent more time at the office."

38

MANAGING, PARTICIPATING IN, AND LEADING MEETINGS

IN CHAPTER 33, WE MENTIONED COMPANIES that have closed periods during which office personnel don't phone one another and don't attend meetings. That gives them a certain amount of uninterruptible time each day. Indeed, the productivity of the entire country would be greatly increased if all office meetings of more than two people, in business and government, were banned for one year. Meetings are very expensive. You are taking people away from their work. Always consider what alternatives you have to holding a meeting. If the meeting is just for informational purposes, you can send out an email with attachments. If you want discussion and decisionmaking to occur, a meeting may still be unnecessary. You may instead be able to use an online document to facilitate a virtual discussion through comment tracking. While this method may not replace a final decision-making meeting entirely, it can allow that meeting to be briefer and more efficient. One-way communication does not require a meeting unless the meeting participants never see each other. Then, once in a while, it is nice to bring the group together.

THE COST OF A MEETING

Can you justify your meeting in terms of its cost vs. the benefits? Let's say you have a meeting planned for your group of ten including yourself. You want to get reactions to new procedures put into place last week and address a few pending items. You have scheduled two hours for the meeting. Let's calculate the cost of this meeting. Assume the average salary of everyone at the meeting is $80,000. Based on fifty work weeks per year, that would make the daily salary about $320 and the cost per person for two hours $80. We multiply that figure by ten and get about $800. Then add on any room rental fees, costs of snacks and coffee, and so forth. Then some of your attendees may have to travel to your meeting location. That takes them away from their work for an even longer period. Ask yourself the same question we started this section with: "Can you justify your meeting in terms of its cost vs. the benefits?" If you can, go forward with it. If you cannot, find an alternative.

ADVANCE NOTICE

One idea that helps generate a more productive meeting is to send the proposed agenda to meeting participants a few days before the meeting. Going to a meeting unprepared is counterproductive. Many meetings are spur-of-the-moment necessities, but a scheduled meeting should have an agenda.

If you are the only person knowledgeable about what is going to be covered, then that might feed your ego but it damages the quality of the meeting. Your agenda should list every topic to be discussed and the time frame for each topic. Whenever possible stick to the time frame so that you can end the meeting on time. Nothing exasperates people more than having meetings go beyond the agreed upon or announced ending time.

If you are approaching the time the meeting is scheduled to end and have more to cover, it is appropriate to let the participants decide whether to extend the meeting, reconvene, or handle the unresolved issues later. At the least, it may be appropriate in this situation to revise the agenda quickly, selecting the most urgent items to address in the limited time left.

It is good to have different meeting participants take the lead on different agenda items. This gets them more involved and helps them develop their leadership and facilitation skills. You can also involve your attendees in another manner. Ask them to contribute suggested items for upcoming meetings. Realize that you are likely not aware of all issues and opportunities within your organization.

Make sure you begin your meetings on time. You are wasting valuable time and resources when you have people sitting around waiting for the meeting to begin. When you become known for starting your meetings on time, people will make note and be more punctual. Plus you never want any of your meeting participants to feel that they are not as important as the people you are waiting for.

Another key thing to remember about agendas is to have the most important items listed and discussed first. You have probably attended too many meetings where the minor items came first, which took up most of the allotted meeting time. When that happens, there is never enough time to cover the important stuff.

MISTAKES MANAGERS MAKE

Many managers who are new to the meeting process feel obligated to have an opinion on every issue. That isn't necessary. Have an opinion where your motivation is the issue, not the perceived need to speak. It's far better to make a few thoughtful statements than to rattle on about everything. It's preferable to have an executive attending the meeting say, "John is a thoughtful person," as opposed to, "John always has something to say, but not necessarily anything to add."

The other extreme of remaining silent during the entire meeting is just as bad. It implies you are intimidated by the situation, have nothing to contribute, or are just plain not interested. That is not an image you want to project. Even if the situation does intimidate you a bit, never let them see you sweat. Chapter 39, which covers public speaking, will help you in this regard.

Never say anything uncomplimentary in a meeting about anyone on your staff. It will be received as disloyalty on your part. Handle situations, not personalities. Managerial careers have been halted by a manager who trashed an employee in front of a high-ranking executive. As with inappropriate humor, this type of behavior reflects poorly on you.

Some managers view a meeting with higher-ranking executives as a place to display management skills and acumen. That is all right if you go about it correctly. However, if you view the meeting as a competition with other managers at your level, your emphasis is wrong. Your goal is to be a productive, contributing member of the team, not to show up other managers. Competition is the wrong element to bring to the table.

Another mistake that many managers make is seeing which way the boss is going on an issue, so that their positions are the same. The idea is that their bosses will think more of a manager who agrees with them, or thinks as they do. Most bosses immediately spot that game, and the manager may be thought of as spineless. Of course, if you have a point of view that is different from your boss, state it in a diplomatic, reasoned way—but you ought to do that anyway. If everyone agrees with the boss, you don't need to have the meeting.

By the way, many managers lack the courage to take a position different from their boss's. Probably in the vast majority of situations, the courage to state a thought-out position, even if different from the boss's, does more for a career than transparent agreement. There are even executives who deliberately throw out a false position to see which sheep will follow, and then agree with someone who had the courage to state the correct position. (Most executives didn't get to their positions by being stupid.)

Any executive chairing a project or a meeting with members she outranks would do well to hold back disclosing her own position until *after* everyone else has given their thoughts and opinions. Example: The president of a company headed up a corporate reorganization project team consisting of seven people. The president wisely didn't announce her opinions until after she'd called for everyone else's. That approach precluded anyone from playing up to the president, or withholding contrary information out of concern for how it would be received.

An executive does not need employees or project team members to play up to him. This approach might also teach new managers that it is okay to have a different point of view. Of course, as mentioned earlier in this book, some executives say they don't want "yes people," but their actions indicate otherwise. These executives end up with rubber-stamp teams and employees who merely provide cover for the executive, and that is a terrible waste of corporate and managerial time.

ADVANTAGES OF BEING ON PROJECT TEAMS

Occasionally, you will be asked to serve on a project team. Often the request is in the form of an invitation that you can decline if you choose. Always be discerning about which project teams and committees you join. They will all place additional demands on your time and take you away from your primary responsibilities. That being said, there are several advantages to being placed on a project team:

First, someone believes you can make a contribution or you wouldn't have been asked. If you choose to join, make the most of it.

Second, you may come in contact with managers and executives across a wide spectrum of the organization. These can be valuable contacts and broaden your exposure.

Third, you may have the opportunity to become involved in decisions that reach beyond your own area of responsibility. This broadens your experience with the organization as a whole and helps you develop a broader perspective of how your team fits into the larger organization.

HOW TO LEAD A MEETING

When you become the meeting leader, you should take it as a compliment: Someone sees leadership or at least leadership potential in you. Don't shy away from such an opportunity.

Some of the best training for leading a meeting is in being exposed to some poorly led ones. Most meetings last too long. You can't help but wonder if some folks think sitting around at a meeting beats working. But probably the main reason meetings last too long is that they are poorly planned and poorly led.

In addition to the earlier suggestion about circulating an agenda in advance, distribute the minutes of the previous meeting. Most everyone then reads the minutes before going to the meeting, and except for a minor correction now and then, approval of the minutes is quickly handled. Contrast that with everyone sitting around for a quarter of an hour reading the minutes and feeling compelled to nitpick them to death.

Obviously, all agendas show starting times of meetings. It adds discipline to a meeting if you also show the expected closing time. People tend to stay focused on the subjects at hand if the meeting has an expected adjournment time.

Most meetings are run rather informally. You'll seldom chair a committee that requires you to be an expert parliamentarian. If it does get formal, you'll have to familiarize yourself with *Robert's Rules of Order.* Having this reference available is a good thought, but you'll rarely need it. In all the years you've attended business meetings, you probably can't recall any parliamentarian questions having been raised, except in jest.

The rules of common sense should prevail when leading a meeting. Keep your cool. Don't let anyone press your panic button. Be courteous to all meeting participants. Avoid putting people down. Act as a facilitator, not as a dictator. Keep to the subject. Don't cut people off before they've had their say, but don't allow them to drift away from the subject. Always deal with the problem at hand. A fair meeting leader discourages the same points from being expressed repeatedly.

Don't get involved in personalities, even if others do. Be better organized than anyone else at the meeting. Develop the kind of thoughtful relationships with participants that will prompt them to come to you beforehand with unusual items, thereby avoiding unpleasant surprises. Be fair to everyone, even minority opinions that are unlikely to prevail. The majority view should not steamroll the minority opinion, at least until that opinion has had a fair hearing. If you are fair to all viewpoints, you'll earn the respect of all the participants and make people comfortable sharing their ideas. An organization that welcomes ideas tends to be more innovative. Being a successful meeting leader is another chance to display the high quality of your leadership skills.

OTHER MEETING TIPS

Establish ground rules at the beginning of a meeting. Ground rules are agreed-upon behaviors that everyone follows. They help the meeting run more smoothly and help reduce disruptive behaviors. Ground rules may include not talking when someone else is, agreement that comments will be about the topic and not the person presenting the topic, agreement to abide by the meeting leader's requests to wrap-up comments, and avoiding side conversations. Meetings have ground rules about staying on topic, allowing everyone to participate, commenting on the suggestion but not the messenger, and so forth. Ground rules are very helpful and you would be wise to develop a set with your meeting participants. The ground rules need to include whether phones and laptops will be used during the meeting for texting and email. To avoid using up valuable meeting time, this can be done in advance in an exchange of emails with the participants.

Asking someone to capture ideas and positions and write them on a whiteboard or flip chart helps participants feel confident that their thoughts have been recognized and captured. It will also reduce the chances that people feel a need to repeat themselves. If someone does, you can just point to where his point has been recorded and ask if there is an additional point he would like to offer.

When you are leading a meeting and multiple participants express a desire to talk, acknowledge their desire and let them know they will be heard in a certain order. This lets them know they will have a turn and can relax knowing it will soon come. The same method works if you have a problem with someone interrupting a participant. Simply let him know he will have an opportunity to speak but, "We all want to hear what Shannon has to say."

If a discussion develops that is clearly just between two participants and does not involve others in attendance, ask the two involved to pursue their discussion at another time. If the outcome of their discussion is related to topics being addressed in the meeting they can report back on their outcome by email or at the next meeting. This way their one-to-one conversation does not eat into everyone else's time. You may be surprised how often this happens and how rarely the two involved realize that they are diverting the purpose of the meeting to address something that just applies to them.

When facilitating a discussion, it is appropriate to ask a person before he starts to speak if two, three, five, or ten—whatever is appropriate—minutes will be sufficient for his comments. That way he has agreed to a "time budget" for his remarks and he knows he needs to be efficient. If he has used the amount of time he agreed to, it is appropriate to gently stop him and ask how much more time he will need. By doing so you have respectfully reminded him that he needs to wrap up so the meeting can stay on track.

Spend five or ten minutes at the end of a meeting to discuss with the group how the meeting went. You want to get feedback so you can improve the quality of the next meeting you run.

Have the purpose and the goals of the meeting on the top of your agenda.

Only invite those individuals who should really be there. As a rule of thumb, have the fewest people possible. Also, individuals do not have to stay for the entire meeting. They may be interested in or need to be there for only a couple of the agenda items.

You want your meetings to be as short as possible. Keep in mind that after about two hours most people's attention spans are shot. If your meetings run longer, you need breaks. That can become time consuming and even more costly.

Prepare a follow-up action plan with action items for the different participants. Make sure everyone gets a copy so each person knows what other people's responsibilities are.

Schedule meetings reluctantly. Pride yourself on making them quick and efficient. By doing both, you are likely to get a higher level of participation and superior outcomes.

REMOTE MEETINGS AND VIDEO CONFERENCING

Often you will be including people in your meetings who are offsite and participating through video conferencing. This situation presents unique challenges to keeping the meeting meaningful and productive. Avoid having people participate by audio only unless the meeting is very brief. Using an audio-only connection deprives both the remote participants and the onsite participants of the vitally important visual elements of communication.

A few of the basics to keep in mind when conducting meetings with remote participants are:

✍ These meetings are not the same as in-person meetings. Do not make the mistake of treating it as though everyone is in the same room.

✍ Remote meetings require more advance planning.

✍ Even with video conferencing nonverbal communication is hampered. That means your communication style will need to be clearer and more specific.

✍ Be sensitive to the local time zones of the remote participants. Try to find a meeting time that is convenient to all. If there is no way to avoid some of the people participating during non-work hours move the meeting times around so the inconvenience of off hours meetings is evenly distributed and does not always fall on the same person.

✍ It can be quite valuable to have one-on-one calls in advance with remote participants to initiate dialogue, set expectations, and get a sense of their goals and concerns. Doing so will allow you to avoid having to clarify their thoughts during the meeting when communication is less-than-ideal.

✍ There are times when remote meetings are not advisable. Lengthy, multi-topic meetings do not work well in a remote format. Brainstorming or strategy sessions that require more of a free flow of information and a lot of idea explanation do not work well with remote participants.

These ground rules will help make your remote meetings more successful:

✍ As always, be clear to all involved on the objectives of the meeting. This is even more important when some of the participants are remotely located.

✍ Distribute an agenda, materials, and ground rules for the meeting to everyone in advance.

✍ Keep the meeting to just a few topics.

✍ Ask your remote participants to find a quiet setting without background noise or distractions. This means their local coffee house or diner is not suitable.

✍ Start the meeting with a pleasant hello to each participant then have them introduce themselves by name and role. This will help to keep a personable tone and keep the meeting from becoming too sterile.

✍ Ask that all turn off their cell phones or at least silence them, as you feel is appropriate. If cell phones remain on remote participants will often send text messages to other remote participants during the meeting. It is up to you to determine whether this is positive or negative.

✍ The meeting leader needs to put extra effort into helping remote participants stay with the flow of the meeting. This may mean they need to occasionally take a moment to report to the remote participants on anything significant they cannot see or hear. They also may want to occasionally ask those offsite if they need any clarifications.

✍ If you will be seeking input or feedback ask each remote participant one at a time to be sure they have an opportunity. Avoid surprising them by telling them in advance that you will be doing so.

✍ The meeting leader needs to make sure that people are not talking simultaneously.

✍ Ask both onsite and offsite participants to identify themselves each time they talk in the event they are not in the frame of the video feed or presentation graphics are on the screen.

✍ Take a brief break every half hour or so to avoid having people step out unannounced.

You will be well-served to set expectations by distributing etiquette for the call in advance. This may seem a bit excessive but it is easy for remote participants to not be aware of how they can negatively impact a meeting. Suggested etiquette for a meeting involving remote participants includes:

- Asking those offsite to log in fifteen minutes early to validate their connection and confirm that the meeting application is working for them.

- Ask participants to focus on the meeting. This means not multitasking by sending emails, texting, or surfing the web while the meeting is underway. Keyboard clicks are an obvious giveaway. Many suggest that notes be taken by hand to avoid keyboard clicks in the background.

- Just like eye contact is important in-person it also is during a video conference. This means look into the camera.

- Dress appropriately. Your people are in a business meeting and should be appropriate. This does not necessarily mean formal business attire, unless that is what all will be wearing, but it means not wearing pajamas.

- Ask that participants let the meeting leader know if they need to step out.

Another tip: Be aware of what is behind you on a video call. You do not want a background that is distracting or unprofessional. If your work setting makes this difficult you may want to get a folding stand-up screen to put up behind you during calls. Finally, be aware of the lighting in the room. Poor lighting can make you look odd or ill. Neither is good.

Even if your team is all in one location you will still likely need to include remote participants into some of your meetings. You owe it to yourself and your team to be thoughtful about how to make such meetings productive and pleasant.

39

TAKING CENTER STAGE
The Role of Public Speaking in Your Career

IT IS AMAZING THAT THERE ARE so many capable managers who can't handle a public speaking situation well. Standing up on the platform they come off as dull, uncertain, and of limited talent. The impression the audience receives is that they're not very good on the job, either. That impression may not be valid, but as we've discussed earlier, people act based on their perceptions.

PRIOR PREPARATION

Many managers are poor public speakers because they wait until they find themselves in a speaking situation before they do anything about it. By then, it's too late. You can be the greatest manager in the world, but it will be a well-kept secret if you don't prepare yourself to be a public speaker.

Because so few people in managerial positions prepare themselves to speak publicly, you'll have a leg up on most of them if you learn how to do it well. Public speaking frightens many people, and so they avoid it. Many people—not just managers—have a fear of public speaking. In fact, public speaking ranks near the top of phobias that people have.

As a new manager, you may have the option of not having to do presentations or public speaking to outside groups but you probably will not have that choice within your own organization. It may be a meeting of your department in which you have to explain a new company policy. It may be a retirement dinner for someone in your area of responsibility, and you're expected to make a "few appropriate remarks." You may have to do a presentation to a client or to the board of directors. Your boss may be ill and you may have to step in for her at the last minute. Managers will often go to almost unbelievable lengths to avoid these types of speaking situations. They will use ploys such as arranging a business trip so they'll be out of town or scheduling their vacations for that time. They'll spend the rest of their business lives plotting how not to get up in front of a group and speak. How much better off they'd be if they'd obtain the necessary skills and turn these situations to their advantage.

What many people don't realize is that learning to be an excellent public speaker will also improve their ability to speak extemporaneously. How do you respond when you're unexpectedly called on to say a few words?

Presentation training won't get rid of the butterflies in your stomach, but it will keep them from making you look less capable than you are.

WHERE TO RECEIVE PRESENTATION TRAINING

There are three specific ways that can help you learn how to be an effective presenter—Toastmasters, training classes, and presentation coaching.

One of the best ways to improve your presentation skills is commonly available. Toastmasters International is a nonprofit organization dedicated to helping people develop public speaking and leadership skills through practice and feedback in local clubs. Toastmasters is a very low cost option and groups are available worldwide. A simple web search will identify clubs that meet in your area. Their website is www.toastmasters.org.

There are neither professionals nor staff members in Toastmasters clubs, only people who have a mutual interest in developing their speaking capacity. For a modest semiannual fee, you receive the materials you'll need to begin the process. You go at your own speed, and you'll find a supportive group of people who help one another not only by providing an audience but also by engaging in formal evaluation sessions when you are ready to receive their input.

Another aspect of the Toastmasters' training that is invaluable is called Table Topics. This part of the meeting is designed to develop your skills in extemporaneous speaking. The Topic Master calls on various people (usually those not scheduled to give a formal speech that evening) to talk for two or three minutes on a surprise subject. You have only a few moments to prepare your comments. It is a very valuable exercise that not only builds your speaking skills, it also bolsters your confidence.

Another benefit of participating in Toastmasters is that you will meet people from other organizations in your area, providing an excellent opportunity for informal networking. With Toastmasters clubs all over the world, it's very likely that you'll find one in your area.

The next way to build up your public speaking ability is to take a training course or a college course in presentation skills. If your organization has an established training program, it likely offers presentation skills training. There are also many training organizations that offer excellent programs. One of them is the American Management Association (AMA), the organization that published this book. AMA has a variety of presentation skills seminars available in numerous locations throughout the year. Their website is www.amanet.org.

The third way to become an effective presenter is to get one-on-one coaching. Here, you or your company hires an individual to give you private instruction and guidance. Professional speaking coaches are readily available and can potentially assist you significantly—not only with your presentation skills but also with the content of your presentation. They are expensive but can be very valuable. Your HR department can help you locate a qualified speaking coach.

By no means are these three suggestions your only alternatives. You can read books, watch professionals in action, find someone in-house whose presentations you admire and ask him to work with you, rent or purchase video training courses, or access online videos of professional speakers. But improving your presentation skills ultimately comes down to getting up in front of people and speaking. All the knowledge and preparation in the world will not substitute for actually doing it. The exciting part is that once you get past any hesitance or uncertainty you will find that doing it is a powerful confidence builder.

NEXT WEEK'S PRESENTATION

You might be saying to yourself that these are all great suggestions for the future, but what do you do if you have to give a presentation next week? Here are some basic things to remember and do when presenting in front of a large group:

✍ **Decide what the purpose of your presentation is and write it out in one sentence.** It should not be longer than one sentence and should be clear to anyone listening to it or reading it. There are two basic outcomes for presentations—information transfer, inspiration, or some of both. If you are transferring information, you may want the audience to remember certain things, know a particular procedure, or physically be able to demonstrate the use of something. If your goal is to inspire, you are seeking to have a positive impact on the attitude of those in the audience. Keep these two general outcomes in mind as you craft the one sentence that captures the purpose of your presentation.

✍ **Develop your subject matter outline.** Most studies have shown audiences remember only one main point and three subpoints. Keep the presentation as brief and tight as possible.

✍ **During the planning for and delivery of the presentation, keep these well-known words about presentations in mind.** Tell them what you are going to tell them (do this in the opening), tell them (do this in the main body of your talk), then tell them what you told them (do this in your conclusion). Though not at all original this strategy will serve you well. The great majority of us need to be told something more than once to retain it. Plus the overview during your opening of what you will be covering helps the people in your audience to be better prepared to receive your message.

✍ **Before planning your talk try to do an audience analysis.** Find out who they are, their reasons for being there, their interest and academic levels, their attitudes, their cultural backgrounds, ages, and so forth. The more you know in advance about the audience the better you will be able to prepare for your talk. If it is vital that you have the benefit of the audience members' thoughts on a specific issue before you present, you may want to query audience members in advance with a few calls or an online survey. The information you get from such an effort can be invaluable in understanding audience members' thoughts and attitudes.

✍ **During the presentation, watch your audience.** Are they smiling and attentive or restless, confused, engaging in chats with their neighbors, texting, emailing, or leaving? You may need to change your delivery style by talking louder or lower, faster or slower, cutting things short or explaining in more depth, changing your tone of voice, and so forth. Be prepared to adapt your presentation as needed.

✍ **If you are using visuals like PowerPoint slides, don't talk to the slides, talk to the audience.** Many new managers make this mistake. Visuals should be a backup for the audience. You need to be the main attraction. Nothing will make your presentation less interesting and make you look more like a total rookie than standing up there and reading your PowerPoint slides. Your slides should only reinforce your major points, not serve as a substitute for your note cards or a script. If you are using PowerPoint or a similar application, keep the content on each slide to a minimum and use large type. Few things will destroy a presentation faster than unreadable slides. One of the worst examples I have seen is someone who cuts and pastes a nearly indecipherable spreadsheet into a slide then stands in front of it pointing to various cells with a laser pointer trying to explain it. Instead they should make a slide that presents the three or four key points derived from the spreadsheet.

✍ **Practice, practice, practice.** If you are prepared and comfortable with what you are presenting, you will come across as much more relaxed and you will experience much less stage fright. However, do not make the mistake of memorizing your presentation. This can be disastrous if you forget your place. There is nothing wrong with using a few note cards or a presentation outline printed in a large font to help you keep your place and remember the next point you will be making.

✍ **Be ready to adapt to all situations.** You never know what might happen at a presentation. The equipment may be faulty, rendering useless your wonderful slides or video clips. You have to be ready to reorganize your presentation quickly. Or suppose your plan includes having the audience break up into small groups for discussion purposes during your presentation—but the auditorium has chairs that cannot be moved. You must have an alternative plan or your presentation will fall apart before you begin. One of the best tests of whether you are well-prepared is to challenge yourself to give the presentation in half the allotted time. Doing so as one of your practice presentations will have two benefits. It will make it clear that you understand the core elements of the presentation and prepare you for the possibility that the time you have for your presentation will be cut at the last minute. This happens often, particularly if a senior executive who does not feel a need to abide by the time limit for her presentation is on the agenda ahead of you.

✍ **Be energetic, lively, and demonstrate to the audience that you are enjoying your talk.** If you don't, you really should not expect them to be enthusiastic and interested. The more it is a conversation rather than a presentation in tone and energy, the better. And smile.

FRINGE BENEFITS

How many outstanding public speakers do you personally know, either inside or outside your organization? Probably not many, if any. Why don't you resolve to be one of the few who are outstanding? Think of the possibilities not only for promotion within your company but also for positions of leadership within the community and your industry. As a matter of fact, the opportunities for leadership challenges may come more quickly outside the company. Consider what that may open up for you: There are many followers out there waiting for someone to lead them. One characteristic most outstanding leaders have is the ability to speak persuasively on public occasions. There is no reason you can't be one of those few leaders.

40

A FEW BODY LANGUAGE INSIGHTS

KNOWING THE BASICS OF BODY LANGUAGE will help you be more effective as a manager. This information is very basic. If you want to learn more about body language there are many good books on the subject.

Having even a basic knowledge of body language will give you advantages in reading other people and effectively conveying your own messages. Simply stated there are two general types of body language: open and closed.

Open body language is invitational and welcoming. It involves movements and vocal characteristics that put people at ease and inspire them to trust you. You have likely been around people who just seem to welcome you with their smile, eyes, and body position. You may be one of them.

Examples of open body language are:

✍ A smile with the eyes engaged. That means you'll see some wrinkles around the eyes.

✍ Gestures that include open palms and arms comfortably away from the body rather than shielding or seeming to protect it.

✍ Head nods and attentive eye contact that encourage continued conversation.

✍ Minimal or no reliance on nervous or self-soothing gestures; a sense of calm in conversation.

✍ Minimal or no barriers. There is a sense of comfort with the other person, a sense of easy interaction that makes barriers unnecessary.

Closed body language reflects restraint, or even avoidance. It involves movements and vocal characteristics that tend to put people on guard. Turn around all the examples above to a kind of opposite body language and here is what you get:

✍ A fake strained smile. Eyes that wander and do not engage.

✍ Gestures that include clenched hands and arms close to the body, perhaps even crossed in front.

✍ Either avoiding eye contact or glaring.

✍ Fidgeting, or actions such as clicking a pen or rubbing fingers together—which may suggest either impatience or nervousness.

✍ Physical barriers between you and the other person, such as a desk, a computer, or a phone. Another type of barrier is turning to the side while the person is talking—that is, giving the proverbial "cold shoulder."

Both styles of body language have a place in management, depending on the nature of the interaction. Open body language is nearly always the better style if you want to engage someone positively. Closed body language could be appropriate for those occasions when you need to send a message that you want distance from an employee. Be careful when you use closed body language in a professional setting. Though it may be subliminal it is powerful and will likely be noticed at some level by the recipient.

Regardless of what message you want to convey, avoid nervous gestures all the time. The best way to do that is to identify all the things you do when you feel uncomfortable or stressed. They may be rubbing your hands, touching your ear, running your hand through your hair, playing with a paper or binder clip, twitching your feet, or many other things. Most of us have them. It is no big deal unless you are unaware of yours. Have someone you trust help you identify yours. These are likely some things you do unconsciously.

In reading people, look for open and closed body language, and note when you see changes from one to the other. Ask yourself what may have occurred in the conversation to cause the shift in the other person's body language. Observe how a change in the pace or tone of your voice, or in your own body posture, might influence the person talking with you.

Again, this is only a very basic start on body language. Pursue more information if this interests you.

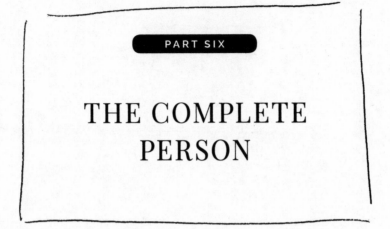

PART SIX

THE COMPLETE PERSON

Managing is challenging. You need to make sure you don't forget to support yourself.

41

COPING WITH STRESS

MANY NEW MANAGERS BELIEVE THEY should be able to arrange their work life so that there will be no stress. Stress cannot be avoided; occasionally, it will come calling. How you react to it is the key. You cannot always control what happens. What you can control is how you react to what happens to you.

WHAT CAUSES WORK-RELATED STRESS?

There are innumerable causes for work-related stress. We all respond to difficult situations differently. Anything that negatively affects our body or mind is stressful. Here are some typical work-related stressors:

- Receiving no direction or conflicting directions from the boss
- Computer failures
- Constant interruptions
- Priorities constantly changing
- Upper management constantly changing
- Mergers
- Downsizing
- Reorganizations
- Organizational politics
- Time pressures
- Performance pressures

- Poor time-management
- Bringing personal problems to work
- Working long hours for extended periods of time

No doubt you can relate to many of these stressors.

SOME RELIEF

Here is an interesting factor about stress that may make you feel better about the stress you feel early in your managerial career: Most of what seems stressful when you're new in management will seem ordinary and even mundane after you're experienced. This possibility reinforces the point that it may be your reaction and inexperience that causes you to consider it stress, rather than the situation itself. That may be a fine point, but the distinction is significant.

Go back in your memory to the days you were taking driver education to learn how to operate an automobile safely. The first time you got behind the wheel was quite stressful. With experience, your ability to drive improved to the point that driving now seems as natural as brushing your teeth. The situation has not changed, but your experience and reaction to it has changed.

How you react to stressful situations is part of your management style. Some managers respond by appearing to be deep in thought. Their brow is furrowed. They are quiet. Unfortunately, this demeanor is contagious to everyone working with you, and it's contagious in a negative way. However, managers who can smile and be pleasant in what seems to be a stressful situation instill confidence in everyone they are leading.

It's hard to think clearly when you are uptight and nervous, so that reaction makes the situation worse. That is a double negative. First you have a stressful situation, and then your reaction diminishes your ability to bring it to a successful resolution.

The third negative is the knowledge that you will be judged by how you handle the situation, which adds even more pressure. Telling yourself not to get uptight is like telling someone not to worry. It's much easier said than done.

There are those who believe that stressful situations get the juices flowing and bring out the best in people. You've heard the old saying, "When the going gets tough, the tough get going." That is true once you get over the fear of a stressful situation. Fear is like pouring the juices of stress down through a very small funnel.

REACT TO THE PROBLEM, NOT THE STRESS

To succeed, you must convert the fear of a stressful situation into the challenge of a stressful situation. If you are going to be a manager who periodically faces stressful situations, here are seven suggestions for you:

1. *Don't make things worse.* Don't be panicked into impulsive action. It may make matters worse.
2. *Take a breath.* Take several deep breaths and try to relax. Speak slowly, even if you don't feel like it. This instills calm in those around you. It says, "He's not losing his head, and therefore I shouldn't."
3. *First things first.* Reduce the situation to two or three key points that can be handled right away to lessen the urgency of the moment. This will then allow you to process the rest of the issues in a timely but non-emergency manner.
4. *Distribute the load.* Assign three or four major elements to members of your team to process in parts and then be combined into the whole.
5. *Seek advice.* Ask for suggestions and ideas from thoughtful colleagues outside your immediate team and from the experienced members of your staff.
6. *Be levelheaded.* Think about the problem and not your reaction to it.
7. *Visualize wisdom.* See yourself as an actor playing the role of the wise, calm, and decisive leader. Play that role to the hilt, and after a while it will cease to be role-playing and will be you.

HAVE CONFIDENCE IN YOUR ABILITIES

As a manager, you handle tougher questions than you dealt with before your promotion. If they were all easy, anyone could solve them. You are there because someone saw in you the ability to deal with these more difficult situations. As you move up the corporate ladder, the problems become more complex, or so it seems. The important thing to remember is that your experience will remove most of the stress. When you've been a manager for a while, you will not react the same way to the same situation as you did the first few months in your managerial career. *It will get better.* And you will be more capable.

In the early days in management, just having the job brings elements of stress. That is why so many new managers look intense, as though they are carrying the weight of the world. While the concern and the desire to perform well are commendable, the intensity gets in the way of getting the job done. You are managing people in the tasks they need to complete in order to achieve a desired result. After all you are not leading them out of the trenches with bayonets at the ready, across a minefield, to engage the enemy in hand-to-hand combat.

The best advice for you to follow as a new manager is: "Lighten up."

42

HAVING BALANCE IN YOUR LIFE

THE FIRST-TIME MANAGER OFTEN BECOMES so engrossed in new responsibilities that the job occupies almost every waking moment. This dedication is admirable, because it indicates that the person is determined to do a great job and be successful as a member of the management team.

A healthy life must have balance, however; while your career is important, it is not your entire life. Actually, you will be a more complete manager if you are a more complete person. You cannot separate the two.

When you ask people what they do, they will automatically tell you what they do for a living. They might be a dentist, accountant, lawyer, salesperson, manager, barber, or truck driver. But we are all so much more than what we do professionally—or if we're not, we should be.

There are many sad stories of people who retire and lose their sense of identity and self-worth. Their job was their life, and when they retire, they lose their sense of purpose. A person who has this reaction to retirement is not a complete person. Their interests, other than their families, all revolve around their careers. It's understandable to miss your work, especially if you enjoyed it, but retirement should never be the end of all meaningful life.

A person whose only interest is the job is one-dimensional, and a one-dimensional person is not as effective a manager as a multidimensional person. I'm not referring to your first few months on the job. But after you have successfully passed through the breaking-in period, you need to broaden your interests and your activities.

COMMUNITY WORK

Those who aspire to management need to be involved in their community. You don't want to take from a community and not put something of yourself back into it. The same is true of your profession. Put something back into your profession through professional associations. These are not completely altruistic recommendations. The primary objective is to be of assistance to your community and the cause of the profession, but there are ancillary benefits. You become known within your community and your profession. You enhance your base of knowledge, and you make contacts and friends. That not only makes you a broader-based manager, but also a more promotable one. And the higher you go in the organization, the more important leadership becomes. Community and professional association leadership positions are good growth opportunities and are viewed favorably in the executive suite of most companies.

There have been countless situations where two people being considered for promotion were both qualified as far as the work was concerned. Although a close call, the difference came down to leadership within and *outside* the company. In many companies today, staff is allowed "release time" to engage in company-sanctioned community service programs.

OUTSIDE READING

While it is vital that you read about your business, it is also important that you are a well-read person. A manager should be a well-informed citizen and should know what is going on in her city, state, and nation. That means keeping up to date by reading news websites, newspapers, news magazines, industry blogs, and trade magazines. A manager needs to be well-informed about the world: What is going on in the world does affect your organization.

It also helps to read a good novel once in a while. Reading well-written books will improve the quality of your writing. In addition, good fiction writers often have great insight into the human condition. Besides, these books are entertaining, and that is positive too. Some managers have their teams read the same book and then the book is discussed at a meeting or get-together. The book can be on leadership, communication, or a subject related to their business. This practice makes for great discoveries about each of the team members and helps build a high-performing team.

All people at all stages of their lives need to stay mentally challenged and alert. It's much easier to do that if you maintain broad-based interests. Reading is just one way to do that.

A HEALTHY SEPARATION

You must have the ability and determination to separate work from the rest of the day. It is important to be able to leave work at work and go on with the rest of your life. We need to have interests, hobbies, and other things to do outside of work. A fitness program that meets your needs and keeps you interested is of great value. Exercise is an excellent way to relieve stress.

You will inevitably need to take work home with you at times. At the very least, you will likely find yourself at home in the evenings catching up on emails. Ideally it would not be necessary to do work at home, but in reality that is nearly unavoidable. Work hard to minimize the work you do at home. Try not to fall into the trap of getting less done at the office knowing you can catch up at home. When you do have to get work done at home, set clear boundaries such as allocating specific time blocks for the work and abiding by them. Above all, do not let the work you take home overtake your personal life, which you need to preserve in order to maintain a healthy balance. Technology makes this even more challenging.

WORK/LIFE BALANCE IN
AN ALWAYS-CONNECTED WORLD

Maintaining balance between your work life and your personal life will require you to be very intentional and specific with your colleagues. For better or worse, we are now accessible at all hours. The challenge of not letting that connectivity take over your life has two components. The first is your self-discipline in deciding when you are unavailable. If you feel a need to check email at all hours and read text messages regardless of what hour of the night they arrive you will never be successful at creating balance.

The second component is training your colleagues. Do not hesitate to make it clear to your colleagues that you are not available at certain hours unless there is an absolute emergency. This may require you to silence your phone at night or keep it in another room so you do not hear it unless it rings repeatedly. Challenges in this realm include colleagues and customers in other time zones. There is nothing wrong with reminding them that during some of their work hours you are away from the office and in need of personal time or sleep.

Another challenge is the inconsiderate colleague who thinks nothing of texting or calling at all hours. It is up to you to make it clear to that type of person that you are not available at certain times. Sometimes the best way to train that colleague is to not respond to off-hours messages until the next business day. Even a clueless and inconsiderate person will figure out with time that they are not going to hear back from you during certain time windows.

This all starts with you. If you are not able to discipline yourself to stay offline during certain hours and be direct with your colleagues you will need to accept that your personal life will not be your own. It is your choice.

43

A TOUCH OF CLASS

THERE ARE MANY MEANINGS TO THE WORD *class*. As a manager, think of class as "style and elegance in one's behavior." Class in a manager or executive consists of what is done and, often of greater importance, what is *not done*:

- Class is treating people with the dignity their humanity deserves and not treating them as objects of production.
- Class has nothing to do with your social status in life. It has everything to do with your behavior.
- Class does not use foul language, even when irritated. Class means having the vocabulary that makes four-letter words unnecessary.
- Class does not have to be the center of attention. It can allow others to bask in glory without feeling slighted.
- Class does not tell off-color or racially demeaning jokes.
- Class separates any sexual desires from the workplace, and would never make a remark to a person of the opposite sex that wouldn't be said in front of one's mother, if she were standing alongside.
- Class does not say anything derogatory about the organization, no matter how justified you may feel it is at a moment of disappointment.
- Class does not allow the unsatisfactory actions or negative words of others to drag one down into that ugly arena.
- Class does not lose its cool. It never burns its bridges.
- Class does not rationalize mistakes. It learns from them and moves on.

- Class in a manager emphasizes *we* and downplays *I*.
- Class is good manners.
- Class means respect for oneself as a foundation for respect for others.
- Class never makes a demeaning remark about one's spouse or partner. These remarks say more about the speaker than the person about whom they are speaking.
- Class in a manager means loyalty to one's staff.
- Class means not believing one is superior to one's employees; each simply has different responsibilities.
- Class does not take action when angry. It waits until cool reason has returned. Class is not impetuous.
- Class recognizes that the best way to build oneself is to first build others.
- Class does not become overly concerned about receiving credit and recognizes that sometimes one receives more credit than one deserves. It helps balance out those times when there are no accolades.
- Class is authentic and works hard at making actions consistent with words.
- Class doesn't build oneself up by tearing others down.
- Class leads by example.
- Class knows the importance and value of a warm smile.

CONCLUSION

A VARIETY OF TOPICS HAVE BEEN COVERED in this book on how to lead people, but certainly not every situation you'll confront in your career as a manager—or even within the first few weeks in your new role—has been reviewed.

There is no way that a book of this sort can be all inclusive. We hope that you have gained some insight into the techniques of managing people that will make the job more meaningful, enjoyable, and understandable. You may think we've spent an inordinate amount of time on attitudes, on how you view yourself and the problems you face, but that is exactly where your success or failure in working with people will be determined—in your head.

If you're the type of person who believes you're primarily controlled by events, then what's the use? In that case you're merely a puppet, with some giant puppet master pulling the strings. But in actuality, it's not that way. Although events beyond your control do have an impact on your life, you can control how and what you think. That in turn controls your reaction to these events.

We have been straightforward in this book. You haven't been told that if you work hard and keep your nose clean you'll rise to the top. However, you'll have a better chance if you follow some of these concepts than if you ignore what are basic truths. You didn't come into this world with any guarantee that everything would be fair and that the deserving would always get what they deserve. They don't! But you obviously have no chance of achieving your goals if you just sit there and wait for lightning to strike.

We must grow. This book is devoted to exploring how you manage your people, but equally important is seeing you grow as a total person. Your career can add to your total growth, since it's such a large part of your life. We shouldn't work at jobs we don't like, but on the other hand, we must be realistic in recognizing that all careers include aspects we don't like. It's the balance that is important. If most of the job is enjoyable, satisfying, and challenging, then you can put up with the parts you don't care for. If it's the other way around and you dislike most of what you have to do, you're obviously in the wrong career and you ought to change it. Life is too short to spend time and energy in a career that depletes and destroys you.

You have known people who stick with a job they don't like because someday it will provide a great retirement benefits. What good does that prospective retirement benefit do if people ruin their health before they get to retirement? What's worse, they might not live that long or the retirement plan may not turn out to be as desirable as they thought.

There are also people who complain about a job constantly but never seek a better job because their fear of change or of the unknown is more powerful than their dislike of the job. Some people prefer the predictable (even if it's bad) over something new or unknown.

Perhaps Abraham Lincoln was right when he said, "Most people are about as happy as they make up their minds to be." That summarizes what this book has addressed about the primacy of attitudes.

Many people, as they approach their middle years, start thinking in terms of the kind of contribution they're making to the world. They often become discouraged because they believe what they're doing is not very important. They ask themselves, "How significant is it that I'm a manager in a company making bolts?" Put in that context, it may not seem terribly significant. But the question they should ask is, "What kind of impact am I having on the people I come in contact with, both in my work and in my personal life?"

If you can answer that question in a positive way, it doesn't matter whether the company you're associated with is making bolts or lifesaving medicines. The system isn't the payoff; the product isn't the payoff; your impact on the people whose lives you touch is what is important. Also, holding a position that is a little higher on the organization chart *does not* make you more important than others. An executive or a manager is a combination of leader and servant. Some executives are not willing to accept the servant aspect of their responsibilities, because it interferes with their elevated opinion of their rank.

In developing systems for your people to use, you're in fact serving them. In maintaining an effective salary administration and performance appraisal system, you're serving them. In thoughtfully finding ways to merge the needs of your organization with the professional aspirations of your people, you're serving them. In working out vacation schedules that allow your people to maximize the benefits of their relaxation time, you're serving them. In hiring and training quality people for your department, you're serving the people who are already there.

Most people have no difficulty understanding the proposition that the president or prime minister of a country has immense power but should also be a servant—in fact, the number one public servant in that country. The same concept applies to managerial jobs. This is a combination of what appears to be contradictory concepts: authority and a responsibility to serve. If you can keep these in some semblance of balance, you'll avoid getting an inflated view of your own importance. You'll also do a better job.

As you progress as a manager you don't necessarily get smarter. You gain more experience, which has the potential to become wisdom. It doesn't matter what you call it as long as you continually become more effective. You can become more effective as you develop a greater variety of experiences in working with people. As you repeat the same experiences you have the opportunity to develop a smoothness you might not otherwise develop.

And this point, although elementary, bears repetition: There is a great deal to be gained from developing empathy for your employees' attitudes and feelings. Can you really sense how you'd want to be treated if you were in their position?

We wish you the best of success as you direct people in what amounts to about half of their waking hours. Your success as a manager starts with you and your attitude toward that responsibility. We hope this book has been of help to you at the beginning of a new and exciting chapter in your life. Good luck to you, and enjoy the ride.

INDEX

accountability, and team building, 61
achievement, need for, 142
active listening, 27–32
agendas, performance appraisal, 187
American Management Association (AMA), 265
appraisal inflation, 189
appraisals, *see* performance appraisals
appreciation, showing your, 23–25
arrogance, 210
The Attacker (behavior type), 69
attitude
  of employees, 98–100
    of job candidates, 72, 81–82
    your, 10–11
audience, of presentations, 266–267
authentic leadership, 216–217
authority, exercising your, 11–12
autocrats (managerial type), 49–50, 137

Baby Boomers, 165
balance, maintaining a sense of, 36–37, 279–282
"barn raising," 136–137
becoming a manager, ways of, 3
behavioral comments, in performance appraisals, 192
best case outcomes, 159, 161
The Bleeding Heart (behavior type), 70
body language, 29, 269–271
breathing, 277
Business Lessons from the Edge (McCormick and Karinch), 233
buyouts, 110–111

career risks, 144
change, resistance to, 91–93
the chosen few, 6–7
class, having, 283–284

closed-office periods, 232
comfort-zone underachievers (CZUs), 78–79
The Comic (behavior type), 69
communication
  and body language, 269–271
  in-person, 12
  as manager's responsibility, 34
  open, 125–127
  and reducing resistance to change, 93
  and risk taking, 148
  team building and open, 58
  via active listening, 27–32
  via grapevines, 241–242
  via writing, 237–240
  when disciplining employees, 97–98
  and your attitude, 10–11
  with your team, 12–13
community work, 280
The Complainer (behavior type), 70
comprehension gap, 28
concern, showing genuine, 34–35
confidence
  building, 19–21
  self-, 277–278
  and self-image, 215–216
consistency, in firing employees, 109–110
continuing education, 221–222
control
  with employees, 50–51
  span of, 15
conversation terminators, 30–31
correcting others, 19–20
costs, meeting, 253–254
creative risks, 144
creative tasks, logical vs., 229–230

deadlines, setting, 234
decisionmaking
  centralized, 151

decisionmaking (*cont.*)
  involving others in, 20
  types of, 215–216
decisions
  delegated, 216
  responding to flawed, 152–153
delegated decisions, 216
delegation, 243–247
  avoiding, 244, 247
  benefits of, 243–244
  choosing employees for, 245
  difficulty with, 5
  and perfectionism trap, 246–247
  steps in, 245–246
  upward, 247
The Deserter (behavior type), 69
diplomats (managerial type), 50
direct reports
  ideal number of, 15
  praising, 23–24
disability, 117
disciplining employees, 95–104
  avoiding personal attacks when, 96–97
  case example of, 100–101
  and communication, 97–98
  and employee attitudes, 98–100
  and feedback, 96
  performance-improvement tool to use
    when, 102–103
  techniques for, 103–104
"dismissal drama," 112–113
documentation
  of disciplinary conversations, 98
  and firing employees, 109
dovetailing, 138–140
downsizing, 111
dressing for success, 222–223

education programs, 221–222
ego, 209
elevated decisions, 216
emotional intelligence, 205–207
Emotional Intelligence (Goleman), 205
emotional quotient (EQ), 205–207
emotional risks, 144
employees
  choosing, for delegation, 245
  correcting or praising, 19–20
  delegating to, *see* delegation
  existing friendships with, 13–14
  with poor personal hygiene, 101
  remote, 169–171

types of, 50–52
  see also disciplining employees; firing
    employees
empowerment, and team building, 58
encouragement, of employees, 50–51
Enterprise Management System (EMS),
  91–92
EQ (emotional quotient), 205–207
Equal Employment Opportunity
  Commission, 115
equity, in salary administration, 196–197
evaluating, as manager's responsibility, 34

Family and Medical Leave Act (FMLA), 119
Federal Rehabilitation Act of 1973, 118
feedback, providing
  during training, 87
  when disciplining employees, 96
  to you supervisor, 42
feelings, managing your, 17
financial risks, 144
firing employees, 105–114
  documentation when, 109
  and downsizing, 111
  and drama of dismissal, 112–113
  flexibility/consistency in, 109–110
  as manager's responsibility, 34
  and mergers/buyouts, 110–111
  questions to ask yourself before, 108–109
  trying to "make it work" vs., 106–108
flammable task lists, 230
flattened organizational structures, 14–15
flexibility
  with task lists, 230
  when firing employees, 109–110
FMLA (Family and Medical Leave Act), 119
follow-through, job candidates', 80–81
friendships, existing, with direct reports,
  13–14

generation gaps, 163–168
  avoiding mistakes with, 164
  and mentoring, 167
  and motivation, 165–166
  and young managers, 164–165
Gen Xers, 165
Gen Y, 165
goal clarity, and team building, 59–60
Goleman, Daniel, 205
grapevines, 241–242
ground rules, meeting, 258–259
group socialization, and risk taking, 146

hiring, 71–82
  and candidate's attitude, 72, 81–82
  and candidate's desire to work, 79
  and candidate's judgment/follow-through,
    80–81
  of comfort-zone underachievers, 78–79
  getting a second opinion on, 78
  and job descriptions, 79–80
  manager's involvement in, 129–130
  as manager's responsibility, 34
  managing the process of, 81
  screening process for, 72–73
  and unemployment rates, 77–78
  use of tests in, 71–72
  see also interviews
honest, being, 10
human resources department (HR),
  129–131, 179, 265
humor, sense of, 249–252

importance, urgency vs., 234
improved outcomes, achieving, 157–162
improvement seed, planting the, 86–87
indispensability, avoiding, 220–221
infallibility syndrome, 212–213
informal interim appraisals, 189–190
informal writing, 239–240
information, providing accurate, 125–127
initiative, rewarding, 154–155
innovation, encouraging, 151–155
in-person communication, benefits of, 12,
  170
input, requesting, 20
intellectual risks, 144
intelligence quotient (IQ), 206
intelligent risk taking, 157–158
interruptions, 231–232
interviews
  as component of performance appraisal,
    183–187
  describing the job during, 79–80
  establishing rapport in, 73–74
  questions from applicants during, 76–77
  sample questions for, 74–76
  screening during, 72–73
IQ (intelligence quotient), 206
irritation, showing your, 16

job candidates, *see* hiring; interviews
job descriptions, 79–80, 177–179
job reviews, *see* performance appraisals
job scores, 179

job titles, 140–141
judgment, job candidates', 80–81
judgment, passing, 68

Kaiser, Henry, 228

laughter, encouraging, 250–251
leaders, 6–7
leadership
  authentic, 216–217
  management vs., 63
  of meetings, 257–258
  and mentoring, 167
  servant, 287
  and showing concern, 35
  and team building, 60–61
left-brain activities, 229
legal issues, 115–121
  disability, 117
  family and medical leave, 119
  with performance appraisals, 182–183
  privacy, 119
  sexual harassment, 115–117
  substance abuse, 118
  workplace violence, 120
Liberty ships, 228
life balance, achieving, 279–282
The Limelight Seeker (behavior type), 69
listening, 27–32
lists, to-do, 228–229
logical tasks, creative vs., 229–230
loyalty
  current state of, 133–134
  to your superiors, 39–40

management
  leadership vs., 63
  situational nature of, 53
management seminars, 4–5
management-training programs, 4–5
managerial role, transitioning into, 35–36
managerial styles, 49–53
meetings, 253–262
  advance notice of, 254–255
  cost of, 253–254
  with direct reports, 15
  leading, 257–258
  remote, 260–262
  tips for successful, 258–259
  your behavior during, 255–256
mental imagery, using, 238–240
mentors and mentoring, 42, 167

mergers, 110–111
methodicals (personality type), 44, 45
middle case outcomes, 159, 161
Millennials, 165–166
mixers (personality type), 44–45
monitoring
    as manager's responsibility, 34
    of social media use, 174
monopolizers (personality type), 44, 45
mood, your, 16–17, 235
The Moonlighter (behavior type), 69–70
motivation, 135–142
    "barn raising" as, 136–137
    and dovetailing, 138–140
    manager's role in creating, 137–138
    and need for achievement, 142
    self-, 135–136
    status symbols and, 141–142
    subjectivity of, 142
    titles' role in creating, 140–141
motivators (personality type), 44, 45

need for achievement, 142
nervous gestures, 269, 270
nervousness, handling, 276–277
new employees, training of, 84
The Not-My-Jobber (behavior type), 70

objective, being, 214–215
office politics, 217–218
omnipotent ones, 5–6
online meetings, 260–262
online performance appraisals, 193
on-time habit, developing the, 235
open communication, 125–127
open-door policy, 190
organization
    improving the structure of the, 14–16
    "publics" of the, 73
    structural changes in the, 110–111
organizational goal clarity, 59–60
organizing, as manager's responsibility, 34
outcomes, achieving improved, 157–162
outside reading, 280–281

participative decisionmaking, 216
perfectionism, 21, 246–247
performance appraisals, 181–194
    agenda for, 187
    and appraisal inflation, 189
    form for, 183–184

informal interim, 189–190
    interview as component of, 185–187
    and legal requirements, 182–183
    manager's responsibilities with, 183
    online, 193
    and open-door policy, 190
    review of, 193
    of satisfactory employees, 188–189
    subjectivity factors in, 190–192
    use of behavioral comments in, 192
personal attacks, avoiding, 96–97
personal hygiene, 101
personality styles, of managers, 43–45
personal problems, employees with, 67–
    68
personal touch, having a, 12
persuasion, as factor in risk taking, 148
physical risks, 144
planning
    as manager's responsibility, 34
    for presentations, 265–268
    of your time, 234
planting the improvement seed, 86–87
POSEMs, 159–162
positive self-image, 209
positive self-talk, 211
power, abusing your, 11
The Power of Risk (McCormick), 143, 157
PowerPoint, 267
praising others, 19, 20, 23–24
predecessor, following your, 9–10, 221
preferences, of your supervisor, 45–47
prejudicial mindsets, 213–214
presentation skills, developing your,
    224–225, see also public speaking
privacy, employee, 119
probation, putting employees on, 104
problem, focusing on the, 277
problem employees, 65–70
    rehabilitation of, 66
    with serious personal problems, 67–68
    tips for managing, 68–70
professional associations, membership in,
    280
project teams, 256–257
promotion(s)
    HR department and, 130–131
    opportunities for, 4
    seeking, 225
"publics," company, 73
public speaking, 263–268

getting training in, 264–265
tips for, 265–268

quality control, 87–88
questions
  answering, honestly, 10
  important, before firing an employee,
    108–109
  in interviews, 74–77
quiet confidence, developing, 215
quiet time, 233

rapport, establishing, in interviews, 73–74
reading, outside, 280–281
rehabilitation, of problem employees, 66
relationship risks, 144
remote employees, 169–171
remote meetings, 260–262
resistance to change, 91–93
responsibility(-ies)
  accepting, for mistakes, 211–212
  manager's, 33–37
  team building and clarity of, 58–59
  for training, 83–84
restating, as listening technique, 30
retirement, 6
rewards, 61, 154–155, 235
right-brain activities, 229
risk quotient (RQ), 143–145, 147–149
risk taking, 143–149
  awareness of inclination for, 145–148
  and group socialization, 146
  and identifying the risk, 158
  intelligent, 157–158
  and persuasion/communication, 148
  situational aspect of, 147
  styles of, 143
  types of, 144
RQ, see risk quotient

salary administration, 195–201
  equity in, 196–197
  and making salary recommendations,
    197–198
  with problem employees, 103–104
  and talent management, 199–201
sarcasm, avoiding, 251
screening, of job candidates, 72–73
second opinions, when hiring, 78
segmentation, of tasks, 227–228
self-confidence, 277–278

self-image, 209–218
  and accepting responsibility for mistakes,
    211–212
  and admitting your shortcomings/
    prejudices, 212–214
  and authentic leadership, 216–217
  and being objective, 214–215
  and confidence, 215–216
  ego vs. positive, 209
  and office politics, 217–218
  strategies for improving, 210–211
self-motivation, 135–136
self-promotion, 223–224
servant leadership, 287
"settling in," 9–11
70/30 rule, 234
sexual harassment, 115–117
shortcomings, admitting your, 212–214
"sink or swim" method of management
  training, 4, 11
skill(s)
  listing of, in job descriptions, 178–179
  required, for being a manager, 3
  showing appreciation as acquired, 24–25
smartphones, 228
smiling, 269, 270
social media, 173–174
social risks, 144
solo decisionmaking, 215–216
span of control, 15
spiritual risks, 144
sponsor, acquiring a, 226
staff reductions, 110–111
starting out as a manager, 9–17
  and communicating with your team,
    12–13
  and exercising your authority, 11–12
  and existing friendships with reports,
    13–14
  and improving structure of the
    organization, 14–16
  and reactions of others, 9–11
  and your mood, 16–17
status symbols, 141–142
storytelling, 238
stress management, 275–278
styles, managerial, 49–53
subjectivity
  of motivation, 142
  in performance appraisals, 190–192
substance abuse, 118